NOW YOU DON'T HAVE TO TRAVEL BLINDLY THROUGH YOUR MARRIED YEARS. NOW YOU CAN SEE WHAT'S COMING IN TIME TO CHANGE THE BAD TIMES INTO THE BEST TIMES!

THE MARRIAGE MAP

QUANTITY SALES

Most Dell Books are available at special quantity discounts when purchased in bulk by corporations, organizations, and special-interest groups. Custom imprinting or excerpting can also be done to fit special needs. For details write: Dell Publishing Co., Inc., 1 Dag Hammarskjold Plaza, New York, NY 10017, Attn.: Special Sales Dept., or phone: (212) 605-3319.

INDIVIDUAL SALES

Are there any Dell Books you want but cannot find in your local stores? If so, you can order them directly from us. You can get any Dell book in print. Simply include the book's title, author, and ISBN number, if you have it, along with a check or money order (no cash can be accepted) for the full retail price plus 75¢ per copy to cover shipping and handling. Mail to: Dell Readers Service, Dept. FM, 6 Regent Street, Livingston, N.J. 07039.

THE MARRIAGE MAP

Understanding and Surviving the Stages of Marriage

MAXINE ROCK

A DELL TRADE PAPERBACK

This book is dedicated to my husband, David Rock, and to the other people who taught me the most about marriage: my parents — Jean and Louis Hochman, Dr. H. Lee Hall and Dr. Ralph M. Klopper.

A DELL TRADE PAPERBACK
Published by
Dell Publishing Co., Inc.
1 Dag Hammarskjold Plaza
New York, New York 10017

Dell ® TM 681510, Dell Publishing Co., Inc.

ISBN: 0-440-55726-7

Reprinted by arrangement with Peachtree Publishers, Ltd., c/o Harvey Klinger, Inc.

Printed in the United States of America

March 1987

10 9 8 7 6 5 4 3 2 1

MV

Table of Contents

Acknowledgements

Two doctors in particular contributed their insight and wisdom to this book and carefully monitored its progress.

H. Lee Hall, M.D., is a former teacher at Columbia University's Psychoanalytic School in New York City and former director of the Emory University Psychoanalytic Clinic in Atlanta. He is now in private practice.

Ralph M. Klopper, M.D., is a graduate of the University of Missouri and completed his residency in psychiatry at Duke University. He now maintains a private practice in Atlanta and is on the staff of Emory University's Psychiatric Department.

The comments and observations of Dr. Hall and Dr. Klopper appear regularly throughout this book. I developed many of my ideas from their thoughts about marriage, which spring from the roots of classicial Freudian theories of human behavior. Dr. Hall and Dr. Klopper also read and approved the final manuscript.

Lloyd Mendelson, Ph.D., a specialist in marriage and family counseling in private practice, guided me during the early stages of the book.

Here, in alphabetical order, are the names of the professionals who helped me research *The Marriage Map:*
Norman Abrams, M.D.
Ann Agnor, Researcher
Jim Bird, M.A., M.S.W.
Gaston de Lemos, M.D.
Marion Glustrom, M.A.
H. Lee Hall, M.D.
Mildred R. Kagan, M.S.W.
Ralph Klopper, M.D.
Rabbi Philip Kranz

Louis McLeod, Ph.D.
Maxine Rosen, A.C.S.W.

   Thanks, also, to Libby Mark, literary agent, for excellent work and for help far beyond the call of business; and to Peggy Hood, who typed and proofread the final manuscript.

   I am grateful to Lauren Rock for helping me select the title for this book, and to Michael Rock, who was helpful in many ways.

Author's Note

I have been married to the same man for twenty-one years. But *The Marriage Map* is not a book about me and my husband, nor an anatomy of any one marriage. It is based mainly on what I learned from marriage experts and from the people I interviewed. Most of these people — like me — are living within what they consider to be a rewarding, mature, legal and socially-sanctioned partnership with a person of the opposite sex.

Because I wanted to trace the development of happy marriages, I usually picked people to interview who placed themselves in that category. Now and then I talked to people who said they were unhappy, or who proved it by divorcing. Most had remarkable insight (after the divorce) into what had gone wrong and how they might avoid it next time.

Except for the experts who shared their professional knowledge, everyone who was interviewed for this book has a guarantee of anonymity. Therefore, the names and some physical characteristics of my subjects have been changed. In a few cases I also changed their professions and locations and made what I thought were reasonable substitutions. I believe these attempts to preserve my subjects' privacy do not interfere with the essential truth of the stories they told about their marriages.

For the sake of grammatical simplicity, I often use "he" instead of "he or she." Used in this way, the word "he" stands for both sexes.

In discussing the stages of marriage, I have assigned a time span to each growth level. That way, readers can gauge the probable stage they will be in according to the number of years they have been married.

Although I have used very specific and detailed case histories to help describe each stage, this book cannot probe the full reasons why certain marriages succeed or fail. Rather, it takes a collective look at marriage as a basic component of growth in adult life.

Preface

This is a book about the process of being married.

We have been wrong in thinking about marriage as a one-time event. It is a series of episodes, or growth stages, which people attempt to negotiate as couples.

Although the joys and problems of marriage are common occurrences, they appear unfamiliar to most of us. Couples flounder — and perhaps divorce — largely because they are shocked by what they find in marriage and feel unprepared to deal with these realities. The stages of marriage, as presented here, provide a "map" for success in traveling along one of life's most basic pathways.

Marriage Is For Adults

When people become adults, they almost automatically think about getting married. "Marriage is something you are programmed to do," says psychoanalyst Dr. H. Lee Hall. "You will do it, unless prevented."

Eventually, about ninety percent of the American public gets married, usually for the first time at about age twenty-two for women and twenty-three for men. More than forty percent of those marriages now end in divorce, but at least half of the divorced people remarry and many remain that way. Although most of the people I interviewed for this book have been married only once and are deeply involved in making that marriage work, couples in second or even third marriages also go though the same stages . . . only faster and with more apparent understanding of the dynamics.

Who Was Interviewed, And How

I found research subjects in New York City, Chicago, Atlanta,

Washington, D.C., and parts of Connecticut, Michigan and California. I have contacts in these areas, and together they represent what I consider a good cultural cross section of the nation. Almost all of the interviews were conducted in the homes of the couples to whom I spoke, except when the active presence of children made that impossible. When that happened, we met in offices, restaurants, hotel lounges or bars.

Most of my subjects live in big or medium-sized cities and enjoy their jobs or careers. They range in age from nineteen to seventy-eight years old, and three-fourths of them have one or more children.

I spent three years interviewing the more than one hundred subjects who participated in this book, enlisting the aid of twelve marriage experts in analyzing the interviews, and collecting statistics and other supporting data. After many thorough interviews, the presence of definite, predictable stages in marriage was clear. And when several experts dug into my notes and picked up the patterns, I became convinced that it is possible to judge the course of marriage and to understand the dynamics of a marriage relationship based on the approximate number of years spent together.

For the interviews, I picked mostly people who were glad they had married their present partners and for whom marriage was one of life's top priorities. About half the time I talked to the wife alone, then the husband alone, then returned to quiz them together. One-fourth of my subjects talked to me without their spouses because their partners (usually the man) didn't want to do the interview or were unavailable, or because my subject was separated or divorced. Another fourth answered the questions only as a couple, no matter how many times I returned. The people who were most honest, I believe, were those who talked to me alone — without a spouse to listen, nod approval, frown, or get ready for a fight the minute I walked out the door.

Battles Over The Book

Some people did have battles over answering questions for this book. I was sticking a big spoon into the melting pot of their marriages, and some husbands and wives didn't like the answers that were stirred up.

I spent one sunny afternoon in the quaint, restored home of an Atlanta couple married for twelve years, watching them get angrier and angrier at one another with each new question and disturbing answer. They had begun the interview being cheerful and aimlessly chatty. After about twenty minutes, the husband responded to my prodding for honesty. He was still happy most of the time, he said, but he was growing increasingly weary of his wife's refusal to shed ten pounds so he could become more aroused in bed. "I particularly like slender women," he told me.

The husband had to decide if this was important enough to fight for, or if he ought to stop harping on his wife's weight and try to accept her just the way she was. He said he feared his wife's enthusiasm for food might be a way of expressing buried hostility toward him, because she knew he did not approve of heavy eating. When this was said, she stiffened, turned to him slowly and hissed, "When will you give up trying to control me?"

This couple had started the interview snuggled together on their living room couch. Gradually, they separated. By the time I closed my notebook and rose to leave, they were perched stiffly at opposite ends of the sofa. When I walked out the door, I felt a distinct prickling up and down my spine, as if I was rushing away from an area that was charged with hostile energy.

The husband called me a few days later. "We had a terrible fight the minute you left," he said.

"I was afraid that would happen," I told him. "I'm sorry."

"Oh, don't be sorry! We really got a lot of stuff out in the open. It didn't change anything, but now we both understand more of what's going on. So we can accept it better. I guess every few months we are just going to have a big fight . . . and this time, you helped bring it out. A buildup of frustration, a fight, and then more understanding and acceptance seems to be our pattern."

Patterns Within The Stages

Such patterns are individualized methods couples devise to deal with the changes implicit in their marriages. Quite a few people described their patterns as an intricate "dance" and told me a good marriage depends on learning the steps well enough to follow the music without trampling too often on their partner's toes. Each couple hears the same music — the stages — and performs basically the same movements in response. But each has different techniques. One couple holds together tightly as they sway; another is at arm's length. They all struggle to find a comfortable way to dance with their mates and occasionally come up with some innovative two-steps in the process. But people fool themselves if they think they are striking out in drastically different directions. The stages are firmly fixed, and they determine the basic outline of every marriage.

These stages do overlap. Few of us leap gracefully from one period of life to another; instead we progress in a series of clumsy lurches. Some people may skip a stage, become confused and have to back-track. Others linger in one place for a long time, afraid to make any move toward growth.

If they get divorced, it seems that many people do so not because they can't get along, but because they keep stumbling in a difficult stage, panic and run away.

People may also revert to an earlier stage during times of crisis, much as children often go back to thumb sucking when they're scared. But if they can successfully negotiate the Marriage Map, with all its intricate turns and bumps, they will emerge with a lifelong love affair that is worth the effort they have put into it.

PART I

1

Steps Toward Marriage

At exactly 10 A.M. I emerge from the elevator in a Chicago high-rise, and before I'm halfway down the hall, Harriett opens the door to her apartment and beckons me inside. She has been looking forward to the interview, she says, and can explain her choice of a mate in very practical terms. "I used a specific method in deciding who to marry. For me, that kind of planning really works."

Harriett is twenty-seven. Tall, dark-eyed, with a figure as sleek as a whippet, she is surrounded by the heady perfume of female self-confidence. When she walks, it is with a purposeful stride; when she talks, there is no hesitation in her voice. She was born and raised in a suburb of New York City, where life goes more easily for people who are not shy. Harriett studied art and art theory at New York University on a full scholarship. She did an internship at the Museum of Modern Art, then worked as a researcher for the art critic of the *New York Times*.

A few years ago Harriett moved to Chicago, went back to school and emerged with an honors degree in architecture. Now she runs her own freelance business from an airy loft with a marvelous view of Lake Michigan. Harriett decorated her apartment in what might be called "contemporary precise." The gray modular sofa fits perfectly against the wall, the hand-painted tiles in the kitchen are the same as those framing the sunny window in the nearby eating area, and even the tulips in a round glass bowl are artfully arranged.

Harriett is a careful woman who likes an orderly life. It is no coincidence that she formulated a set of standards for her selection of a future husband and stuck by them. She had become engaged the week before.

"He is Jewish, like me. That's very important. I wanted a man who shares my religious and ethnic background," Harriett says.

"He is my intellectual equal, and we like to go to the same cultural events. Nathan is also a product of an upper middle-class family, where the stress was on getting an education and bettering yourself through professional achievement. So he understands and shares my feelings about how to live. It would be hard to raise children with a man who couldn't relate to the same kind of family values.

"Nathan looks like what I wanted my mate to look like. He's not handsome, really, but he's got what it takes to turn me on. So there's sexual chemistry.

"On top of it all, Nathan was available. You know what I mean. He was not married to someone else, not serious about anyone when I met him, but definitely looking to get married, too. And he was where I could meet him in the first place, which is right here in Chicago. He likes it here, so we share a sense of being comfortable in the same city. There won't be hassles about him wanting to be in one place and me in another."

Harriett says her realistic approach to the selection of a mate was deeply influenced by the example of her parents' marriage. Her mother and father "seemed welded together in a very good way." When she was small, Harriett accepted their compatability as something that just happened; it was, to her, the way every married couple had to behave. But when she became a teen-ager and began observing the marriages of neighbors and friends, Harriett slowly came to the conclusion that her parents had something special. She decided this was because her mom and dad had deliberately picked someone to marry who complemented and enhanced their own ideas of life.

Harriett grew up in a tidy brick house on a traffic-plagued street named Union Turnpike. Her father was a doctor. She loved to visit his nearby office, perching on a three-legged stool in a back room and sorting out the paper clips, thumbtacks, rolls of gauze, and safety pins on his cluttered supply tables.

"He would get a break between patients and poke around to find me. Then he'd lean against the door, looking regal in his long white doctor's jacket, and tell me that I was being very helpful," Harriett recalls. "He didn't gush over me or call me a good little girl for being so quiet. He simply said something like, 'It's helpful to have my things sorted out that way,' or, 'I'm glad you're here. It puts more fun in my day.' And I believed him. He was very sincere. It helped give me a real sense that men don't have to fall all over you to be appreciative, to show love or need. All they have to do is be honest and give credit where it's due."

Harriett's mother was an artist who worked in a big studio at home. Her huge modernistic canvases were sold on commission through fine art shops. Harriett vividly remembers her mother's tall, strong body leaning over a workbench nailing canvas to wooden frames, or arched toward the easel as she concentrated on her painting.

"I always admired her body, especially her hands and arms. They were thin but solid; it was a beautiful combination of strength and grace. I was an only child, but my mother wasn't the type to spend much time worrying about me, telling me to eat all my vegetables or put on another sweater. She assumed I had enough common sense to survive, and she usually didn't give much advice unless I asked. What she gave was plenty of hugs . . . with no strings attached.

"She related to my father in the same way. Mom and Dad got along very well. They had nice discussions. I do remember fights — everyone has to fight sometimes — but not screaming fights. More like disagreements over specifics, not philosophy. As far as I know, when they did disagree, nothing festered. They seemed to get things ironed out. They were both happy people, secure about themselves, and they helped show me that I could be happy and secure, too.

"But the good things in life, like a solid marriage, don't just happen. I think you *make* them happen. My parents believed you could have control over your own life, and part of the way to do that was to set out a plan, sort of a list of goals in your head. Oh, the plan changes, the goals might be replaced with others, but at least you have something solid to work for. You go from point A to point B, as it were, until you reach your first goal, then your second, and so on. Doesn't that make sense to you in the context of finding a marriage partner?

"I thought this marriage thing all out in advance," Harriett says with a luxuriant smile. "I knew the sort of man I wanted to marry — one like my dad, actually — and I was prepared to go for it when I met him."

Harriett tells me she keeps in close touch with her parents. They are her friends, she says. Her interview is a mellow tale of contentment, presented carefully within the framework of a common sense, I-can-do-it attitude toward life.

After a few hours, Harriett sees that my wine glass is empty, unfolds herself from the sofa and pads in red Chinese slippers across the loft to a serving cart. She has thoughtfully set out a basket of fruit, a chilled bottle of Liebfraumilch and a plate of crackers and Brie. Harriett leaves very little to chance. She is prepared.

"Are you dying to ask me if love plays a part in all of this?" she teases, pouring the wine and flicking the bottle rim deftly with a napkin. "Do you want to ask if I *love* Nathan?"

"Okay. Yes."

"I don't want to sound . . . uh . . . clinical or passionless," Harriett says, her brow creasing for a moment into tiny furrows. "But to my way of thinking, what I've been talking about is a definition of love. I mean, if a man meets all your standards or comes close, how can you miss? In my own mind, I set out the qualities I wanted. Along comes Nathan, and he has those qualities. I meet his standards, too. All the ingredients are there for a good marriage. I figure we have a pretty reasonable chance."

Harriett is probably right. The qualities she describes — and which Nathan possesses — parallel the answers people most often give to sociologists who ask, "What qualities determine who you select for a lifelong mate?" The answers usually include mutual respect, trust, shared goals and interests, a common family background and religion, and agreement on philosophy of life. The process of courtship and partnership selection is not, as romance novelists would have us believe, a crashing discovery made while people are drenched in sexual sweat. That sometimes happens, of course, but it's amazing how fast that kind of sweat evaporates. Lust is fun and has its place both in courtship and in marriage, but it is only one component of mate selection.

What Is Courtship?

Before people can accept and manipulate the changes that occur in a healthy marriage, they need a lot of practice. That is part of the purpose of courtship.

We step into courtship while we are still very young. When Spanish philosopher José Ortega y Gasset tried to categorize the growth phases of human beings, he said childhood occupies the years from birth to fifteen, and one remains a "youth" until the age of thirty. By this reasoning, we begin seeking a mate while we are barely noticing the new fuzz of pubic hair, and we court and marry far in advance of our emotional ability to withstand the pressures and responsibilities of a lifelong commitment.

Young middle- and upper-class men are especially unprepared for early marriage. It takes longer these days to gain the basic education, upper-level academic degrees and professional experience necessary to get a solid footing in the career world. And without that, hard-driving men don't feel ready for the personal responsibilities of marriage. Still, they cannot ignore the persistent tide of sexual and emotional energies that trickle, then flow, in early and late adolescence. When these energies finally rush over them in swirling waves as they hit their early twenties, it leads to the passionate selection of a marriage partner long before they have a mature concept of what being married will require of them. For the love-swept youth who finds that marriage is forcing him to be a workhorse instead of a frisky stallion, there is much self-doubt. Did he do the right thing?

Does he really love the woman he promised to cherish forever? Is it all for real — for *life?*

Young women take just as long getting their resumés together, but when their sexual energies emerge, they seem better equipped to regulate them. When a woman looks for a husband, she usually has a few other things in mind besides biceps and bedrooms if she is reasonably mature. She wonders if the man under consideration is stable, if he can be a provider when necessary, if he shares her ideals about male-female equality. This is not to imply that men are coasting blissfully into marriage with only sexual attraction as an emotional lubricant. But for men, being married is not a time-honored method of gaining social status, as it still is for women. Females have been conditioned by centuries of need to select the mate who is seemingly best equipped to anchor them safely in society. Men have always had to provide their own anchor; the notion that women also can stand alone is fairly new.

No matter how far we have come, marriage still determines a woman's destiny far more than it determines a man's. It brings more changes into a woman's life because marriage usually involves career compromises that come with family responsibilities. It is a near-sighted woman who ignores this knowledge, gained from simply looking around at all the young wives struggling to juggle both family and job while their husbands claim to be satisfying responsibilities to both simply by carving out a good career.

The women's liberation movement has taught young females to be more careful about getting married. Many women now look very critically at a man's value system before leaping into matrimony. By and large, women are more aware of the consequences of an injudicious choice of a mate, more conscious of their options in today's society, and far more determined to exercise them.

For these reasons, young women may tiptoe into marriage now, instead of leaping as they once did. But they still are forced into the rituals that will lead them to the altar, just as young men are forced. These rituals are called courtship. This is not a stage in marriage, of course, but it is a crucial "stage before the stages" — something people have to go through in order to travel the road to social maturity. And the "forcing" into courtship comes from a society that shows us, almost from birth, that marriage is expected of every male and female.

"As soon as I graduated from college...honest, as soon as I had that degree in my hands...I thought, 'Well, the next important thing I have to do is find a husband,' " a twenty-seven-year-old office manager told me. "I had my own apartment and was certain I could support myself. But I kept feeling very alone, and I was calling my mother at least three times a week. All the ads for video dating services got to me, too. At singles bars, sometimes, if I couldn't connect with a man, I'd just sit and talk to the other women there, and we'd say how nice it would be to find a husband and not have to look around in the bars anymore. The world seems to be built for pairs.

"As soon as I found a steady boyfriend, I relaxed a lot. I certainly do want our relationship to go on into marriage. I've also noticed that I don't call my mother as much now. If that means my boyfriend is a substitute for the security I got from my mother...yes...I think that's true to some extent. I just know being married seems like the natural thing to do."

Marriage Is Back In Style

In 1950, the median age of marriage for females was slightly more than twenty years old. For males, it was about twenty-two and a half. Courtship was usually brief and to the point. This median did not change substantially during the 1970's, although fewer people married; prolonged dating or "living together" were popular. Now, according to Peter Francese of American Demographics in Ithaca, New York, people wait longer to marry but *more* marriage is slowly coming back into style. He says the rituals of courtship and some living together are still popular as brief intermediate steps before marriage, but people are definitely groping their way back to traditional family structure...and that means marriage. According to the U.S. Census Bureau, the median age of first marriage is now twenty-three for females and almost twenty-five and a half for males.

Evidence of this return to the values of family life among the young is shown by a recent survey conducted by National Research, Inc., of one thousand Americans born between 1946 and 1964. The survey shows that seventy-six percent of this group (the baby boomers) favor marriage over other options, provided it is an equal marriage where work, childrearing and homemaking responsibilities are shared.

James Ogilvy, director of SRI International, a research group, thinks young men and women are going back to "old-fashioned" life structures such as marriage because they're fed up with the self-ishness and empty lifestyle of the "me" generation. He says, "The large crop of baby-boom kids are maturing now . . . they're settling down into communities and longer-term relationships and recogniz-ing that their private desire for self-realization can't be carried out without acting on some concerns for our social organization."

What goes into the decision to marry? Until a few decades ago, marriage was an economic necessity for everyone except the very rich. There was virtually no other way for women to get money except from a working male willing to support them. And men needed wives to perform household chores that were too expensive to dele-gate to others or which they couldn't do themselves and stay on the job. Of course, marriage also filled other needs, as it does now: providing a "nest" and training ground for children; assuring security and care in times of illness; and easing the boredom of living alone. In earlier times, if love, respect and good sex came along with the marriage, so much the better. Now we ask for love, respect and good sex first. These demands provide the chance for a far more equal and rewarding relationship than our grandparents or even our parents might have hoped for.

So we are programmed to marry partly because we know, from history and tradition, that in terms of keeping society together, marriage works. The current conservative fear that feminists are anti-marriage and that women — once freed by their own paychecks — will turn away from marriage is unfounded. The women's movement was never out to sink the marriage boat. It just wanted to redefine the terms, so that husbands weren't always captains and the wives first mates.

Sizing Up A Potential Marriage Partner

Bernard Murstein, author of *Who Will Marry Whom*, says we all go through a precise sequence of sizing up a potential mate, testing him or her for fatal flaws and then making a decision. First comes the stimulus, says Murstein. You are drawn to a person because he or she looks good and acts in ways that are pleasing to you. You may also know something about this person's fine reputation or well-heeled family. That helps. If you think the attraction could be mutual, you'll have the self-confidence to make an approach.

Next comes value comparison. You talk and find out the person's attitudes on everything from politics to childrearing. Do you share the same religion or philosophy of life? Are you both interested in the arts or in deep-sea fishing? This process of mutual discovery may take minutes or months.

If there are enough shared values, the relationship gets deeper and couples start discussing roles. Now you're asking for vital information on whether this potential mate shares your ideas about the roles men and women should fill in modern society. You won't go further if she's a career woman and he wants a stay-at-home wife. But if you both get this far and find shared perceptions about gender roles, you'll probably get married.

Nobody goes through this process every time they hear a seductive laugh across the room at a party or head out for a casual date. Plenty of youthful man-woman contacts take place only for sex, fun or something to do on Saturday night . . . with no serious thought tossed in to mess up a good time. But when people become aware of being on the prowl for a lifelong mate — when they're ready to marry — they probably go through a selection process like the one described by Murstein. The plan doesn't have to be as well thought-out as Harriett's, but it usually does include finding someone who fills specific needs such as sex, shared interests, or an income that assures a lifestyle that is at least equal to what your parents enjoyed.

Because Harriett is educated and financially secure, she can afford to be choosy about whom she will marry. People like Harriett can also afford to wait and go through the selection process carefully or repeat it several times if the first few tries don't work.

Among the very poor, however, marriage can be much more of a hit-or-miss proposition. People handicapped by poverty don't feel as if they have many options in life — including the option to carefully select a mate. Testing a potential partner's reaction to one's lifestyle and value systems is a practice of those who think they have at least a reasonable chance of manipulating life events to their satisfaction. Poor people don't think that way. Many of them have been conditioned to *accept* what happens, not to engineer it.

For the huge numbers of people who belong to the nebulous group we commonly call the American middle class, however, the rituals of courtship are like the unfolding of a hothouse flower. First we go to the movies or basketball games in packs, finding safety from embarrassment in the nearness of other teens of our own sex . . . even though we're keeping our eyes glued on the opposite sex in the crowd. From this or similar group encounters, we eventually select one boy or girl we like best and progress to single dating. If the involvement is serious, we'll abandon other potential mates and "go steady." Next is engagement, which announces our intentions to parents and to society at large and formalizes the romantic involvement.

There might be a period of living together tossed into the courtship somewhere along the line, often as a test ground for marriage. Some sociologists think new marriages have a better chance these days because more couples are living together before taking the final step. That could be true if the arrangement is clearly defined as a pre-nuptial stage. But it doesn't seem to work for people who use living together as a substitute for marriage, claiming loudly that fancy weddings and legalized vows are silly social trappings that only muddy the waters of pure love.

Living together can be an exciting voyage of discovery, and it could be a practical method by which one can ease into the day-to-day responsibilities of marriage. According to the most recent Census Bureau studies, the number of unmarried men and women living together has more than tripled since 1970. Now about 1.6 million unmarried couples share living quarters, at least partly because they are postponing marriage in favor of testing their compatibility while they concentrate on careers or higher education. But many studies show that living together without being married is a game that pays off only if it culminates in marriage after a few months, or a year or two at most. The longer people live together unmarried, the less likely they are to ever commit to the real thing.

People who cohabit cannot duplicate the rooting process of marriage. They usually don't buy a house or make other major investments as a team. They don't often take the chance of having babies. They don't pool paychecks or get deeply involved with one another's parents. They are, after all, "free." It is not hard to pack up and get out, and people who live together always hold that possibility of hassle-free escape in the back of their minds. A popular song of recent years was singer/songwriter Paul Simon's "Fifty Ways to Leave Your Lover," in which he sings, "... hop on the bus, Gus, don't need to discuss much... drop off the key, Lee, get yourself free!"

People who need freedom without marriage may live with many partners during a lifetime without ever making a firm commitment. But those who seek the comfort of marriage must also accept its rules, many of which are unspoken and simply handed down from generation to generation. These rules are based largely on tradition, such as appointing women as family cooks and men as financial problem-solvers. But the rules do eliminate the confusion that would paralyze us if we had to ask, "Who does what?" at every turn. At the same time, traditional marriage rules are now mostly arbitrary and often unfair to both men and women; but couples who accept them at first, and then gradually work together to make changes that are comfortable to both, are couples who say they get along well. They call themselves a team, and after a few years of marriage they seem proud of the way they have been able to make changes, no matter how small, in the way they divide life's daily chores.

2

Why Do We Marry?

In the groggy light of an Atlanta morning, I stumbled out of bed and turned on my television. The lovely face of Anne Bancroft appeared on the screen. There she was, sharp-featured and raven-haired, explaining to an ardent morning anchorman why she married the boisterous, homely writer and comedian, Mel Brooks.

"Oh, it was love right away. Mel looked just like my father . . . and he acted like my mother. What else could I do but marry him?"

I laughed out loud. Anne Bancroft had made my morning. With one deft on-the-air retort, she summarized the subconscious flash of recognition we all experience when we meet a potential mate. "He reminds me of Daddy." "She looks just like Mom." With few exceptions, this is the reason for the beginning — and perhaps the end — of most American marriages.

The subconscious cause for getting married is to recapture the unconditional acceptance of early childhood. That is a fantasy; it never materializes again. People who cling desperately to the fantasy and keep trying to force their mates to act like parents will eventually erode the relationship.

Our first intense love affair is with the person who holds us tenderly in the dark night of infancy, who comforts us when we tumble, who appears magically to ease the pains of hunger and the terror of being alone in a huge, confusing world. Most often, that person is mother. Yes, father is very important, too. He serves as a role model for little boys, as a love object for little girls, and has many other vital parental functions. But the immediate care-giver and prime love object for most people before the age of four is a female, who is usually the biological mother. From her we experience the overwhelming pleasure of single-minded devotion. Her tenderness helps us form the mother-child bond, which will be modified in later life but never broken.

As we mature, we remember how wonderful it felt to be loved by mother. The feeling is buried deep in our subconscious minds, perhaps, but it is there. We want it again. And we know, through instinct and by the prodding of a social order that says we cannot stay with mother forever, that the best way to recapture the feeling of that unconditional early love is to get it from a marriage partner.

If mother was even a barely adequate parent, the bond with her will form. The better the bond, the easier it is for us to fall in love at a later, appropriate age and get married. If the bond was weak — if, for example, we know mother just barely tolerated us and couldn't wait to be rid of her child — we mistrust ourselves and others. How could we be lovable if mom didn't love us? Who would marry such an unlovable person? Those are the tormented emotions of the adult who was unloved as a child.

Still, the human psyche is wonderfully resilient, and if we have been loved at all, by mom or perhaps by a surrogate who nourished our emotions and encouraged them to expand, we will be able to fall in love and marry. The early experiences of love are imprinted on us in much the same way as the mother-image is imprinted on ducklings when they struggle, wet and gummy, from the prison of their eggs.

"You're Not The Woman I Married!"

I told psychologist Dr. Lloyd Mendelson about Anne Bancroft's cheerful public admission of her reasons for marriage. He laughed hard, because he said it reminded him of a recent and similarly penetrating remark made by his beautiful Iranian wife, Nahid. One time, after they had an especially stormy disagreement, Dr. Mendelson marched angrily around the house. When he confronted his wife again, he blurted in frustration, "Damn it, Nahid, you're not the woman I married!"

She just looked at him with wide black eyes and let a faint smile curl up from the corners of her mouth.

"I never *was* the woman you married," she said.

That story illustrates Nahid's quiet wisdom and pinpoints her husband's realization of the truth in her answer. We are never the people our mates think we are when they first marry us. And our mates are never what we think *they* are. We all marry an illusion, a fantasy. It is the phantom of our nurturing parent we crave, and for the period of courtship and very early married life our subconscious needs take over and tell us that we indeed captured true love... again. Mother gave it to us once. It was grand. Now our mates will blend into us, become one with us and give us the same kind of love. Says Dr. Mendelson, "That's one origin of the old folk saying, 'Love is blind.' We are blind to the truth that nobody can be mommy for us. We can't ever get her back again. But the reason we marry is because it's just not normal, when you're young, to stop trying."

Growing Up, Growing Out

Marriage is the pot of gold at the end of childhood's rainbow. It is a social reward for letting go of mother. In a thousand different ways, society and family send messages that we must find another love object, for we cannot retain our infantile control over mother. With each new birthday, she does less and less for us. First we have to feed ourselves, then go to the potty alone, then tie our own shoes. Soon the school system conspires to force even more of a separation. At each new withdrawal of mother's overwhelming power, we resist. If growing up means going it alone, who needs it?

We do. Growing is an undeniable urge, an inescapable set of bridges over which we must all pass in order to achieve full potential. Oh, we can grow *up* easily enough; with good food and reasonable care, our bodies can become adult. But we cannot grow *out* — expanding emotionally — unless we're willing to take the chance of leaving mother, doing things on our own, and facing the bold truth that makes us adult: We can't suck energy from others. The strength that sees us through life has to be our own.

Emotional growth is scary, but it is such a powerful urge that healthy people overcome the fear at each stage in life and push on to eventual maturity. We may not progress at the same speed; we all know people who seem "mature" or "immature" for their ages. And we certainly use different styles. But one universal method of growth, says Dr. Mendelson, is to get married.

"That's why I count marriage as almost a biological urge," he says. "Marriage is virtually the only safe arena where an individual is able to shed childhood fantasies and grow to real adulthood. In marriage you are able to develop humility, differentness and tolerance. That kind of growth just isn't possible without the push and pull you get from trying to live with a marriage partner. You can't do it alone."

In the 1920's, it was fashionable for sociologists to believe that marriage, or formalized mating, contained a strong biological component. Some observers felt that marriage served somewhat of a Darwinian function, perhaps as part of the basic theory of survival of the fittest. People who are emotionally healthy, said the sociologists, are the ones who get married and successfully stay that way. These people are able to perform the essential task of growing up. If a person is good at growing up — if he or she is able to become emotionally mature — that person does well in stressful society. By this reasoning, the sociologists felt that happily married people might be the most able of the species, and their offspring could be expected to rise to the top of society.

Today, says Dr. Mendelson, this idea is still valid but needs modification. He says, "I think of it this way: If children observe love, trust and affection in the home, they will tend to view social institutions this way. However, if they observe mistrust, abuse of love and hostility in the home, they will take this stance with society.

People who are comfortable with society, who can be said to fit in well, usually aren't afraid to achieve success and be creative. They have good careers and may wind up as pioneers, mold-breakers, not because they reject traditional patterns but because they are secure enough to experiment with them. Those who view social institutions with fear and anger are often the people we call failures. They are men and women who just can't stay with a good job, for example, because they balk at the rules in a hostile way, or they get in trouble with the law."

This is a modern interpretation of the theory that good marriages can produce the most productive citizens. As people obey the subconscious and deeply powerful urge to grow, the solid emotional underpinnings provided by the example of their parents' healthy marriage will help them through.

Obeying The Urge To Grow

Growth can be painful, and we all resist in a variety of ways. Some people delay the acceptance of formalized education, career goals and marriage until they get bored with a floating, self-centered lifestyle. Others marry and then refuse to continue the growth pattern by behaving like children rather than spouses. They shrug off their share of daily chores, for example, pout when a child is born because *they* want center stage, or threaten to abandon their mates in favor of spending a lot of time with single friends.

When we resist growth within a marriage, it usually boils down to fights over who will take care of whom, who will give in, which one gets his way. Baby stuff. At first, it happens to practically everyone, but immature adults just can't get past it.

Emotionally healthy people, however, go through a brief period of this sort of resistance, then accept the growth urges over the baby urges and nourish joint development by progressing with the marriage stages. True adults may grieve for their lost childhood, but then they put the demise of immaturity behind them.

These are the people who can get past the tough spots, work

through them, and emerge after about twenty years of marriage and family life knowing they are a viable unit. Each of them — husband, wife and children — is a strong individual. The parents are still in love and content. The offspring are capable of meeting both career and personal challenges. They are all survivors of life's inevitable hard knocks.

But to put a label of "survivor" on contented couples and their well-adjusted children does not imply that unmarried people cannot be successful in many ways. Single and divorced people are increasingly accepted in modern society. Many of them are single by design, although increasing numbers — especially women — say they remain unmarried because they simply can't find a suitable mate. It is true that there aren't enough males to go around.

According to 1980 U.S. Census Bureau figures, the ratio of males to females at age twenty-two is about even, and it stays that way roughly until both sexes reach the age of twenty-nine. At thirty there is a jump to 102 unmarried men for 114 unmarried women, and from then on it's a male's market. By the time a woman is in her early forties, the ratio is 135 unmarried women per 100 unmarried men. Those men are often unwilling to hook up with women of their own age, who probably are financially successful, independent and difficult to please. Dr. Anna Grant, an Atlanta sociologist, says middle-aged men — if they want to marry at all — are looking for marriage partners who will pamper them at home and not bring their own career ambitions to bear on a relationship. This gives one answer to the question of why men of that age tend to marry women who are much younger than they and who are only mildly interested in worldly activities, if at all. Dr. Grant says bluntly that these men ignore mature, experienced potential marriage partners and "turn to women they can feel superior to."

More and more, this means forced singlehood for ambitious women who delayed marriage in favor of career development. They might marry men who are younger than they, as did some of the professional women I interviewed for this book. But it isn't easy to find a young man who is ready for marriage and unthreatened by an older, successful female. Journalist Maureen Downey, who recently conducted newspaper interviews of single career women on their marriage prospects, makes the point that today's educated, achieving women have a hard time finding males of any age who can accept and encourage their demands for full equality within marriage.

"In the past, women brought little history to a marriage," she writes. "Like clean blackboards, they waited for their husbands to scrawl in their futures, to add and subtract the sums of their lives. A career woman today is less flexible and compliant because she has invested more in her lifestyle and exercises control over her life."

Unmarried people, male and female, find ways to enjoy a solitary life. Many of them are at the top in their careers because they are free to pursue work with single-minded devotion. But singles may miss out on the full range of human emotion. Life for them can be terribly lonely. If single people have delayed marriage because of the inability to find Mr. or Mrs. Right, as they grow older they modify their expectations of what they demand in a spouse and find a more realistic partner. Those who avoid marrying because they think being single offers a more colorful lifestyle are often disappointed.

"When the glitter is gone," says Dr. Mendelson, "there is no one in their corner. Staying single, especially if you do it to avoid all the trouble of adjusting to marriage, is a bad trade-off. Unmarrieds and even non-parents sometimes maintain the illusion of youthfulness, but they grow old anyway — probably without ever having grown up."

Dr. Mendelson adds, "It is often the immature people who resist the growth of marriage, and the resistance costs them dearly. They are robbed of the deep inner wisdom of that growth, the peace of maturity, the real intimacy of stage-negotiation with a partner. Unmarrieds are not survivors in the same complete way that married people are, because unmarrieds can't tolerate emotional turmoil on an intimate level."

We all know people who seem so emotionally frail that they can be crushed by a misinterpreted glance, a seemingly harsh word or even an unexpected touch. The strength of these people seems fleeting.

They may get married, but their lives are marked with pain and the debris of many divorces.

We also know people who seem strong, secure, "all together," and who stay blissfully single. Perhaps they are very wise. They know that if they cannot have full success as happily married people, they can get by nicely on the partial success of career, friends and the accumulation of material wealth. For them, these are hassle-free attainments. It would be destructive to attempt marriage or parenthood and put themselves into what they inwardly know are no-win situations. Usually, it's not hard to construct a value system, with the support of peers and the increasing acceptance of a more liberal society, that says it's "better" to be single or childless. And for these people, it *is* better.

Robyn's Story

Robyn curls her tongue seductively around a scoop of fudge-swirl ice cream and nibbles playfully at the sides of the cone. She is in a small neighborhood luncheon spot — the kind of place with billowing lace curtains at the windows and earnest waiters who tell you their first names and recite the daily specials. While she enjoys the cone, Robyn also enjoys watching two young men in a nearby booth watch her. She is full-figured and stunning, and her provocative ice cream manners, plus the bold stare in her green eyes, say she is "available."

And she is. Robyn, in fact, is one of those rare creatures young men say they want but have so much trouble finding: a terrific looking female who is single and very happy to stay that way. She is a no-strings-attached woman. Robyn is thirty-seven years old, never married, and says without hesitation that marriage would be death for her.

"Being single is my way of surviving," she murmurs dreamily. All of her words come out in a purr of contentment, mingled with the barely audible rumble, underneath, of someone who knows exactly what she wants in life and has already come far in getting it. "I am a very happy person with my own business, my own in-town condo, and more boyfriends than I can fit into my schedule. I mean, to get married now would be the death of the beautiful and successful Robyn and a transformation to a Robyn I wouldn't care to be at all. I like my life just the way it is."

Robyn's talent agency books television commercials for stars — "personalities," as she calls them — and serves as professional casting director for actors and producers. Robyn also finds models, male and female, for people with jeans or cowboy hats to sell and who want an appealing body to show off their wares. The agency is Robyn's lifeline to much more than money, although it has supplied her with plenty of that. It is also the source of her many lovers, an endless supply of people she can call friends and a way of life that keeps her busy and excited without demanding commitment to one person or even to one career. "I'm the Jill-of-all-trades in there," she says of her agency. "I'm the head administrator, the person who screens the nice faces and asses for advertisers, the one who reviews the photos and looks at the ad copy. So who needs one man on the scene complicating my existence? I'm not looking for a deep relationship because I don't have the time or the room in my life for anyone to make demands on me."

Robyn's parents were moderately successful stage and screen actors who lived with her in a Los Angeles split-level, when they weren't off on location somewhere or doing a show-biz tour. Robyn says she had a nice childhood. She was raised by an indulgent nanny who liked men, booze and Robyn — in that order. The nanny never abused her and was actually a lot of fun; Robyn remembers plenty of circus popcorn, dancing lessons, French poodles and walks in the park. But she can't recall many childhood kisses or hugs. Her mom and dad would sweep her into their arms when they got home, but they were always tired after being away and would soon send Robyn back to her nanny. The nanny always came up with the idea for a shopping trip or a new toy to keep Robyn from nagging her parents for more attention.

Robyn says she knew what was going on, but the nanny's diversionary tactics always worked. After a while, she didn't notice much difference between the times mom and dad were home and when they were away.

Robyn grew into a woman with long red-brown curls that framed a ravishing face. People told her she was a knockout. Movie agents came to call. Lovesick boys wrote poems that said Robyn's eyes were like emeralds, her lips like rubies. She took a screen test, did very badly, and went to college instead, where she majored in public relations. After graduation she landed a job in Los Angeles with a top PR firm and met all the "biggies." She had lunch with such stars as Paul Newman, Cliff Robertson and Robert Redford. She made contacts. But she found California's market too hard to crack. She went to Nashville in 1970, when it was becoming a mecca for country-rock singers and other people who wanted a break in show biz. She opened her own agency there in 1971. By 1980, she was a millionaire.

"This life is right for me," she says with a satisfied sigh, dabbing at her lips to remove the sticky traces of ice cream. "I don't care that I'll never get married. I honestly wouldn't know how to go about *being* married, and having children is out of the question.

"Do I worry about being alone in my old age? No. Honestly, no. Most women wind up being alone anyway, either because their husbands die first or because they get dumped for some young chickie who lures hubby away and gets him to feeling his oats again. I figure if I take good care of myself, I can have male companionship literally into old age. And I have plenty of money, so there won't be fears of how to take care of myself.

I have been in love a couple of times. Sure. Listen, I'm a norma woman . . . at least in some ways. But being in love just didn translate into marriage for me. It meant good sex and a lot of fun and a steady companion until it got to be a drag. Then it was on to someone new. It's true; I am not the type to commit. I'm happy that way. Go sue me!"

Robyn laughs and reaches into her purse for a tiny silver makeup kit. She flips it open, surveys her face in the mirror and rolls on "Kiss Me Pink" lipstick. She snaps the kit shut and just before tossing it back into her purse, she leans forward with a big-toothed smile and whispers, "Look. Those guys still have their eyes glued to me. Their ice cream is melting. Isn't that funny?"

Robyn, the woman who has it all, is functioning just fine despite what I'd call a vacuum, an emptiness, in her life. She has no capacity for intimacy. Her glamorous mom and dad, so wrapped up in themselves and their bright-light careers, had little energy or inclination to act as parents for Robyn. What chance did their little girl have to develop a true sense of belonging, of feeling that she was a person who could be intimately connected to others? Today, despite her cheerful overlay of self-confidence, Robyn is insecure about forming a bond with another person. Her sense of self is permanently blurred. Who is she? "Not the type to commit." What is she? A self-described "Jill-of-all-trades." Those broad, nebulous definitions of self keep Robyn comfortable as a free-wheeling single. Ask her questions about trust, about devotion, and she'll cringe. Try to pin her down, and she slips away with a wink and a laugh. If Robyn knows what she's missing, she won't admit it . . . to herself or to anyone else.

Vera And Antonio

Vera says she went through three lonely but defiant years, right after her divorce at the age of twenty-five, when she acted just like Robyn. She calls it her "tough broad stage."

It was a time when Vera went into a funk about men and figured that true salvation lay in career success. She stopped writing free-lance articles for local magazines, bought herself some raised-letter stationery and sent out flyers to big corporations announcing her availability as a communications consultant for executives. She landed accounts with big firms such as Coca-Cola and Georgia Power. In a few months she had swapped her jeans and baggy T-shirts for dark suits and a leather briefcase. She acquired an office and a secretary. She cut her scraggly brown hair into a stylish pageboy and experimented with pancake makeup. Vera went from an annual freelance profit of about $6,000 per year to $24,000 for her first six months in business. And she hardened her heart against marrying, ever again.

"That first marriage was such a disaster," she says, wrapping her fingers around a ceramic coffee mug and letting the steam rise from the mug to warm her face. "When it ended, I went on a major crying jag. Gosh, I was such a kid. Married at twenty-two, divorced at twenty-five, tossed out into the world with nothing to show for my efforts. No children, no money, no man. I felt like a nothing, a failure. I started sleeping around with a lot of real losers, because I thought I was a loser, too.

"Then I got tired of the jeans-and-beads-scene, the drinking and drugs part of it especially, and figured I'd get into something that could at least give me material comfort. That's when I switched from freelance writing to consulting. I think my parents were instrumental in making me see that I was on a downhill slide with the other lifestyle, because I was using it as an excuse to hang around all day and get high at night. They didn't nag me into changing, though. They really helped me most by having me over to dinner a lot and letting me come back to the house whenever I felt like it. I saw how they were doing so well — my mom with her job as a department store manager and my dad still going strong as an engineer — and them being able to share the ups and downs together. They never said, 'Vera, shape up.' But after a while I felt like I wanted to be more like them, so I just did it."

As soon as Vera's business took off and she gained enough confidence to date again, she found herself looking for a very different man from the bearded, hazy-eyed youths she had bedded right after the divorce. She accepted the advances of the cleanshaven executives she met on the job, allowed them to pour wine in glitzy hotel restaurants, made sure each little "fling," as she called it, was cheery, under her control and brief. "I avoided intimacy," she says. "It had hurt me too much."

Antonio was the first man who invited — then insisted on — a more meaningful relationship. He was five years younger, just out of engineering school, and working as a junior partner in the same firm as Vera's dad. She first saw him on a sunny Sunday morning, looking lithe and trim in tennis shorts, caught up in practicing his swing on the front lawn of her parents' home. Antonio was waiting for Vera's dad to join him for what had become their ritual Sunday morning match.

"I didn't know who he was, but he looked young, so I didn't get flustered, thinking, 'Oh, darn, here I am in my ratty jogging outfit, just dropping in for a casual visit with my folks, and there's this guy who's going to see me all sweaty and everything.'"

As she talks, Vera and I are sitting on the patio of the two-bedroom house she now owns with Antonio. They are renovating it themselves on weekends, and the newly-painted white patio glitters in the morning sun. Antonio pokes his head in from the kitchen, where he is preparing another pot of coffee, and bellows teasingly, "I knew Vera thought I was too young to bother about!" Then he adds thoughtfully, "Yeah, and that's what probably made me like her. That day we met, if she had been in a suit of armor, like she usually was in those days, I'd have been scared off. You could say I met her when she was in a vulnerable moment."

Antonio steps gingerly onto the patio carrying a tray jammed with the still-bubbling coffeepot, a tower of mugs, napkins, spoons, and a huge pile of honeybuns. He makes it to a side table without spilling anything and triumphantly plops down the tray, grinning at his wife. He and Vera have been married almost a year. Already they have adjusted to the gentle seesaw of healthy married life, opening themselves to the shared emotional ups and downs and the increasing intimacy that will enable them to grow.

"I was sort of untouched in life, compared to Vera," Antonio admits. He has a round, boyish face, a mop of curly black hair and an endearing grin that seems to underscore his opinion that life is pretty good for him. "Vera had been hurt by her first marriage, and she was down on love, so to speak. I wasn't. I'd had a few relationships, especially one when I was in college, and I lived with a very nice girl for eight months. But I don't think I was ever willing to spend the rest of my life with anyone until I met Vera. She needed me, but she wasn't helpless. That was an appealing combination. I was really attracted. And in my family, when you like somebody very much, you get to know them, and if it works out you get married. I never considered anything less.''

Antonio's father immigrated from Italy to America in 1938. He got a job as waiter in an Italian restaurant in downtown Chicago, married the dark-eyed daughter of his Italian boss and inherited the restaurant with her when the old man died. Antonio was the last of five sons, all of whom helped poppa in the restaurant as they were growing up. "We were a big, noisy, full-of-fun family," Antonio says happily. "Sure, us boys had fights; one time I dumped a plate of hot meat sauce on my big brother because he was teasing me. Mama made me clean up the floor and wash my brother's shirt. Then she kissed me and said the next time I threw meat sauce around, try and do it after it gets cold! Poppa really roared when he heard that. He told me, 'Listen to what she says, she's a smart woman.' We were together a lot as a family, all busy with the restaurant, and I grew up with a nice warm feeling that marriage and family life was the only thing that could make a person really happy.''

Vera laughs, although this is not the first time she has heard Antonio's meat sauce story. She says it represents the sort of jovial, relaxed family life she would like to build with her husband. Vera and Antonio are in a good stage. After an initial rejection of intimacy resulting from her first, failed marriage, Vera is opening up. Her contribution to Antonio is her response to his gentle demand for commitment; she is giving him the gratification of feeling that he has made a major difference in her life. Antonio's gift to Vera is his enthusiastic assumption, based on a secure childhood, that they can and will be happily married. Although Antonio had to draw it out of her, Vera always had the capacity for intimacy because the rewarding marriage of her parents supplied her with a good foundation for personal growth and an example of how that growth could continue through marriage. Antonio's lusty childhood gave him plenty of emotional fuel to keep a relationship energized.

By turning away from the single life in favor of marriage to Antonio, says Vera, "I realize now that I was saying no to being closed up inside and yes to trusting and sharing and making room emotionally for another person in my life. We plan to have children, so I will be making a lot more room. I can see now how being married opens you up to really meaningful lifelong relationships with a lot of other people."

3

A Triumph of Change
Over Fear: An Overview

The seven stages of marriage have definite characteristics.

Stage One: FANTASY TIME (years one to three) is when you think everything about your new mate is wonderful . . . and if it isn't, his or her faults are "cute" rather than annoying. This foggy stage of young marriage is commonly known as the "honeymoon period."

Stage Two: COMPROMISE (years two to seven) is the couple's first encounter with mutual disappointment. You realize that you are, indeed, annoyed or hurt by certain of your spouse's traits or habits. This is a dangerous time, when many marriages dissolve in divorce. You begin negotiations aimed at persuading the spouse to change, and you promise to make changes of your own in return.

Stage Three: REALITY STRUGGLES (years five to ten) brings the realization that while some compromises may stick, you and your spouse aren't going to change much at all. You must force yourself to understand and accept the other person's limitations. The reality is that he or she cannot live up to your ideal. More permanent bonding takes place here, often produced by having children and further combining finances.

Stage Four: DECISIONS (years ten to fifteen) comes right after a person accepts reality... and doesn't like it very much. Now that you know the partner's bad points are here to stay, can you honestly say his or her *good* points make up for them? Can *you* change enough to cope with those bad points so they don't interfere with the continued growth of the marriage?

Stage Five: SEPARATION (years twelve to seventeen) often seems like the only option when you can't make up your mind to cope... or to flee and perhaps divorce. Separation could mean living apart for a while or living together but feeling aloof and alienated from one another. This stage, perhaps the most painful point on the Marriage Map, ends when couples start talking about specific ways to alter their lives so they can remain married. There is great relief in knowing the other person cares enough to make the effort of such discussion.

Stage Six: TOGETHER AGAIN (years seventeen to twenty) begins when you realize that despite what may be some irreconcilable differences, you *want* to stay married. The commitment is not only to one another but to the concept of preserving and enhancing your growth as a couple — no matter what. People in this stage usually stop thinking or talking about divorce. It is no longer an option for them.

Stage Seven: NEW FREEDOM (years twenty to twenty-five and beyond) is a release from the pressures of making up and trying to fit comfortably into the new emotional lifestyle you have created with your spouse. Now the relationship flows quite naturally. People stop wondering what the husband or wife is thinking and stop trying so hard to please. It really doesn't matter, because you are — at last — fully accepted and accepting. This is a time of surging personal growth. Both partners are free to explore new ways of fulfilling themselves, instead of pouring so much energy into the marriage. The New Freedom marks what many people consider the beginning of the best years of marriage.

ONGOING GROWTH continues the expansion of personal horizons within a marriage that has successfully gone through all the stages. Ongoing Growth is not a stage itself, because it has no end. It is the rich, ripe reward for growing together while remaining enough of an individual to grow separately as well.

No Skipping Allowed

These seven stages follow a fixed sequence, progressing in tight order like acts in a play. Some people claim, at first, to have skipped one or two stages. But later, when they think it over, they usually decide the stage slipped by unnoticed at the time because it was brief, relatively trouble-free, or because it was overshadowed by disturbing events outside the marriage, such as the death of a parent.

Because the stages must progress in an orderly march toward maturity, it doesn't matter how old a person is at the time of marriage or how many times he or she has been married. For people who marry late — in their thirties or forties — for the first time, the initial stages often zip by until they catch up with people who married at the more average age of twenty-three or so. Then they progress at a normal pace. People in second or third marriages also may go through the stages quickly until they reach the point at which their previous marriages dissolved. Then they, too, slow down and continue the pattern with their new partners.

Some people can reach only a certain point in marriage because they keep faltering at the same stage with each new partner. A tall, platinum-haired artist, married three times, says each of her marriages went through the same stages, only faster than the time before: sexual attraction, a period of cooling off, being disillusioned, trying to work things out, getting exhausted and needing separation, and a final breakup. After we talked for a while, this woman decided she is stuck on the idea of working things out. It's so hard, she complains. Why? Well, she really doesn't love any man; she just loves the idea of love. She grins broadly when she says this, as if it is a deep secret she has shared with herself for a long time, and it is a relief to admit it, at last, to somebody else. She never tried hard enough to make any marriage work, because she really didn't want to be married at all. Now she has a new lover every year and rushes through the same stages with them.

But for people who want to be married, the important component in healthy unions is change that leads not to divorce but to greater intimacy. That is the premise of this book; the "map" is the route along which such changes take place.

It is impossible to remain at a fixed point in any healthy marriage. People grow into evolutionary phases of the relationship and then almost immediately begin the process of growing out. If we fear change and try to ignore the ebb and flow of marital stages, turning away from the idea of successive periods of adult growth, we are depending almost entirely on luck to keep a marriage alive. If a couple is very mature, very flexible, or not too fussy about the quality of their marriage, luck might see them through. But it doesn't happen often.

"My wife was very sweet when I married her right out of high school," a thirty-year-old electrician told me. "Then, I wouldn't say she turned bitchy, but she started sort of trying to do things differently. She didn't like it that I wanted to keep my own hours. You know — working overtime, then going out with the guys when I felt like it, or going to the races or something on weekends. She wanted me to live by a schedule. But I never lived like that. She wanted me to change, and I didn't want to. I was comfortable like I was. We had some pretty bad fights, starting about the third year of our marriage. I took it for about a year, and then I felt like, 'Well, if she can't let things stay like they are, screw it.' We got divorced a month after our fourth anniversary."

A wife and husband also can be in different stages. They don't necessarily develop in the marriage at the same speed, although if one spouse is too far behind or ahead of the other, there is an uncomfortable feeling of being "out of sync." If that feeling drags on, it means trouble.

The stages are often subtle, and they overlap. That's why it is difficult to pinpoint a specific beginning or end for each stage. Many stages creep up, grow, then slide away into the next stage. The early years — when the urge to marry might be overpowering — is an exception. So is Separation; that stage can come on like a thunderbolt, and when it leaves there is a distinct rush of gratitude. But most of the other stages wash up and over couples like a wave. It might be clumsy, but it has a distinct and individualized beat. After a while, people can sense the pulsing rhythms.

No stage of marriage just comes, then collapses, and is never seen again. It hovers, ghost-like, around the fringes of marriage and can erupt in times of crisis. And while most stages seem to last from three to five years, many people told me they experienced a stage (such as Separation) for only weeks or months. One couple went crashing through *all* the stages in eight months, ending with an explosive divorce. A thirty-three-year-old art critic told me the stages in her marriage last only from six months to two years, because that is how often she and her husband change the way they look at the world. Their separation came after three years of marriage, because they were both eager to buckle down to a lifelong commitment to one another or find somebody else.

"The shit really hit the fan just as we were coming out of the first, intense, 'got-to-have-you' stage of being madly in love," she says wryly. "It was a real shock to start into the disappointments and compromises. We got panicky and separated. I think because we were both very aware of ourselves and our marriage, very analysis-oriented, we were able to see what was going on and get back together again."

This woman's husband is a psychiatrist. "We are constantly analyzing ourselves, each other and our marriage," he says. "It's an ongoing process in an evolving relationship."

"Yeah, and if you don't change, it's all over, because there's nothing worse than the living death of a marriage where all the growth, all the excitement is gone," adds his wife.

No one stage is more or less important than the others. Some stages are definitely more fun, such as Fantasy Time and Together

Again, but each is vital to a healthy marriage. You can get stuck in a stage and stay there because you're afraid to progress and make an even deeper commitment. At that point the marriage will stop growing. It may even end. But to stay solidly married, people have to push through each stage, no matter how frightened they may be.

A Life All Their Own

Some psychologists say the stages of marriage are formed around crises, such as the loss of a job, moving from one city to the next, or the strain imposed by the birth of a child. If you're hovering on the brink of a stage, a crisis can certainly push you over. But plenty of people I interviewed never changed jobs or cities, had no children, and the stages came anyway.

This points to the unnerving conclusion that the stages of marriage have a life all their own. We just haven't explored them until now; and we've had no names for the good and the bad times. We don't know what to call ourselves when we enter a stage, or how to describe the process when we're bawling our eyes out because the whole thing has become so confusing.

Why are things so bad for some people and so great for others? Don't they know there is a better way? Perhaps people who have less than satisfying marriages stay that way because they are intoxicated by the power marriage gives them to make another person happy or unhappy. There is an odd stability in conflict. As long as you fight with your husband or wife, you are actively *engaged* in a marriage. It might be hell, but at least you know you're not alone. That's how some marriages get bogged down in a difficult stage. If these couples were more aware of the good times that could lie ahead, I believe it would help propel them into a better stage.

It is not unusual or damaging to get stuck in a stage now and then, as long as a couple isn't entrenched for too long. Some people become determined to succeed when this happens. They pull harder and get through. Others give up and storm out the door. That's easy to do, especially when it seems that everyone else is getting divorced instead of working hard on the marriages they have.

Silence and a feeling of isolation from others make the stages more difficult. Married people need to share their experiences. Practically everybody who has been through at least one stage wants to talk about it, to compare notes, to find out if they're the only couple struggling this way. But discussion with friends isn't always enough. The people I interviewed said it would have been much easier to go through each stage if they had had some reliable help in charting the probable times of pain and pleasure.

"Figuring it out yourself is so damned lonely," says a thirty-two-year-old medical technician who has been married five years. She lives with her husband and young son in Michigan, has a lot of friends, and isn't afraid to discuss marriage with them. But she says friends don't help much. They're usually the same age, in the same stage, and having confusions of their own. She says, "Friends can sympathize, but they're just as dumb as you are in knowing what to expect down the line. The hardest part of marriage, for me, is trying to decide when to let go of certain habits so my husband and I can progress to something better. For example, I would like to experiment with giving him more freedom so I can take more freedom for myself. We're used to checking in with each other before we make any plans; it's a way of asking for permission, like, 'Can I eat out with my female friends tonight?' I'm ready to go on to, 'I'm eating out with my friends tonight, and I'll be home late.' I sense that would be a step toward another kind of relationship. But it also scares me. There's a certain security in being tied down and in keeping my husband the same way. I'm not sure I want to let go of that."

The Terror Of Letting Go

Letting go, in the way described by this young wife, can evoke growth-related fears that have nagged silently at us since childhood. Psychologists have a name for the terror that accompanies giving up relationships or behavior patterns that are no longer suitable for a person's age or stage in life. It is called *separation anxiety*.

The story of healthy human development, from birth to death, is a story of separation and one's triumphant battle over separation anxiety. As people mature, they trade childish pursuits and fantasies for adult occupations and a more realistic grasp of the workings of the world. Those types of tradeoffs — which are essential to survival — do cause stress. But usually the major traumas of growth are associated not with separating from ideas and ways of acting but from people.

When we're children, we fight hard to hang on to people who are meaningful in our lives because we think we cannot live without them. We are dependent, and the desire to cling to others for safety lasts long after we've already made our own lifestyle decisions and are searching for ways to carry them out. That's what makes adolescence so tough. We must separate from our parents, and we know we can. Still, it's scary. And it's hard to decide on the right time to shift responsibility for survival from their shoulders to our own.

Said a frail-looking blonde housewife, "I still think that if I get sick or I get into any trouble, like if Frank and I run out of money, my parents will save me. They're my safety net. I don't feel safe by myself. I don't even feel safe with Frank. I suspect this is keeping me immature. I'm twenty-five. What is the right age to stop depending on your parents? I don't know."

Gradually, most people shift those dependent feelings from parent to spouse and then to themselves. Under ideal circumstances, a person should feel strong as an individual *before* he or she marries. But according to the people I interviewed, this doesn't happen often. First marriages usually take place before a young man or woman has had time to develop a secure sense of self. So they trade mom and dad for husband or wife, and like the blonde housewife, they spend a lot of time asking themselves, "When should I stop being so dependent?"

It may take a long time to find the answer. Every married person has gnawing insecurities about dependence versus independence in the relationship. The urge to cling to the spouse for safety is always playing tug-of-war with the urge to separate and achieve independence within the marriage.

Separation first begins at birth, of course; it develops steadily through infancy and reaches an explosive point at about the age of three. At that time, the toddler matures from infant to child, as he subconsciously confronts what experts call "the separation individuation process." Successful negotiation of this process leads to the eventual development of a firm sense of identity.

The more secure a person is about his own identity, the easier it is for him or her to select a mate and tolerate individuality without hysteria. But if a person is unsure about his own identity, he will rely heavily on his mate to provide it for him. If his spouse tries to break away, perhaps even for something as simple as a night out with friends, he panics.

Psychoanalyst Dr. Ralph Klopper says this kind of smothering dependency is common in people who somehow failed, very early in life, to develop enough emotional distance between themselves and their mothers. He says the theory comes to life so often in the flesh and blood of his patients that it cannot be denied. Over and over again, says Dr. Klopper, people get into trouble in their marriages — or in being unable to find suitable partners — because they could not separate from a powerful mother when they were very young.

"Two things might happen to a person who is prevented from becoming individuated from the mothering figure," he says. "When he [or she] grows up and gets married, he might never feel secure enough to let his wife become a person on her own. It would be too threatening, because he feels that if his wife doesn't support him emotionally at every turn, he'll crumble. He will become listless, depressed, have a feeling of emptiness. These symptoms are a result of what he experiences as the painful loss of a vital support. If the wife gets tired of holding him up, he may divorce her and find a wife who *will* devote her life to little else but his comfort. He thinks the divorce is the first wife's fault; after all, she is the one who separated, right? So he'll go her one better. He'll finish the job with a total rejection, a divorce.

"The other thing that might happen is that such a person will shy away from marriage altogether. For the man or woman who rejects the warmth of marriage, something went very wrong during the separation individuation process. It was so tough to break away from mother that the person is left with a deep-seated aversion to getting too close to anyone, ever again. There is fear that they will be suffocated, that their wives or husbands will not let them be individuals. These people don't realize a marriage characterized by two autonomous individuals maximizes the potential of each person within the context of that marriage."

Most marriage books, and people who give advice about marriage, don't spend much time — if any — on the topic of autonomy within marriage. However, I view each stage in the Marriage Map as one more step toward separating emotionally from one's spouse so a person can become a full, whole individual on his or her own while still maintaining the warmth and intimacy of being married. Sex, money, communication, sharing and all the other oft-discussed aspects of a good marriage are important, in varying degrees, depending on each couple. But I think they will come naturally, as part of the friendship between a wife and husband. The real challenge in being a married person — the challenge so often overlooked — is in the process of separating from a spouse. And healthy separation is the key to success in every stage.

Mitchell's Story

Forty-one-year-old Mitchell is a man who interprets autonomy and separation not as a process but as an end . . . the end to his twenty-year marriage.

Mitchell is a tall, thin physician who says he has been a hard worker, a devoted father and a "damned good" husband. His divorce is so recent that there is still a pale strip of skin around his left index finger. He is sitting in an Atlanta singles bar, his long legs wrapped around a chrome and leather stool.

Mitchell has a boyish, craggy face topped by a surprising thatch of steely-white hair. He jokes grimly that his hair was black before the divorce; aggravation turned it prematurely grey. His conversation is pocked with such jokes, each announcing his bitterness over a divorce he says he didn't want but had to carry through.

Mitchell's wife, also forty-one years old, told him one day a few months ago that the law degree she had earned was not merely for adornment. She had been offered a job in one of the city's top law firms and was going to take it. Despite Mitchell's stunned expressions and angry demands that the job must not be accepted, because he feared it would put him in a No. 2 spot in her life, Mitchell's wife became a practicing lawyer. Five months later, says Mitchell, they were divorced.

"I simply could not get used to the idea that my wife was going to take that damned degree of hers and *use* it. She was going to be a lawyer. I never thought it would actually happen. We both had a good setup, and just like I said she would, she ruined it. Before this happened, she was always there when I needed her. But when I wasn't around, her time was her own. If she wanted a job so badly, why didn't she do something part-time? We sure had enough money. Her needs were all being met, for chrissake!"

Mitchell's anger seems to bubble up from his chest, and he is gasping for air. A tiny bead of sweat seeps from one of his sideburns and trickles down the side of his face. He wipes it away with a paper napkin, then crumples the napkin in his hand and starts shredding it, bit by bit, as he talks.

"My world was shattered. I mean, my wife just turned my image of her inside-out. When we got married, she was a loving, responsive, caring wife who always had a hot meal waiting for me and the kids. But she certainly was no dummy. She had ideas. She went to school. She could hold a conversation with the best of 'em. Everything was wonderful, and it stayed that way for almost twenty years.

"And then the kids got into high school, and she tells me it's time for a change in her life, too. She's going to take a job in a law firm, she's going to have some influence in politics, she's going to look into the judicial system. Does she think she'll change the damned world? And at *my* expense?

"Well, I just couldn't handle it. I just refused to take a back seat to her damned career. So we got divorced. She changed all the rules. She deserted me. Man, it kills me."

Mitchell calls to the bartender and orders a Black Russian. Talking about marriage depresses him, he says. He just feels so bad. He clutches the damp stem of his glass and mutters angrily about how women have gone too far these days, overturning the apple carts of a lot of faithful husbands like him.

But he will get even. He is already dating. Mitchell vows to find another woman — cuter and younger — who will treat him right. Not a "deserter," like his ex-wife. How dare she pull away from him like that!

Mitchell says his wife insists she didn't want divorce. When I telephone her for an interview a few days later, her voice quivers and she begs off; the pain is too fresh to re-examine. She will say, however, that she still loves Mitchell. "All I wanted to do was to be my own person a little bit more," she adds sadly.

Later, Mitchell ponders his ex-wife's claims. "She can *say* she didn't mean to break up the marriage, but I know better," he concludes grimly. "I know rejection when I see it."

Some Astonishing Patterns

Author Robin Morgan, who looks at some of marriage's inevitable hurdles in her book *The Anatomy of Freedom: Feminism, Physics, and Global Politics*, says she's astonished by the discovery that couples play out essentially the same patterns when a woman married to a traditionally-thinking man attempts to equalize their marriage. Many of these men are so threatened by separation that they seem to prefer divorce. It is an acting-out of the old dramatic saga where the lover kills his woman rather than let her desert him, crying, "I'd rather see you dead than let you leave me!"

Some people do go crazy and actually commit murder when their loved ones attempt separation. We read about these fatal affairs in the daily newspapers. But in Mitchell's case, the "death" is divorce.

The fiery passions of the spouse who imagines himself abandoned when confronted by separation are far more understandable in light of Dr. Klopper's explanation of what might have happened to these people when they were very small. Never having become individuals, or "full people" in their own right, the Mitchells of the world cannot face what they think might be the loss of the mate who makes them whole. If Mitchell's wife had gone further in reassuring him, or if Mitchell had not been so hasty in acting out his fears through divorce, perhaps he could have discovered that her kind of separation would lead to a far more rewarding and intimate relationship.

Intimacy and separation don't sound as if they go together. But in marriage, they are essential emotional twins. People need both. There is a great parallel between individual growth (separation) and growth within a marriage (intimacy).

When children are successful at becoming what Dr. Klopper calls "individuated," they no longer find it necessary to cling to mother. They have matured to the point where mom's physical presence isn't their only stability in the world; at individuation, babies can carry a mental image of mom around with them as they explore. This is what makes it possible for a three-year-old to go alone into the next room, or even down the block, without panicking because mother isn't at his side. The child now trusts that mom will be there when he returns. He doesn't have to physically hold on.

The ability of a child to form a mental picture of his beloved parent, and to use that picture as security instead of the real thing, is sometimes called the *holding introject*. It is critical to maturity. In the first months of marriage, we may cling to our new mates in the same way we clutched mother, relying now on our spouse to provide her kind of warmth, nourishment and stability. That's the prime reason newlyweds are always touching one another (it's more emotional than sexual) and get uncomfortable if one of them leaves the room. But if they have gone through a successful individuating process in early life, the young married couple soon will be able to repeat the miracle of the holding introject. It then becomes okay to leave one's spouse and pursue interests of one's own, because it is possible to carry his or her image subconsciously within one's brain. We're no longer afraid the beloved will abandon us the minute we avert our eyes.

When married people are strong individuals, they will begin the normal process of separating almost at once. Even on the honeymoon, these people have no fears about doing their own thing. They trust their mates to welcome them back after brief periods of absence; and the mates, if they are healthy, too, aren't concerned or fearful about being alone. At each new stage in the marriage, such people feel a growing freedom to learn, expand their personal horizons and thus mature. They don't nag, whine or get into fights where they scream, "How *could* you go without me?" or, "If you loved me, you'd stay home!" When they have reasonable and legitimate things to do alone or with other people, they leave without guilt...and return with pleasure. Then husband and wife share information and feelings about their separate experiences. This exchange, possibly over dinner or while cuddling in bed, leads to more intimacy.

Two Chicago physicians, both in their early thirties, told me their marriage is rewarding despite schedules that prohibit them from being together frequently during the week and rarely for more than one full day on weekends.

"I don't mind because I love my work," said the wife, "and frankly, it's a pleasure to come home to an empty house after a full day and just put up my feet and not have to make conversation. When we are together, Jeff and I have a lot of fun, but I also have fun being by myself."

"She's more independent than me," the husband admitted. "I feel myself getting angry if more than one day goes by when we can't have dinner together. But I try to remind myself that this kind of life was my choice; I am very happy being a doctor, and if this is the sacrifice it takes...well...I knew and she knew what we were getting into. Sometimes I have fantasies that she quits to stay home for me. But I don't think I'd really want that. No...this is reality. I'll take it like it is. I feel very close to my wife when we do see each other, because we have a lot to talk about, and we fill each other in on every detail of what happened during the time we were apart. Then we usually have sex."

A lot of people interviewed for this book linked the sharing of intimate conversation with the sharing of physical intimacy. And when people couldn't or wouldn't talk, sex was infrequent and joyless.

A beautiful thirty-year-old Connecticut lawyer says she rarely told her husband about her innermost thoughts and concerns. Their sex life was a disaster. When we talked, she had been divorced for two weeks following a seven-year marriage.

"We really got married because our parents were best friends, and they had prayed for it, and we had dated since we were kids... and... well, you know how it is. You kind of get in deep before you realize it.

"We were both very good-looking. People, our parents especially, were always saying we made the perfect couple. So we got married. Then everybody looked at me and saw a great-looking woman and they looked at him and saw this handsome man, and I guess they figured, Wow, this couple must really have a fabulous sex life! But in reality we had almost none. Despite his physical looks, I couldn't get very sexually interested in my husband. And the physical distance between us underscored an emotional chasm.

"I thought I could overcome this. But I think now that if you can't be best friends, you can't be lovers, either. I would rather fight, then make up and have sex than just not talk at all."

According to David and Vera Mace, an older married couple who in 1974 wrote *We Can Have Better Marriages,* the way to get happily through the marriage stages is by sharing conflict as well as intimacy. Having a fight isn't much fun, but the Maces say it can't be helped. The trick is to realize that some confict may be part of each marital sequence and that fighting often helps people to better understand their partners. That way, problems have less chance of festering and sending out hostile fumes to poison the relationship. But newlyweds, especially, hate the idea of fighting.

"The moonstruck young couple, beginning their life together, are appalled when conflict raises its ugly head," writes the Maces. "It seems to them that some sinister force from the outside has invaded their relationship and is threatening to destroy their love. Not having been warned to expect this to happen, they panic and make every effort to evade and suppress it.

"What they *should* be told is that conflict, far from being a hostile invader from outside, is in fact an integral part of a healthy marriage relationship. Indeed, it provides the essential information the couple needs for the sequential growth of their marriage; and if they suppress it, they are actually denying themselves the chance to deepen their involvement."

Only one couple told me they refused to fight. At first it sounded like a charming idea. But when I saw them, this couple provided a perfect example of how a marriage gets mummified if you can't trust yourself or your spouse to withstand the battering of disagreements and gradual separation.

Rita And Howard

Rita and Howard, who are both high school math teachers living in a New York City apartment, just celebrated their thirty-third wedding anniversary. Except for a brief tiff long ago over whether to buy a new dining room table, Rita and Howard *never* had a fight.

"We're just like one person," Howard says. "We have the same ideals and the same outlook on life. Why, there are times I even think we have the same exact thoughts."

Howard is curled on the floor of his book-stuffed living room. He has just finished frying doughnuts in a wobbly pan, and the sweet, sticky aroma is wafting from the tiny kitchen into the room where we sit. He nibbles a doughnut, likes it, and bolts it down, immediately reaching for another. He holds out the tray in his pudgy, ink-stained hands and says, "Try one. They're great. Just *try* one!"

A one-eyed cat is dozing fitfully at Howard's feet, its pink snout resting precariously just at the tip of his toes. Rita is sitting on the couch above Howard. Her naked, blue-veined thigh is pressed against her husband's shoulder. She is wearing wrinkled shorts, even though it is a chilly fall day in Manhattan. People scurry by, clad in overcoats, in the street ten stories below. The apartment is stuffy, the furniture threadbare and sparse. The books, records and even the art hanging lopsided on the cracked walls are all on loan from the nearby 42nd Street Library. Howard and Rita do not like to think of themselves as poor; Howard calls it "living in a position so as to be very aware of expenses." It has to be that way, he says, because he and Rita teach in ghetto schools, and the pay isn't so hot. Howard didn't want to be a math teacher, but he drifted into the profession because it gives him lots of time with Rita.

"We do everything together. We each have given up our own ambitions in life pretty much to accommodate the other. I had some thoughts about going into law, but she was a math teacher, so that's what I am. I don't regret it. She and I get long vacations together. We have the same hours, and we can walk back and forth from school together every day."

Howard goes on for some time, recounting all of the things he and Rita have given up so they could preserve their togetherness. More money is one of those things. So is an independent view of how to face the world; Howard and Rita face it together, together, together. They are both Democrats. They are now both staunch Catholics, although Rita was Jewish before she met Howard. She decided that having two religions in one family would bring about conflict. So she converted to her husband's religion, because "he was more deeply into that sort of thing." She also cut her long auburn hair, which she once displayed proudly in cascading curls. "Howard likes it short," she says sweetly, "so now I wear it short."

Howard and Rita never had a fight because they are terrified of conflict. They maintain stability only by avoiding any show of independence or self-assertion that might annoy each other. And they have avoided fights so often — and so well — that it is by now a deeply ingrained behavior pattern, insuring them a highly dependent but conflict-free marriage. They have become clones of one another, avoiding arguments through a long marriage and the raising of a son and daughter who are also very bland, compromising, I'll-do-any-thing-to-please sort of people.

"It is foolish to fight," Rita says flatly. She briefly exchanges a reassuring glance with Howard, who pats her knee and urges another doughnut on her. At first she shakes her head no. She is already overweight. But Howard insists. Rita takes the doughnut and bites around the edges, licking her fingers as she nibbles. Howard slides the plate of doughnuts in my direction and pouts with rejection when I refuse. Then he reaches forward and takes a particularly large doughnut for himself, breaks it in two and hands half to Rita. She sighs and accepts it.

"Our little spat over the buying of the dining room table was nothing," Rita goes on. "I remember it so clearly because it was our only fight, you see. It happened when we had been married... oh... about five years. Five years is right, isn't it, Howard?"

"No. More like six or seven years."

"Yes. It was six or seven years." Rita smiles, having found the truth through Howard, and gulps down her half of the big doughnut. "Anyway, I wanted a new table because the old one was cracked. Of course, it was a big expense, but I was willing to spend the money."

"I wasn't," says Howard.

"We went around a bit about it. Oh, it was nothing very bad. No screaming or anything like that. But Howard and I were mad at each other, and I just *hated* that feeling. I couldn't stand it. It made me feel as if the whole world was falling apart. Then I realized nothing, absolutely nothing, was worth feeling that bad. So I told Howard to forget about the table. Period. We never had another fight after that."

Rita says she doesn't think Howard controls her. He just has a lot of common sense. He often listens to her advice ("Yes, indeed," says Howard), and the marriage is pretty much a two-way street. Life is very simple for them, and there's nothing much to fight about.

It is a brief, pleasant interview. Howard is cooperative and charmingly scruffy. Rita, equally relaxed about her personal appearance and the condition of their well-worn apartment, has a personality as comfortable and as yielding as a goose-feather pillow. They are insulated by their relationship against much of life's storm and thunder. Even their cat is contentedly half-blind, happy to doze through life at Howard's feet. After about an hour, we all run out of things to say. Howard is yawning, and Rita fights to keep from slumping sleepily against the sofa cushions. When I leave, the cat disturbs herself long enough to slink forward a few feet and lick the last crumbs from the empty plate of doughnuts.

If Howard and Rita enjoy burying their individuality in favor of a seemingly faultless marriage, so what? The marriage works well for them. They are comfortable. We can look at them when we're in a rough spot in our own marriages and be envious. But we can't learn anything positive about a vital marriage from Howard and Rita. They can only teach us about avoidance, not creativity.

When you attach electrodes to the human heart and watch its movements on a screen, you can see great peaks and valleys on the screen if the heart is beating healthily. That is the same pattern you'll see in a vibrant marriage. It goes up and down, up and down. When you see a flat line on the screen, the person is dead. Just like Rita and Howard's marriage — a steady, no-hassle, flat line.

In the early stages of marriage, fighting seems to be a way of trying to gain control. Later it can become a learning experience, if couples can back off from the fight after a while and view it more objectively. Fighting also can help couples expand the room they have to grow as individuals within the relationship. It means separating while getting more and more involved with each new stage.

PART II

4

Stage One: FANTASY TIME
(Years One to Three)

"The marriage seems to be shaping me, rather than the other way around." — *a twenty-four-year-old lawyer, married one year.*

In the first stage of marriage, people think all their plans will work precisely. The "fantasy" of this chapter's title is partly in assuming that life does, indeed, turn out exactly as you dreamed it would.

Right after the wedding and up to about the third year of marriage, people concentrate heavily on specific ways to achieve long-nourished goals of career advancement, furnishing a home or apartment, purchasing a car and settling into a community. The young couple is consumed by the details of acquiring material goods and forging a common social identity. Few people make a conscious effort at this time to adjust to the concept of an evolving marriage; for the newlywed, all you need is love, and life's puzzle will arrange itself at your command.

Success in stage one is defined by many young people as a long staircase: They get to the top simply by taking it one step at a time.

People can't imagine complications at this innocent stage because their life experience is limited. Secure within the illusion that marriage provides an armor against failure, people in their late teens and early twenties rarely admit that their staircase might bend in unexpected directions. They cannot yet undersand that to a great extent it is the marriage itself which will outline the patterns of their lives.

"I felt like once I was married that was it, and I could devote all my energy to the law and to making partnership in my firm," a twenty-four-year-old California man told me. "Now our first anniversary is coming up. I've gone from feeling like my emotional life was settled to seeing that a marriage is not something that you just accomplish and then it's going to be the same from that time on. It's not like taking the bar exam. Once I passed that, I was a lawyer and would probably remain a lawyer forever. Marriage is much more complicated. It is demanding. I actually have to think about it, think of how I'm relating to my wife and how a fight with her churns me up inside in a way that losing a case, for example, never could get to me.

"The marriage seems to be shaping me, rather than the other way around."

The new partner — who is also "shaping" you — may begin displaying flaws, but the normal reaction at this stage of marriage is to deny them. That is another part of the fantasy: People refuse to look at problems within the marriage because that was not part of the plan. It is much easier to worry about getting a promotion or a good used Chevrolet. *Those* were challenges to be expected.

So if the new mate isn't exactly Mr. or Mrs. Perfect, you are quick to overlook grievances as merely annoying habits or problems that can be dealt with later. People push away the pain, consciously trying to dispel all doubts. And they blow their partner's good points out of proportion to justify the process.

This is a crucial defense mechanism for the newlywed which must take place during stage one of marriage. Because people marry a dream, it is unthinkable to wake up too soon. It is not in the best interests of a young married person to hang on to his fantasy for very long, but human nature compels us to try.

Nancy And Monty

When I visited them in Connecticut for an interview, Nancy and Monty had been married four months. Monty, twenty-four, has the swagger and assurance common to young American men who are well-nourished in childhood by generous parents and a social system which coaxes them into developing big dreams. Nancy, twenty-three, has dreams of her own, but they are not as secure, for they are less supported by an educational network of schools, churches and other institutions that in many parts of this nation still reserve real responsibilities, and thus real goal-planning, for males. Nancy and Monty typify two emotionally healthy people going through stage one, the Fantasy Time of marriage.

As I approach our meeting at Nancy and Monty's house site in the countryside, the whine of the buzz saw is deafening. Chunks of wood fall from the roof's skeleton, where Monty straddles a beam, his husky body outlined against a blue-gray summer sky. A fine mist of sawdust drifts down to where Nancy waits below, squinting up at the sun and calling to her husband.

"Turn off the saw!"

"What? I can't hear you!"

"Oh, silly! I said, TURN OFF THE SAW!"

At once the noise stops. Monty flips up his protective glasses, grins and waves and inches his way to the ground. Nancy watches him closely, almost quivering with pride and delight. She loves the way his muscles ripple, she says. She thinks he's *so* good-looking . . . even coated with grime, as he is now. She is even oddly charmed by the foolish mistakes Monty has made on this house: the purchase of lumber that turned out to be rotten, the lost application for a city sewer line, the miscalculation that cost them an extra $300 in bricks.

Nancy turns to me and says, "This is a lot of fun, building our own house. Oh, once in a while I get annoyed at Monty. He goes ahead and does things without asking me. And I find out later that we're in a mess, like with the bricks. But . . . well . . . that's okay. He's doing a wonderful job, don't you think?"

Monty bounces to the ground and strolls over to us. He shakes my hand and tries to kiss Nancy, pretending to smear her with sweat and sawdust. She fakes a grimace and playfully shoves him away. We find a shady spot for the interview and sit down, our legs stretched on the ground, our backs resting against a pile of sweet-smelling lumber.

Monty and Nancy say they couldn't wait to be interviewed. They have a *spectacular* marriage, Monty tells me. This is one in a million. Everyone should be this happy.

Nancy is an executive secretary in a Connecticut shipyard. She is a blonde twig of a woman who has never weighed more than ninety-eight pounds. Her mop-headed husband just got out of the Navy. He doesn't have a job; finishing the house is more exciting, he says, than being stuck in an office. Monty describes his building project with wide-eyed gusto, painting vivid mental pictures of the peaked roof, the bay windows in the den, the kitchen with built-in cabinets and a real brick floor.

"He is a dreamer," chuckles Nancy. Monty agrees. They have very little money now, and he has spent almost all of their savings on building materials for the house. He's handy, he says, but adds with a trembling grin that he never took on a big project like this before. Sure, it's a little scary, but so what? Nothing bad will happen. They can live on Nancy's salary for a while. When the house is finished, they will move in and start a family. They will all travel. Nancy will grow a garden, and he will buy her two fine white horses. What a lovely life it will be!

Monty insists he is one man who can make dreams come true. After the house is done, he's going to take a trip to Alaska. There he will find a job — just for a few months — driving a truck or working on the oil pipeline. A fortune can be made in that wild, howling land. He'll save his money, and when he comes back to Nancy, they'll be able to use it to furnish the house. In the meantime, Monty says he will see a place of majesty, maybe visit Eskimo villages, learn to cross-country ski....

"And fall in love with a moose," Nancy interjects with mock horror. There is a faint, faraway tone of impatience in her voice.

Monty looks at her, flashes a little-boy grin, and both of them erupt into laughter.

"I would never take advantage of a helpless moose," he says. "I'm a married man!"

They laugh again and fall into each other's arms, tussling briefly on the ground. They are newlyweds in love, full of energy, plans and sky-high expectations. Maybe some of their hopes will solidify into reality. Very slowly, Monty and Nancy will sort out the "real" from the "hoped-for" and learn to focus on an attainable future. Some of their fantasies will fade.

But that doesn't matter now. For the moment, they are nourishing themselves on the sweet nutriment of mutual affection. Later they will replace the fantasies of the first stage of marriage with the even more exciting challenges of real life together.

In the early days of marriage, both husband and wife assume their lives together are unique and permanent. When sociologists Philip Blumstein and Pepper Schwartz talked to newlyweds for a study on American couples, they found that young married people said their feelings of togetherness would last forever.

"The American tradition is to hope for the best, which means a lifetime of loyalty to and from one's marriage partner," say the sociologists. And part of that tradition is an obligation to share all resources. Blumstein and Schwartz note, "In traditional marriage, it is simply assumed that the couple will share almost everything, even if one or both partners is not really willing to do this."

When we have a chance to talk alone, Nancy tells me she didn't want to turn over all her savings to Monty because she was afraid he might squander it on building supplies. He is going on and on about constructing such a *grand* house, she says. It is not what she had in mind; her tastes run to smaller, less expensive dwellings. But before she knew what was happening, Nancy found herself enmeshed in a joint savings and checking account that quickly slipped from her control. She says with a shrug that she doesn't really mind, because Monty is using the money for something that will benefit them both. Then she adds, "But shouldn't he talk it over with me before he drains the account for more supplies?"

Nancy is already sensing the loss of self that plagues most newly-married people . . . especially women. This happens almost immediately after the honeymoon, experts say, and in some cases it happens right after the wedding ceremony. Often the process has its quiet beginnings during courtship. Monty has also surrendered part of his individuality with the marriage merger, but he is less aware of the event because for now, both he and Nancy have silently agreed to let Monty maintain control of the relationship. Later they will both recover their "lost selves," reassert their individuality in new ways and thus move into another form of personal and mutual maturity.

But for now the subtle loss of self, as shown by the way she voluntarily gave up control of her savings, is getting on Nancy's nerves. She may not know it consciously, but her overanxious smile and the flippant, almost sarcastic comments she makes when we talk about Monty's dreams show that her fantasies of eternal bliss with a perfect partner are slowly tarnishing. She is starting to fret at the way *their* dreams are so often expressed in terms of what Monty wants to do . . . and the way he assumes she will play a supporting role in all of this. Full of the bluster and strength of young manhood, Monty is racing joyfully into a future he perceives is his alone to shape. He plans to conquer the world on his own terms and manage at the same time to merge with Nancy in perfect union.

But Nancy is typical of the female's more realistic approach to the future, especially as it so often materializes for the married woman. She is slowly coming to grips with the notion that unless she fights hard to maintain her own outlook on life and engages in some emotional wrestling with her husband, merger with Monty will be achieved only at the cost of her own autonomy. He is already setting out plans — and attempting to carry them through — as a team leader, not as a team *member*.

Nancy is strong, however, and that strength is a victory flag for the future of any marriage. She does not wait long to voice disapproval if she feels it, and she is not afraid to gently demand that Monty pay attention to her point of view.

"I don't think we should spend any more money this month," she says.

"But I have to buy bricks for the patio!"

"Suppose we let the patio go for now. Can't you finish it later?"

"Well... yeah... okay. You're right, I guess."

Monty is flexible enough, even at this early stage, to rein in his self-centered enthusiams in favor of a more balanced partnership with Nancy. I can see his budding maturity in the way he is willing to listen to her doubts, think about them and make significant changes based on his wife's reasoning. When Nancy admits her ambivalence about Monty's withdrawal of their savings, Monty almost immediately promises to check with her before he spends any more money on supplies. Later Nancy questions the huge freezer space Monty is planning for the kitchen, and they compromise on a combination freezer-refrigerator. Monty and Nancy are enjoying their fantasy time, but neither one, it seems, will be swallowed by it.

Monty is Catholic. He met Nancy when his sister brought her to a party for the family's new priest; he didn't find out she was a Baptist until several days later. By that time, he says, it didn't matter. He was already in love. He found himself sending flowers, begging the young woman for a date every night, panicking at the thought of having to go back to his ship after leave and not seeing Nancy for several more months. When they did part, he says, he cried. On board ship he wrote to her every day, penning long, smudgy paragraphs in the dim light of his cramped bunk. He wrote of love and marriage and children. He promised to build a house for her with his own two hands. Monty says he was overcome by a forceful, mysterious urge to melt into Nancy's life. This urge is typical of the young person's need to replay his earliest instincts when he desperately tried to merge into mommy and daddy, seeking full security in them.

Like all of us, Monty wants the same things from his spouse that he once asked of his parents: keen emotional and physical gratification; the satisfaction of knowing at least one really understanding friend; the security of having a partner with whom he can challenge the world; and the feeling that he has found a soul mate. But it is the all-encompassing nature of these early urges that gets people in trouble. It makes newlyweds think, however subconsciously, that they really *can* find all this in another person. To Monty, his urges meant that Nancy was the hoped-for mate who could fill all his needs. In one of his passionate ship-to-shore letters, he proposed.

Nancy says she wasn't surprised. It was a swift courtship, but she was ready to get married. She had gone through college majoring in English, then took a job at the shipyard because her boss promised consistent raises and a chance to write all the public relations releases for the company. He kept both promises, and Nancy went ahead with her plan to create a position for herself as in-house public relations officer. She felt settled, secure in her job, and okay with herself as a person. Yet she was terribly lonely. In this little Connecticut town of Ledyard, where she lived in a rooming house, there were plenty of Navy men but nobody who attracted her as did Monty. The night she met him she went home, telephoned her parents in Hartford and told them, "I think I got lucky tonight. I met a man who is for real."

She was nervous about the wedding ceremony. Her mom and dad and Monty's parents met frequently, trying to work out the finances, the religious differences, a place to have the wedding, even the color of the tablecloths. The work seemed endless, but these gatherings carried with them the glow of real cooperation, and there was growing fondness between the two sets of parents. Monty and Nancy both told me their parents are warm, outgoing people whose attitude about nearly everything is, "We can work it out." They put their heads together over the kitchen table while Monty's mother unwrapped her delicious brownies, and Nancy's father kept the meetings fueled with brewed coffee laced with his favorite brandy.

After a while the meetings took on a festive air. Once the prospective newlyweds came home from the movies to find their parents laughing together and telling old stories. Monty recalls that his father rose from the chair, wrapped his arms around his son and declared, "You're getting a wife, we're getting some great new friends, and this is a damned good idea for everybody! We're all going to have a wonderful old-fashioned wedding."

Philip Kranz, an Atlanta clergyman, says religious ceremonies "with all the trimmings" are back in style now. He is a rabbi, but he knows priests and ministers who concur, saying the rebellious days of barefoot weddings are past. It also seems obvious to him, says Rabbi Kranz, that an openhearted, cooperative attitude on the part of the parents of the bride and groom goes far in contributing not only to the joy of the ceremony, but to an easier start for the young couple. Newlyweds have a far better chance for a successful, long-lasting marriage if they have had a good relationship with their parents and there is parental acceptance of the proposed son or daughter-in-law. One way to show such acceptance is in a lovingly planned and executed wedding ceremony.

"If the feelings are good all around between the sets of parents and the bride and the groom, people want to walk down the aisle with their parents these days," says Rabbi Kranz. "Five years ago, I couldn't have sold that notion if I had stood on my head. And this isn't going on just among Jewish people, because my Christian colleagues say the same thing. Lace and satin is in. White is back. The brides want veils and the grooms want to be in tails.

"I think it means a renewed dedication to the seriousness of marriage. I'm glad to see that young couples are crying at their own weddings. It means a lot to them again. They don't even want to write their own vows. Everything is going back to the traditional, the known, the tried-and-true. What it says for society is this: Marriage is important again."

Monty and Nancy wanted everything about their wedding to be very traditional. Nancy wore a flowing white gown. Monty was in a white dinner jacket with a single rosebud pinned to his lapel. Nancy's hands were shaking, and Monty gave her a yellow Valium tablet he got the day before from his doctor, who said the tranquilizer wouldn't hurt as long as they didn't ask for refills on the prescription. Between the two of them, Monty jokes, they could have finished the whole little bottle of Valium on their wedding night. They weren't afraid of one another, he says, but they had the jitters because it was all so important. It was *forever.*

They are determined, like their parents, to be the sort of people who work things out. Monty and Nancy both agree that their own concept of religion, plus strong family ties, preclude divorce as an option for them. Says Monty, "That means we'll go all the way to make it good."

Monty has already changed his life for Nancy's sake. He liked the Navy; his dad was a Navy man and his grandfather was, too. Perhaps he would have stayed in the service, pushing his way up through the ranks and retiring at forty, if he hadn't met Nancy. Here again is an example of marriage as a shaping force in one's life. Nancy wanted a man who wouldn't have to travel at the Navy's whim and who could be at her side when their babies were born. "So I quit," Monty says flatly. "I wasn't going to lose Nancy on account of the Navy. No question in my mind about which comes first. It's her."

At noon the three of us pile into Monty's truck and head for a sandwich shop in Ledyard. In the truck, Monty chatters on about the house. He says this is *his* project. He always dreamed of building his own home.

"Finish it quickly," says Nancy, "and get a job."

Monty glances at her, surprised at her seemingly sudden criticism. He sighs, pouts for a moment and repeats his plan of going to Alaska.

"That is unrealistic!" says Nancy. She looks pleadingly at me. "How can I feel secure like this? How can I be sure he can make a living at all? We both want children, and since I'm the one who has to get pregnant, I want to be sure that I can quit work and he can take care of me."

"I'll *always* take care of you," Monty insists. "Only let me do it in my own way."

"How?" Nancy wants to know.

"I don't know, yet," says Monty. "But somehow."

Nancy looks at me, shrugs, and says, "See what I mean?" Without waiting for an answer from me, Monty puts his arm around Nancy's shoulders and nods. "I do see what you mean," he tells her softly. "If the Alaska thing doesn't seem right to you, I'll give it some more thought. We can talk about it."

The wind comes up, blowing sawdust from the hood of the truck through the open window. We can feel the grit between our teeth. For the rest of the ride, Nancy and Monty unfold the story of two young people feeling their way through the first, rosy stage of marriage, with its heady mixture of extreme pleasure and impending pain. Doubts are creeping in and fears and confusions are dimly making themselves heard, but for the moment uncertainty flies away as easily as the wind transports the sawdust. In this early stage, Nancy and Monty cannot afford to see one another's flaws too clearly. They are not ready to cope with them.

Another reason newlyweds live in a time of fantasy is because they imagine their mates are perfect people and insist others must share that view. People in stage one react with hostility to any criticism of their partners from friends or family. The couple perceives itself as an isolated unit, apart from and in some cases pitted against the outside world.

If Monty buys a load of rotten lumber, Nancy thinks, "It's the lumberyard's fault." If Nancy displays a willingness to take three-hour lunches in order to drive to the house site with a picnic basket and tells her trusting boss that she was really running an errand for the company, Monty will excuse his wife's dishonesty as loyalty to him. Never mind that she is cheating her company, risking her job and doing something that Monty secretly feels is wrong. He forms a protective barrier and circles the "home camp" like a wagon train under siege, telling himself and others that such behavior is necessary because Nancy can't get as much time off as she'd like, so it is the restrictive lunchtime policy of her company that is responsible.

Newlyweds are quick to take their mate's side in any dispute without dwelling on the merits of the case. This is a throwback to childhood's loyalty to a parent who is seen as all-powerful and never wrong.

On the surface, of course, a person can be quite aware of his partner's annoying traits. Nancy and Monty joke about one another's "silly little habits." They stifle some appropriate anger now and then or let it leak out in minor squabbles. During our long interview, there is a harsh word or two, and from time to time Monty and Nancy engage in earnest but well-controlled discussions over differences of opinion.

By and large, however, newlyweds keep tight rein on their anger toward one another because they are unable to cope with a full-scale admission of their partner's unpleasant traits. This is another way in which love is "blind." To take a good look at your partner and unmask serious and probably permanent faults is far too much of a threat at this stage. It is easier to wish those faults away, force them out of your mind, and pretend that admiration surges unimpaired from your soul.

Deep down, people know this thin crust of utter approval is a lie, but they invent excuses to take care of the problem: The faults aren't that bad; they will go away in time; you can "cure" them (this is the fatal reasoning of the person who marries an alcoholic, for example, and tries to reform him); or the faults one perceives in a mate are really your own flaws, because you are a picky person.

My visit with Monty and Nancy is relaxed, and when we part there are hugs for everyone. So far, this young couple is doing well. Nancy and Monty are following the normal pattern of the first stage of marriage by avoiding overt clashes of will and temperament. We all learn this avoidance mechanism when we are very young. It is done by perfecting the subtle art of lying.

Acceptable Lies

In our vocabulary, the word *lying* carries an unpleasant connotation. But it is meant here as a constructive, necessary and normal form of denial. This is part of how we all cope with new events in our lives, absorb and attempt to master them, and thus mature. It is part of the process of stage one. Acceptable Lies start in stage one and continue throughout marriage.

One example of the process of forming and dispensing Acceptable Lies is the way a newly-married person denies his own needs in order to satisfy the spouse. He lies both to himself and to the loved person.

"I adore Chinese food," says the wife.

"Then let's go to a Chinese restaurant tonight!" the husband exclaims, dismissing his own desire to feast at home on fried chicken.

"I got us two tickets to the baseball game," he tells her with glee. And the wife forces a smile and shares a hard bench with her husband for endless innings, even though she is bored by spectator sports.

Such "lies," many of which are subconscious, are the way we all avoid endless fights over small matters — pleasing our spouses with a denial of our own urges to be selfish. Such denial lubricates the wheels of all human interaction and is often difficult to distinguish from compromise, which takes place in stage two. Compromise is far more deliberate and thought out and takes longer to achieve.

Injecting some lies into everyday life is a way we must all behave in order to get approval and love, both as a child and as an adult. In a good marriage, this type of denial will continue in modified form for a lifetime.

People learn to make *conscious* use of denial in marriage and thus employ Acceptable Lies. A medical researcher, married for fifteen years, told me that for a long time she was annoyed by her husband's pleas for her to be home every evening waiting for him so he didn't walk into an empty house. Finally she decided to admit her anger and confront her husband. His reaction surprised her.

"I know it's silly," he said sheepishly, "but I really feel much better if you're home. I don't know why."

The wife answered, "If it means that much to you, you don't have to explain why. I can't be home all the time, but I'll make a real effort to be here most of the time. You're worth it."

"Did you really mean that?" I asked her.

"Not exactly. I mean it's worth saying so, even if it's not quite true."

The wife still doesn't enjoy being home almost every evening for her husband, but she knows it is a small sacrifice for her and a major need for him, so she will comply. She will never tell her spouse that she sees her behavior as placative. Such information would probably inflict needless damage on her husband's ego. Withholding it is a form of Acceptable Lies.

People who have been married for many years are aware of Acceptable Lies and use them to keep the marriage as pleasant and as uncomplicated as possible. In a good marriage, Acceptable Lies eliminate some disagreements but are never used to mask major disputes. Pretending you want a baby just because he insists on becoming a father, for example, is such a major decision that it cannot be covered by Acceptable Lies. It must be discussed and hotly disputed, if necessary.

Newlyweds are usually unable to tell the difference between Acceptable Lies and major disputes. They either fight over almost everything in an attempt to find out who has the power in the family, or they go overboard in giving in to the spouse. As the couple becomes more experienced, both people learn to tell the sometimes subtle differences between Acceptable Lies and major disputes. Then the process becomes conscious and can be called compromise. At that point, the couple is ready for stage two of marriage.

Lies which make it easier for a person to gain approval — those involving denial of a spouse's faults — are a necessary part of early marriage. A young husband, whose wife is a journalist, told her he enjoyed reading the *New York Times* but confessed to me that, "I'd rather watch television, except I know she thinks TV is dumb." Some lies will disappear and be replaced by overt assertion of individual needs and wishes as each partner becomes more secure and independent. Other lies, such as deciding to be home when your husband arrives and never telling him it is inconvenient, come into play over the course of a lifetime. Each person learns to make conscious decisions about which lies to keep and which to discard, according to what makes him most comfortable within the marriage.

People who marry for the first time when they are older (past twenty-five) are quicker to detect faults in their mates and to make good use of Acceptable Lies. Still, they go through some of the same psychological phenomenon of hoping for perfection. This is also common among divorced people who swore they'd never fall for the same fantasy again. They *do* fall for it, tumbling willingly into the trap of believing that all of life's storms are over and they are riding the rainbow at last. These feelings are normal. They are part of what we call love: nature's grand, if somewhat muddled, reward for being human.

In the first few months after the wedding, especially in first marriages, couples usually exist in a happy fog. In addition to the leftover narcissism from childhood that makes you believe you can mold your mate like a willing lump of clay, you find bliss in acting like a lump yourself. The first impulse of the newlywed is to become immersed in the mate's personality, lifestyle and desires. Women are especially prone to give up their feelings of selfhood and try to submerge in the partner like grateful mermaids sinking into a warm pool.

Does Sally like to read? Then Sam rushes to renew his library card, even if he has not used it for five years. He's a runner? She dutifully buys a jogging suit and puffs alongside him. If the proud new husband knows that his wife likes to cook — but cannot — he will choke down the most abominable meals in order to please. And if her career plans are a bore, he will nevertheless listen intently and feel compelled to provide constructive guidance. It is all part of Acceptable Lies: partly conscious, partly subconscious, but normal and very necessary as the newlyweds shield themselves and one another, for a time, from realities that will require much adjustment in the next marriage stages.

The Myth Of Marriage

In the first stage, both partners try hard to carry out the myth that marriage is a perfect union between two imperfect people, who will be *made* perfect by the union. Before people get ready to compromise and start untangling the spiral of that myth, they have to come to grips with their own expectations about achieving perfection in anything. People who think of themselves as achievers tend to see life, when they are young, as a split between total success or total failure. And that's a dangerous part of the fantasy of early marriage . . . that unless it's perfect (a total success) you'll get divorced (a total failure).

John Petit, a marriage counselor who has been married three years, uses an example from his own marriage to illustrate how dangerous it can be to expect perfection in a spouse.

"You *do* expect it, even though you can consciously say, 'Oh, of course I don't think in terms of absolute perfection.' But you do. And you are disappointed when each little thing, each little experience, blows up in your face and leads to the inevitable conclusion that your marriage partner — like you — is a bundle of annoyances and contradictions as well as a source of great comfort and happiness.

"For example, Cindy always leaves her shoes in the living room. I'd just pick them up and carry them to the bedroom closet, to keep the living room neat. But I was getting more and more irritated. Why? Because, I have to admit, I expected *her* to keep the place tidy. And if she wasn't going to live up to my expectation, for a little while there I saw it as a great disaster.

"I truly felt the marriage might explode over Cindy's shoes. I wrestled with myself over whether or not to pick them up, if I should ask her to pick them up, if I should *demand* it, or if I should just let it go and get used to the idea of shoes in the living room.

"I recently decided just to pick up the shoes when they bother me and let it go other times. Whenever you get upset at your spouse in early marriage, it means an unmet expectation. And since you expect the sun and moon at this stage, it's only natural to think, consciously or otherwise, 'Hey, wait, I can't handle all these disappointments so soon. So I'm going to ignore them for now.' "

Pushing away problems may be a natural defense mechanism, but it is one that must not last long. Dr. H. Lee Hall, whose forty years of experience as a teacher and practitioner of psychoanalysis has given him rare insight into the coupling process, says the fantasies of early marriage are best dispelled quickly, before two people allow themselves to be crushed by unmet expectations.

"The first stage of marriage is actually a regression," he says. "It's a return to a very early phase of your childhood when you expect the same thing from your husband or wife as you did from mom or dad. What you expect is that this wonderful person, your new mate, will be perfect. You think, 'He will satisfy all my needs. Wow, are my troubles over now!' Newlyweds have lousy judgment."

Togetherness Is Dangerous

Locked away in their first apartment or cottage, playing with new wall-mounted coffee makers and electric woks, newlyweds are blissfully content to believe that the glow of perfection and togetherness will never fade. But, says Dr. Hall, togetherness in every aspect of life is a dangerous concept. It feeds the fantasy that you have merged into your spouse and that individual growth is no longer necessary . . . or perhaps even no longer possible. Although this is often a relaxing and comforting fantasy, it has to end quickly so individual differences in marriage can be used as fertilizer for each partner's separate growth.

"This idea of merging, of being one person through marriage, is a foolish notion pushed upon young people by society," says Dr. Hall. "You hear about it from novels and in movies and songs. It's part of our cultural fantasy life, like Mickey Mouse. 'Two hearts shall beat as one,' everyone tells you. Even the ritual and language of the wedding ceremony reinforces the notion that marriage is like an egg beater: It mashes you up together so you can't tell which ingredient is which.

"The honeymoon is another devastating part of this cultural heritage. You go away together, hide away on an island or somewhere alone and practically breathe for one another. But all of this shores up the fantasy of the early stage to a point where, when reality comes, it can be devastating. And it *must* come."

When reality knocks at the newlywed's cottage door any time from several months to three years after marriage, it does not mean they will open it to find a villainous stranger. If people are capable of maturity and independence, reality simply means getting on with life both as an individual and as a couple.

The best way to enjoy stage one and use it as a strong foundation for marriage is to gradually allow yourself to accept the faults you see in your partner. At the same time you must accept your own limitations — both in dealing with those faults and in achieving perfection in the marriage. When disappointment strikes, ask yourself, "Did we agree to do things that way, or did I just make the assumption?" If you agreed and your partner is breaking the agreement, it is time to assert yourself and either demand compliance or renegotiate the agreement. But chances are you simply *thought* he would do the laundry, or she would spend every evening at home.

Often the mate's assumptions are based on a childhood that was different from yours. Only time will give a young couple the opportunity to discuss each mismatched assumption as it arises and reach an agreement that satisfies both parties. By then people are usually in the third year of marriage, at least, and their agreement process is called the stage of Compromise.

"It took us at least two years — maybe longer — to quit jumping all over each other because Sheila didn't dress the way I wanted, or because I had a pot belly and I wasn't going to stop drinking beer in order to get rid of it," admits a twenty-five-year-old insurance salesman. "See, we each thought as soon as we were married the other person would jump over the moon to please. But you can't do that. What a disappointment."

"He's not kidding," says his wife. She is a twenty-seven-year-old graphic designer. "It hurts to know your spouse doesn't want to go all out for you. You have to work your way into the *idea* of compromising, because at first you don't dream that it's necessary."

People can let go of fantasy if they realize that "reality" is not a code word for "trouble." Among other things, reality means accepting the fun of planning a future with another person you respect and love. It is the joy of living with your best friend and the security of catching a whopping cold and having a spouse on hand to make chicken soup without complaining. Reality is having a disagreement and coming to grips with the notion that you and your spouse may never see eye-to-eye on a number of issues.

One way of clinging to the non-reality of the "honeymoon mode" is for couples to lock themselves away from other people, to engage in isolated romantic behavior again and again, as if intercourse itself could provide a shield against having to cope with life. Sex is much on the minds of couples in Fantasy Time — and why not? — but when it is used as a substitute for reality it becomes frantic and tiresome. Making love never seems to be quite as much fun as you imagined it would be, say newlyweds. It's a strain. It's another expectation.

Later in marriage, people learn how to please one another, how to say no with kindness and how to tell the difference between having sex because it seems like something you should do and having sex because it brings genuine relaxation and pleasure.

But in stage one, people often forget their friends, refuse to visit parents and try to exclude everyone else from their lives except one another. Often they say this is the only way to steal enough time for sex. Later they realize that being alone together too long tends to force agreement on every issue and increases dependency. It also reduces self-esteem and creates an illusion of physical and emotional fusion. The real job of the newlywed is to enjoy a brief period of such fantasy and then re-establish contact with other people as quickly as possible. This will give you enough distance from the partner so you can gradually confront his assets and liabilities and deal with them realistically. And it won't damage a couple's sex life.

The Great Fantasizers

Some people, however, view a return to reality as terrible punishment for not being perfect. I call these people the Great Fantasizers. They are men and women whose expectations are so unrealistic that any slip-up (theirs or their spouse's) leads to disaster.

For the female Great Fantasizer, a man who is late for dinner at home is akin to Jack the Ripper. The male Great Fantasizer sees a wife who won't have sex with him on demand as being as murderous as the infamous axe-lady, Lizzie Borden. Mood swings, failures or even being silent for part of the evening is taken as a personal rebuff. The partner doesn't want to give his all. He is imperfect! For people who have fantasized too much and whose expectations of married life are far off the mark, this is a horrible discovery.

The only way to dodge this discovery is for one spouse — still, most often the female — to remain a clinger and stay voluntarily blinded by fantasy. This is the spouse who silently agrees to go through life almost totally dependent upon and obedient to the other. There probably will be no early crisis in such a marriage, but there will be no growth either. One common pattern in such a marriage is for the husband to gradually become bored with the clinging wife and to initiate separation after about twelve to seventeen years of marriage. It may take that long for the husband to outgrow his own need to dominate such a pliable spouse and to try for a more equal, and thus more exciting, relationship.

Science writer Maury Breecher says a recent study of thirty-five couples married for fifty years shows that when people describe themselves as happily married, it is because they always shared decision-making. Unhappy marriages are characterized by men who make all the important decisions and women who do little more than stay at home and provide custodial care for children and houses. When decision-making is shared, each partner learns to respect the other. When it is not shared, one partner feels there is no one to shoulder life's burdens with him, and the other partner feels worthless.

It is probably easier in our society for the clinger to be female, because she can still hide behind claims that dependency is forced upon her by the demands of small children and running a household. These shields, however, grow weaker and weaker through the years and leave the clinging spouse with very few excuses for not going out with her own friends, pursuing interests apart from her husband and otherwise growing as an individual.

There is no love coming from a clinger; there is only extraction. The clinger will suck out all the vitality from his or her spouse, forcing the stronger partner to face the harshness of the world alone. The clinger depends on a mate to tackle all the serious decisions and responsibilities of adulthood for them both.

The spouse stuck with a clinger, male or female, has two choices: He can go along with the arrangement and shoulder all burdens in exchange for unlimited power within the marriage, or, he can allow himself to become disappointed and attempt to force his mate into equality and maturity. This is difficult to do unless the dependent spouse seeks professional help, because a clinger is a person who has little self-esteem, and it is impossible for the mate to provide it.

The clinger is counting on the strong partner to become addicted to the clinger's adoration . . . so much so that he's willing to become exhausted in order to get it. If the arrangement works, it's because the person being adored also has low self-esteem and needs constant ego feeding from the clinger in order to feel worthwhile.

This is a stagnant marriage, and it starts in stage one, providing another reason why it is important to end the fantasy fast. This rule applies not only to youngsters embarking on their first marriage but to people of any age who may have been through several marriages and acted out the same fantasies in each one. They may be two seemingly independent people, but they are unable to put an end to their fantasies about unlimited joy and total perfection in marriage. They refuse to settle for anything less than the stuff of their adolescent dreams.

Usually these marriages start off with romantic fireworks and fizzle fast, because fantasies, by their very nature, are short-lived. And once the fantasy is gone, such people become dismayed and don't want to progress to the other stages of marriage. This is why some people cannot stay married to the same spouse for very long. They are unable to learn the rules for self-development within marriage and are unwilling to abandon the fantasy that another person can supply happiness for them.

These people marry and fail, marry and fail. Their lives become revolving doors of divorce.

Frank And Lisa

Frank and Lisa are both physicians and both on their third marriage. While they might appear independent because of their successful careers, they illustrate what happens to the emotionally-stunted man or woman who demands perfection from a mate and who wants the mate to assume responsibility for making them feel good all the time.

Frank is thirty-seven. Lisa is thirty-nine. Neither has been able to stay married for longer than two years, nor to seriously plan for having children.

When they met not long ago on a romantic Colorado ski trip, Frank and Lisa thought their troubled lives as divorce-prone people were finally taking a turn for the better. The ski trip was a courtship in the snow, complete with moonlit sleigh rides and picnics on the slopes.

After the trip, Frank and Lisa made a point of seeing one another every evening. They also took time from their busy medical careers to telephone each other at least twice a day. Frank sent little gifts of flowers and stuffed animals by messenger in the morning and purchased extravagant sweaters, furs and jewelry so he would be able to lavish them upon his beloved when she greeted him at her door each night.

In return, Lisa wrote endearing poetry. This convinced Frank that she was astonishingly multitalented and put him in awe of her abilities. All lovers endow one another with inflated abilities, but Frank went overboard. He told me he believed Lisa could be a prize-winning poet as well as a brilliant physician, and he insisted she was also a likely candidate for any beauty contest. He pursued Lisa with vigor in what he now remembers as a "whirlwind courtship." They decided to get married after about six weeks, and Frank says he and Lisa convinced themselves that perfect love was at last here to stay.

They were wrong. After a lavish satin and tuxedo wedding and a gleeful shopping spree for a new brick and glass house and art deco furniture, Frank and Lisa are splitting up. They have been married seven months.

"I can't believe I'm going to go through another divorce!" were the first words Frank said to me when we began our interview. "This can't be happening to me again. I swear, God has cursed me. How could Lisa be so perfect one month and so awful the next? I tried so hard to treat her special!"

Frank keeps blinking his eyes hard to squeeze back the tears. "I'm sorry. . . ." He says it half-choking and pulls a frayed handkerchief from the pocket of his blue jeans.

Frank invites me to look around the home that he and Lisa so joyfully decorated together. There are ornate brass floor lamps, fine oil paintings and twin staircases that wind enticingly to the second floor. There, in the master bedroom, the bottom mattress of the new king-size bed is still wrapped in its protective plastic shipping case. "We didn't use it much," Frank says with a wry laugh.

Frank has a thick mane of wavy blond hair and very clear blue eyes. He knows that his rugged good looks often tempt female patients to say they're sick, just so they can feast for a few moments on Frank's smile and his deep, soothing voice. He says he never had *real* love . . . only distant adoration of that sort, first from the women who raised him and then from the women who married him. Now that he looks back on those women, Frank says, they all seem the same: shallow, selfish, out to suck him dry.

He was raised in an orphanage. His parents divorced when he was still an infant, and neither one wanted to keep him. Nor were there relatives willing to do the job.

"I don't remember the orphanage as a bad place, really. It wasn't a big old dirty building, something you'd think of as being out of *Oliver Twist*. It was a series of very cute little bungalows with about twelve kids in each bungalow and a housemother. You started in the babies' bungalow, and every three years or so you'd move to the older kids' bungalow and a different housemother would take over.

"They were nice ladies. I was always their favorite, probably because I was a quiet boy who did all his homework on time. I never got wild, never was a troublemaker. I got to college on a scholarship, then worked myself through medical school. That was *very* hard, and it took me twice as long as the other students. But I was really determined.

"I'm a workaholic," Frank says with an apologetic grin. "I really knock myself out. I did the same thing for Lisa, treating her like a queen. Then she turned on me and . . . really . . . now I am disgusted by the thought of her."

Frank's rapid swing from adoration to disgust is typical of what can happen to people who fail to use stage one as a time to begin modifying their childish demands for perfection. Because he treated Lisa unrealistically — "like a queen" — he expected a royal response. Frank's assumption was that Lisa was so special she deserved superhuman attention from him and would play out her role as perfect wife and professional peer. His expectations were so outlandish that his fantasy about Lisa could not be sustained for longer than a few months.

Frank's habitual response to a new lover is to wind his life so tightly to hers that all independent thought or emotion is lost. Since he has experience only with adoration, not love, he chooses women who appear willing to surrender themselves almost completely to another person. The combination of two adults with no basic sense of self-esteem clinging to one another leads to inevitable disappointment.

Several days after I talk to Frank, I travel to a Chicago suburb to interview Lisa. She has her own interpretation of their story. It is filtered through the eyes of a woman who, like Frank, never experienced unconditional acceptance as a child. As a result, Lisa's definition of loving behavior is a person who acts exactly as *she* believes he should and who never makes mistakes.

Lisa says Frank let her down. She tells me this as she sits stiffly on a hard-backed chair in her mother's formal living room. Now that divorce from Frank is looming, Lisa has moved back to the home of her parents. The house sits on a acre of manicured lawn in a fine old neighborhood that boasts its own police force and a privately-hired sanitation department to keep the streets spotless.

It is early spring, but the midwest is still in the grip of cold weather. Outside, huge wet snowflakes slam angrily against the windowpanes, making noise like a million tiny fists. It is chilly in the living room, but neither Lisa nor her mother makes a move to light a fire in the big marble fireplace. The room is as cold and inhospitable as Lisa and her mother.

Mother is on the sofa, hands primly folded in her lap, bony legs crossed tightly. Lisa is a younger copy of this woman. Her blonde hair is pulled back from her face and tortured into a tiny bun at the nape of her pale neck. She will be interviewed, she says, only "to set the record straight." Mother is there to make sure it goes well.

"I thought Frank had it all," Lisa begins. "He seemed to me to be not only a very successful physician but a handsome and charming man of the world. We had a lot in common besides our profession. We both love to travel, to ski, to shop for fine furniture and art."

"She was taken in," Mother barks.

Lisa accepts the interruption. She waits a few moments to make sure Mother is finished, then goes on.

"The reason I married Frank is because, first, I thought I was really in love."

A snort of disdain escapes from Mother.

"I *did*, Mother."

There is silence. Lisa sighs and continues.

"I was madly in love, as a matter of fact. We had a really wonderful time together, and Frank was very nice to me. How was I to know it was all an act? You know, I have a medical practice of my own and plenty to keep me busy, but I am not immune to being swept off my feet by a handsome man who says he loves me and who does all the wonderful things Frank did. He brought me flowers and gifts. He *loved* my poetry. There wasn't anything he wouldn't do for me, and I adored him for it."

Lisa says everything changed after the wedding. Frank turned away from her and back to his medical practice, where his patients seemed to come first. Sometimes he came home at night, plopped down on the sofa and began to snore. He put his elbows on the table at dinner, was careless about clearing his spot after eating and was simply awful about washing his own dishes. He wanted sex but was a clumsy lover. On weekends the scrubbed, well-tailored physician gave way to a grubby, middle-aged man in faded jeans and an unkempt beard.

"Frank didn't care about helping with the yardwork," Lisa complains. "He'd say, 'Let's pay a yard man to do it.' " She shakes her head in angry disbelief. "How could he suggest that, when he knows perfectly well that if you want a thing done right you must do it yourself!" Lisa says Frank also had the nerve to tell her to forget about housework and hire a maid. She tells me Frank had no sense of what his responsibilities were to her or to their things.

"A slob," says Mother.

"Really," Lisa agrees.

The wind is gusting now, and tiny puffs of frigid air find their way beneath the doorframe. There are goosebumps on Mother's thin arms, and Lisa hugs herself to keep warm. I ask for a cup of hot coffee, but neither Lisa nor Mother is willing to extend her hospitality.

Their conversation becomes a long tirade against Frank's many real and imagined faults. He is careless, forgetful, boyish, clumsy and sometimes silly, says Lisa. In short, Frank is human. That is an error Lisa cannot accept.

After little more than an hour, Mother looks at her wristwatch, glowers at Lisa and tells her daughter it is time to say good-bye. Lisa rises, smooths her skirt and dutifully delivers a parting peck to Mother's cheek. Then she disappears into the swirling snow.

Lisa and Frank are both the products of loveless childhoods, where they were prized not for their human characteristics but for the ability to toe the line, to be "good." We all learn to be good so mommy and daddy will love us and so that parents will not become exhausted by the endless demands of their offspring. Remember the Acceptable Lies? We learn to invent them ("No, I'm not scared of the dark") in order to agree with our parents that our childish fears are, indeed, unjustified. We learn to flatter, cajole, hold in our true feelings ("Oh, it's okay that you can't take me to the circus, Daddy. I understand"). These are trial attempts at maturity which will serve us well in later years. They also help us get to the point where we can make our first compromises in marriage and begin the difficult process of seeing our partners not as we wish they were but as they really are. Acceptance of this reality is the first step toward the deepening intimacy of married love.

People like Lisa and Frank, however, are unable to love. They can only *adore*. Never having received unconditional affection, they do not know how to give it. So their adoration comes with many strings attached. Frank adored Lisa only as long as she paid homage to the same good qualities in him that were applauded by his orphanage housemothers. Lisa's adoration of Frank ended when she made the discovery that he was, after all, sloppy on weekends and human enough to scatter crumbs over the kitchen floor. To her, these failings were not trivial. She said again and again, "He let me down!"

Of course he let her down. He showed himself to be less than flawless. Lisa was terrified by that and almost immediately ended the marriage.

Lisa and Frank illustrate the extreme dependency needs of the adoring spouse. It is far easier to adore than to love, and while love gets deeper and expands on itself, adoration is like a hot coal held up in the wind: It can't ignite anything else, and it cools off very fast.

The sensation of overwhelming adoration for a potential marriage partner is the only way the emotionally empty human can carry through with his biologic urge to marry. Like the rest of us, such a person will initially see his or her mate as a perfect being and imagine great gushes of love for such a flawless creature. But when reality comes through in the form of broken promises and dirty laundry, the adoring mate is crushed by disappointment. He or she cannot learn to manipulate Acceptable Lies, nor abandon fantasies of perfection. The adoring mate is eager to punish the spouse who let him down. Divorce is often that punishment.

The rest of us also quickly spot the flaws in our beloved, but we can withstand the disappointment. After a while it is possible for us to accept the annoying habits or foolish personal characteristics of the new wife or husband and not condemn the spouse for being less than godlike. Experience with our own parents has taught us that although we believed mom and dad were perfect when we were very little, bit by bit we discovered that they acted foolish at times and also made mistakes . . . like other mortals. We accepted that. We didn't quibble about the little disappointments after a while, because as we got older, we learned that they appeared to be universal in human life. And we also noticed that mom and dad accepted *our* faults, too. It was okay to wet the bed, bring home a "C" report card or forget to wash the dishes. As long as we adhered to basic rules of conduct most of the time, infractions now and then were acceptable and didn't affect the long-term love of our parents for the basically good people we knew ourselves to be.

But Frank and Lisa didn't grow up in such an accepting atmosphere. If Frank wasn't good all the time, his housemothers could find some other little boy to adore. If Lisa showed Mother that she wanted to be naughty now and then and leave the bed unmade, Mother was quick to withdraw her approval. For Frank and Lisa, there was no room for childhood's mistakes. They had no choice but to grow into "perfect" adults who left no room for the mistakes of others.

Momentary Suspension Of Disbelief

What makes people like Frank and Lisa decide to marry? Experts call it a "momentary suspension of disbelief." Such people simply deny any flaws in their marriage partners before the ceremony and for as long as possible thereafter. But that's usually not very long; marriages between people like this are shockingly brief. We have all read about movie stars who marry one day amid the promises of heaven-sent love, only to split the following day shouting curses at one another. Of course they are furious! They believe their own fantasy of a perfect person. When the realization of imperfection comes crashing in on them, their adoration turns to fury.

Adoration has to end. And when it does, it turns to hate. You hate the partner for letting you down, and you hate yourself for being imperfect enough to believe this would not happen. Also, the Great Fantasizer is so insecure that he or she assumes most of the responsibility for the failure of the marriage. Frank told me, "I must be pretty bad for Lisa to have treated me that way."

When you adore someone, you depend on them far too heavily. Adoration *is* dependency. That is why Frank and Lisa's story comes to a sad ending. They got stuck in the very early part of stage one, which is the phase of strong attraction. Once that wore off, they could not progress.

If we are healthy, stage one coaxes us all to mature in several ways. It is usually the first opportunity to learn day-by-day sharing with a peer. When we are living under the care of our parents, it is natural to expect full devotion from them with very little sacrifice on our part in return. In marriage, however, a person our own age is willing to give love, help and money only if we repay these gifts with contributions of our own.

Another advantage of stage one is to serve as a gentle bridge between passionate romance and long-lasting friendship. This is a time of transition, when young people can combine sexual delight with intimate conversation and learn that each activity complements the other. Couples gain time in stage one to mellow and to discover how their new mates will influence their goals in life. When they are ready to begin pursuing those goals as individuals, they can progress to stage two.

5

Stage Two: COMPROMISE
(Years Two to Seven)

"You can share! You can do it!" — *a twenty-eight-year-old woman, at her fifth anniversary party.*

The fantasies of stage one are powerful and alluring because they are built on the expectation that a spouse will take care of all our needs. But the only way such a fantasy can be fulfilled is for one or both partners to remain infantile. Since most of us want to grow, we pull away rather quickly from stage one and march into the next developmental phase of married life, which is the stage of Compromise.

Compromise is an exciting time, characterized by surges in personal development. People come face to face with the reality of married life as it impacts their jobs, their view of the world, even the way they learn to share everything from a paycheck to a tube of toothpaste. At her fifth anniversary party, a twenty-eight-year-old woman told me, "I was an only child, and I guess I grew up a bit selfish. I never knew how wonderful it felt to share daily life with someone else on a very intimate basis. Even the fights I have with my husband — the bad times — teach me something. Sometimes I just get up in the morning and look in the mirror and congratulate myself, saying, 'You can share! You can do it!' "

The stage of Compromise is also filled with doubts and worries somewhat reminiscent of a child's adolescent years, when he tries to balance a surge in self-sufficiency with the fear that independent thought or action will alienate him from the people he loves and depends upon — his parents. New and frightening questions arise: Is it all right to disagree with Mom and Dad? How far can I go in asserting my individuality before they get mad at me? If I grow up and display a mind of my own, will I still be loved?

The same emotional tug of war takes place in marriage when the first stage is over and two complex individuals try to become self-sufficient adults while still maintaining a high degree of attachment to one another. It is a juggling task that takes skill and patience and a lot of the same inner confidence that helped them through the puzzling adolescent years. People who accomplished a smooth transition from utter dependency on parents to a more adult partnership with them will be more likely to manage a similar transition now.

In marriage, we spend stage one blissfully assuming our partners want nothing more than to think, feel and act exactly as we do. This is a subconscious replay of the infant's symbiotic tie to mother. After a year or more it becomes obvious that husband or wife does, indeed, have strong individual desires that do not coincide with ours. This can be frightening. At first it seems as if something has gone terribly wrong, because we have been taught that differences of opinion aren't supposed to exist in a happy marriage.

"I wondered if we were going to break up, because after a while, I found out Lila and I disagreed about a lot of things," a thirty-year-old salesman told me. "We've been married about four years. When we don't see eye to eye, it makes me nervous."

The normal coping response to such fear is to try and modify both our own and our partner's behavior to dampen the development of individuality. If a young wife wants to start a business of her own, for example, the husband who assumed they would always be in business together may feel rejected. Instead of encouraging his wife to explore her potential, he rushes to find out how he can change his methods of operation so the wife will be tempted to stay. Or, the husband who is making some moves toward going out one night a week to enjoy an all-male poker game will probably spur his wife into frantic dinner preparations on that night, because she is hoping to lure him home. She sees not a healthy desire for peer companionship on his part but a threat to her status as her husband's only object of attention.

Both the businessman husband and the dinner-making wife are denying growth — their partner's and their own. Instead of fighting change, they must accept the emergence of individuality. At the same time they will learn to *like* these changes because they add interest to the marriage and give each person greater freedom. Pushing away fear and accepting change with an open heart takes courage and self-esteem. In marriage, this great task starts in the stage of Compromise.

Patterns Of Compromise

Three patterns of compromise became apparent during my interviews.

Some people correctly see this time as the real settling down period. They get ready to give up their fantasies of an all-encompassing lover who will supply their needs and start adjusting to the more mature idea that each of us must supply our own needs in life. These people can compromise quickly within marriage as a way of adjusting to adult goals and responsibilities. They look to their partners not as substitute mom or dad but as other adult people who can help them grow up.

Others learn to compromise more slowly. They tell their spouses rather openly about disappointments but have to work hard to accept them. Their compromises are characterized by a great deal of ambivalence because one or both partners may be terrified by the idea of individuality within marriage. At first the couple struggles to find ways of agreeing with one another virtually all the time. They are afraid of fighting. It takes practice and trust to convince themselves that it is not dangerous to disagree.

The third pattern of compromise takes shape in a rush, as a result of some crisis or external force that pushes people into change. The death of a parent, job loss or the birth of a child can bring about attempts at compromise in a couple who otherwise might try to avoid this stage of marriage and the growing maturity it represents.

Each form of compromise is necessary but in a greatly modified form. Most people gradually learn to incorporate a little of all three into their lives, depending on the mixture that works best for them. At the same time, most people grasp the idea that some compromise is necessary because in marriage — as in all other major life processes — some issues never will be resolved. We must all accept arguments without resolutions, struggles that don't always have a happy ending. This realization helps people rely on their own judgment and accept the fact that their decisions often may be less than perfect. Mistakes will be made, but that's the chance a grown-up takes when he accepts responsibility for his own actions.

It is certainly possible to stay married and avoid that responsibility; some people manage to avoid all or most of the stages, too. But their marriages are lifeless or filled with discontent... or, they are battlegrounds where one or both partners are continually abused. The Marriage Map is not often followed by people like this. It is a map for success in marriage, not avoidance of the trouble it takes to achieve that success.

Larry And Millicent

His biggest mistake, Larry tells me, was in thinking Millicent could make a lot of money. He smiles at his wife when he says this, squeezing her hand as if to reassure her that he is not criticizing... just telling the truth. Larry and Millicent are examples of the first pattern of compromise: strong people who face reality quickly and without too much regret, adjusting their roles within marriage to conform not to what they wish would happen but to what is really going on.

They have been married two years. Life together has been good, but Larry and Millicent are not without problems. The photography equipment company they own together is in serious financial trouble. It was just last month, says Larry, that he finally admitted to himself and to Millicent that it was not wise to be in business together unless *he* controlled the finances.

"She is a wipeout in the money management department," he says. "And that's ironic, because I married Millicent thinking she could earn a substantial living with the financial end of this business, and I could devote myself to the artistic part of it, which is what I really wanted to do. I'm not saying I made a mistake marrying her; the mistake was in endowing Millicent with talents and powers she just doesn't have."

Millicent is a pretty twenty-nine-year-old who smiles easily but who betrays some insecurity with hands that flutter like restless birds. Larry, thirty-one, is a tall, husky man whose smiles are slower coming. But his eyes, behind wire-rimmed spectacles, are warm and encouraging. We are sitting together at the card table that serves as their desk, surrounded by boxes of cameras, lenses, printing paper and other equipment. Outside, the muted roar of delivery trucks reminds us that we are perched near a loading dock in Boston's tough, run-down industrial section.

"I'd like to get the office out of here to some place nicer," says Larry, "but we can't afford to move. We have some big money problems. We're just beginning to look realistically at them. Until now, Millicent thought I was going to rescue her, and I thought *she* had everything under control. We each wanted the other one to be the responsible person. Oh, were we both wrong!"

Millicent's childhood had prepared her to be responsible. She was the oldest child in a boisterous family of nine. She remembers a pot-bellied father sucking on a pipe, candy spilling from his baggy workman's overalls as he hugged each sticky-faced younger sibling, then approached Millicent shyly with a more subdued kiss on the cheek and a special gift of flowers or fudge. "Daddy always said I was the little mother of the house," she tells me proudly.

Her own mother was tired a good deal of the time, always clucking with a mixture of delight and impatience as she tucked yet another sandwich into a child's schoolbag or searched vainly for someone's missing socks. The house was a mess. Millicent says the noise and confusion sometimes got to her, so she spent a lot of time after school voluntarily arranging piles of tiny T-shirts or mopping trails of milk from the refrigerator to the kitchen table.

The house never got clean and the confusion rarely abated, but Millicent drew great satisfaction from her efforts to bring some order to the chaos. For one thing, her two younger sisters adored her and pitched in to help. That gave mother time to fix her hair or sew new curtains for the living room windows; Millicent saw results from her labors.

"I would say I had a very satisfying childhood," she explains. "I wouldn't call it totally happy, because as I said, the disorder in the household really got to me sometimes. Mother was sweet, but nine kids ... well ... she was in over her head. Daddy was always nice. He brought home good money from his workman's job, I guess, but he'd just flop on the couch when he got home and didn't lift a finger to help with the dishes or anything. There were six boys, and they all followed example. So that left Mom and the three of us girls, and my sisters were really too young to do very much, so if anybody was going to make some sense of it all, it had to be me. The experience gave me a sort of exaggerated sense of my own abilities to run things, to *manage*. I thought it carried over to business. Now I know it didn't."

Larry was cast from a different, but just as sturdy, mold. His father was a lawyer; his mother made a small freelance salary giving museum tours and lectures on art and art history at one of the Smithsonian museums in Washington, D.C. When Larry was two years old, his mother's lecture was cancelled because of bad weather, and she trudged home through the snow to find her husband in their second-story bedroom fondling his secretary. Larry was asleep at the time, but he thinks he remembers his mother's angry screams. His parents were divorced, and Larry's father slipped out of his life. Larry concentrated on emulating his mother.

"She was very strong, very competent," he tells me. "She kept at her work, expanding it to full time, and with her fees and the alimony, we got along pretty well. We stayed in the big house, and my life was perfectly normal. Mom loved me like crazy and let me know it; that made me feel very secure, very worthwhile. She never remarried, but she did have men friends, so I had enough exposure to male role models to grow up feeling I wasn't deprived of anything because I didn't see my dad. He was a jerk anyway, to cheat on my mother like that and then just abandon the family. I grew up with the understanding that the best person in the world to rely on besides my mother was me."

Larry's choice of career was also influenced by his powerful mother. He enrolled in art school and later specialized in photography. He was twenty-eight when he met Millicent and felt the familiar tug of affection for a woman who seemed to be competent, useful, in charge. He was struggling at the time to establish himself as a freelance photographer and working part time as a photo equipment supply salesman to make ends meet. By then he was lonely, feeling the need to anchor himself in a secure, long-lasting romantic relationship. He wanted to get married. When Larry proposed after about ten months of dating, Millicent said she would like nothing better than to be his wife.

Millicent listens to Larry tell his story. She clasps and unclasps her hands, leans forward and silently nods agreement when he says they each thought the other would take charge of the necessities of life.

"All along I was earning money, but not much," she says. "My fantasy was that as soon as we got married my troubles would be over, because Larry would come into the business with me and somehow magically transform it into something the size of AT&T." She laughs and draws a faint chuckle from Larry. He squeezes her hand again, encouraging her to go on.

"I had the business first. Then Larry lost his sales job and since we were dating pretty steadily at the time and photography was his field, it seemed natural for him to become my business partner. And I simply wasn't comfortable with that idea unless we got married, too."

She stops and looks at Larry, who picks up her silent cue and continues. "I liked Millicent a lot. Our sex was good, and we enjoyed one another. Also, I thought the business would really be successful under her guidance if only I could free her to really go at it, by taking over the creative part. I'd be the idea man, and she'd handle the money. You might say we got married because it was a convenient time for that to happen. We were both ready for a secure friendship."

But Millicent and Larry's subconcious agenda included much more than friendship. Like so many other young people, each of them was looking for a savior who would release them from the tiresome responsibilities of adulthood. As Larry says, "I was hoping Millicent could take care of me, because I was not so sure I wanted to be doing it for myself."

It didn't work. Larry did attract some new customers, but he was not the creative genius Millicent fantasized. Millicent showed she had little capacity for running a business. Money problems erupted almost at once.

"It happened both in our business and in our personal lives," says Millicent. "For example, when we got married, I moved into Larry's condo and *hated* it. It was too small and stuffy. I wanted a house, and I convinced both of us that it would be the best thing, both financially and emotionally, to take on a mortgage. Larry seemed worried, but he agreed. Well, the down payment was too small and the mortgage was *much* too big, and neither of us realized it. That was the first big signal that we had been wrong in our assessments of each other's ability to manage money."

Larry says he suspected the house might be too much of a financial burden, but he didn't want to rob Millicent of a pleasure she craved so badly . . . and he was still sailing along on his dream that, "Millicent knows exactly what she's doing." Two months after the house purchase, they were deeply in debt, their cash flow had shriveled to almost nothing and Larry and Millicent were both frightened and angry.

"We were going down the drain financially," says Larry, "and I suddenly realized that I would have to take charge because Millicent just couldn't do it. In the past in our relationship, it was always me who would be passive, who would worry but not do anything to correct the situation. I was always thinking Millicent could pull us out of the fire at the last moment. I can't tell you how upsetting it was for me to confront her last month and say, 'I'm taking over responsibility for the money in the house and in the business, because it's clear that that's not your bag.'

"I was frightened about saying that to her but also exhilarated. I stood up for what I believed was right. I remembered that I promised myself not to rely on other people and to trust my own ability to get along. I said good-bye to my fantasy of being the little cuddled boy. That is a wonderful growth experience."

After just two years of marriage, this is a swift compromise for Larry and Millicent. Their first and most important adjustment has come from within, as they each agree to drop fantasies about themselves and one another — without blaming their partner for not being perfect. More external compromises may be coming: Larry says his preference now is to have Millicent leave *all* the business decisions to him because she had her turn and failed. Millicent still clings to the concept of sharing both a marriage and a business partnership with the same person, although she admits, "We don't make a very good business team. It might be better if I took a photo equipment sales job myself. I got an offer last week, and it was tempting."

I ask Millicent if she worries that a business split might signal a split in the marriage, too. She shrugs and says yes, that might be what is bothering her. But even more, she needs a chance to adjust to all the rapid changes.

"The balance of power in our relationship has shifted very suddenly and very dramatically from me to Larry," she says softly. "It's odd, but I think I like it that way. I have a tendency to push hard, to demand things be done *my* way. With Larry holding firm, it gives me some limits. I know where I stand.

"Still, I'm not ready to go all the way and get out of the business. After all, it was mine before it was ours, and I'm having a hard time looking at this objectively and saying, 'He's better at this, and we don't do well at it together, so I should find something else to do.' For now we have compromised with him taking the lead in financial affairs, but we'll give it a try. If it really can't work, I'm willing to look at other options.

"Who knows what will happen?" Millicent asks. "But I think we know this much: We got through the bursting of the first big bubble, which was our fantasies that the other person had magic to make money out of thin air and to take care of us both without effort. It's a disappointment to find that's not so and to arrange a compromise that will give us a chance to be successful.

"Okay, I can't have my dreams of this marvelous business partnership that just clicks along. I don't know how it will work out, but just making this one big adjustment to reality shows we can do it without blaming each other and without either one of us being made to feel defensive. For now, that's the important thing."

How Compromise Pays Off

Learning to compromise removes many of the insecurities of young married life. Millicent realized that allowing Larry to take control of the company finances did not mean loss of individuality for her nor abandonment of her ideals; she merely readjusted the methods by which her goals might be accomplished. Larry discovered he could love Millicent despite her inability to provide for him . . . and that he got a boost in self-esteem by stepping forward to try his hand at money management. Now both partners know they can stumble, fail and set off to explore different options without destroying their marriage.

There is another payoff in successfully negotiating this type of compromise: People learn the limits of their own abilities and are able to deal more realistically with them. They get encouragement to explore new horizons, too, and test previously undeveloped talents.

A married person tends to unfold in new directions, if only to compensate for a spouse's deficiencies. This makes the Compromise stage an exciting journey into self-discovery.

Most of the people I interviewed who have been married for two to seven years are still experimenting with ways to compromise. Much of their time together turns into practice sessions; they dabble with taking turns at everything from childcare to initiating sex until they find the proper combination of roles and patterns to make them both comfortable.

But a secure sense of self, which comes with adopting suitable roles, doesn't emerge in marriage until much later. In the second to seventh year, husband and wife are still confused about who does what, so they may try to find a middle ground on every issue. It seems important to agree on *everything*. Little by little all that head-nodding becomes terribly boring, and the couple learns which issues they can compromise on and which ones must be disputed. This enables them to take individual stands and create roles that suit their own personalities.

A grocery store manager, twenty-three years old and married for three years, told me, "My wife used to say, 'We have to share all the chores.' Frankly, I hated it. It wasn't *me*. So I finally said, 'Look, I make all the money. I don't want to split the chores fifty-fifty.' She cried and cried, but in the end we decided it really was fair that I get to rest at the end of my day. I'm glad I stuck to my guns, because I'm being honest on how I feel."

When a marriage is fully mature, both partners have compiled a long list of topics on which they can fondly disagree, such as politics, opinions about people, work methods, and leisure time and other issues that don't directly impact day-to-day married life. Topics like this, if they are approached with good humor and a willingness to learn from the opposing point of view, can be building blocks for an even more secure marriage. It's much more fun to be married to someone who has a strong sense of himself apart from you and whose differences stimulate thought rather than keep you plodding in the same intellectual and emotional circles.

There are also topics which people learn to avoid. Perhaps nothing in marriage — or in friendship — is so needlessly damaging as the brutal "honesty" displayed when you simply *must* tell the other person, "Oh, you look so old because of that receding hairline," or, "I have to confess that I was really tempted to sleep with your sister last week."

Nothing is gained from wounding your partner with these confessions. They are hostile, not honest. People in mature marriages share many of their thoughts but not *all* of them. They know when to keep quiet. Not everything in marriage is open for discussion; there is room, too, for intellectual and emotional privacy.

"It took twenty years for me to learn that," a forty-nine-year-old editor laughed. "During a week-long fight between my husband and me, I had a little fling with a young lifeguard at my country club. I never told my husband; I won't ever tell him. What's the point? We're fine, and it would only bring him pain. There are times you have to keep your mouth shut."

In the still-young second stage of marriage, however, many people assume they are so compatible with their partners that differences in viewpoint are virtually inconceivable. It is common for them to either blurt out everything or to back away from speaking out on many issues, because an open discussion might bring an unwelcome surprise: the beloved doesn't agree. To guard against this, such people protect themselves with a subconcious barrier against self-expression. The result could be a tense, cold relationship marked by mistrust and fear. Such marriages are prime targets for divorce.

Other people feel compelled to solve all their problems at once — an exhausting and impossible task. They know the fantasy of stage one has dissolved. Frightened by the loss of what they thought was a perfect love match, they struggle to fill the void with endless discussions about how to recapture a totally harmonious relationship. When disagreements arise during such discussions — as, of course, they must — one or both partners may panic. Still wanting to think of themselves as one person, the couple blurts out together, "We can find a compromise!"

What is often meant by "compromise" here is a mythical meeting point halfway between two opposing desires. But sometimes such a meeting point is elusive or entirely absent. Then man and wife must at least realize that some problems in marriage never can be resolved. Both parties must simply decide to live with the situation, making whatever arrangements they can to provide as much comfort as possible for both people.

This is a long process. The next couple I interviewed was going through it when they talked to me. They characterize the second pattern of compromise, where people talk openly about their disappointments and slowly help one another accept what cannot be changed.

Arnold And Rose

Arnold and Rose have been married three years. Arnold is twenty-six years old. Rose is twenty-five.

Arnold says he wants more sex, but Rose just doesn't have the same kind of biological drive. Yes, it bothers him; when they fight, he says, it's almost always about his disappointment when Rose drifts off to sleep before he can slip under the bedsheets beside her, or because she mutters, "Let's just snuggle tonight, but nothing more, okay?"

It's not okay. Arnold burns with barely-contained nervous energy, which is expressed partly in a strong sexual drive. He is tall and very thin. Rose has a slim figure and shoulder-length brown hair that excites him. She is wearing a white cotton dress that shows off the suntan she acquired during a Bermuda vacation last week. She says the vacation relaxed her, but it didn't work miracles for their sex life.

"I sort of hoped it would, for Arnold's sake," she says.

Arnold tells me Rose is affectionate, just not much interested in sex. But she is eager to let Arnold caress her, and once or twice a week his trembling, urgent pleadings melt what seems to be a habitual resistance on her part. She likes sex once they're into it, but her need is not the same as Arnold's. He has to get it started and keep it going, for the most part, and she can enjoy its pleasures after she warms up to the idea. After intercourse, Rose will rub Arnold's neck and offer a smiling, sleepy kiss. Then she will wriggle over to her side of the bed and Arnold soon will hear the soft, measured breathing of Rose's sleep.

"Well, let's say it's not a shock that Rose isn't as hot in bed as I'd like her to be, but it is a disappointment," Arnold admits. "I would like to have intercourse every night. She's more into touching. I knew it before we got married, but I kept telling myself sex isn't everything. And I figured that Rose was holding back until our wedding night, maybe because she was insecure. We did live together for a couple of months before we got married. One of the reasons for that was to get a lot of my immaturity out. I used to scream 'This is mine!' if she touched my stereo, or 'I worked hard for that money!' if I felt she spent too much. I got over it, and for the most part we learned to live together pretty well.

"The first year was hard on us both because Rose was studying for her MBA and I was coping with a tough new job, my first position of real managerial responsibility. Still, it was like a lovely dream. Rose is beautiful in so many ways. I kept thinking, 'She's not very much into sex, but that will change.' Also, I figured I was oversexed. I believed the old wives' tales about men wanting intercourse more than women."

Arnold stops and flashes an insecure grin at his wife. They are curled together on a wicker sofa in their plant-filled apartment. I sit on a chair beside them, listening quietly. It doesn't take much prodding to start the words flowing from Arnold.

"I don't think now that it's true about the different sex preferences in men and women," Arnold continues. "I think it's more a matter of personality, not gender. Rose will never be a nymphomanic — too bad! — but I guess I'll learn to live with it."

Arnold shifts uncomfortably on the sofa, reaches for a cigarette and lets the smoke curl in lazy patterns around his head. He tells me how he and Rose met at a noisy Fourth of July block party. They danced and laughed together all night amid the exciting blast and crackle of firecrackers and stumbled home at dawn dizzy with beer, exhaustion and romance. Rose postponed intercourse until their fifth date. Both of them remember that first time as a little clumsy but somehow endearing and wonderful.

Rose was a virgin at twenty-one. It wasn't that she was against premarital sex, she explains, but she never wanted it enough with any other man to take the chance of disease or dissatisfaction. Arnold had been sexually active since he was sixteen, he says, but "not in a very big way; just with girls now and then who I really liked." He says he dreamed of a beautiful wife who would have sex with him every night. He got the beautiful wife, but he is struggling to abandon the dreams of nightly lust and reconcile his disappointment enough to arrive at a suitable compromise. Rose is cuddly, loving, bright, pretty, loyal . . . he lists her virtues proudly. Now he must believe that such virtues are enough.

Arnold has thought about this for a long time, and he is eager to share his struggles with me and with Rose. Every glimmer of doubt, every twinge of pain and its balancing sense of pride, is spread before his wife so she will understand and sympathize with the intricate weaving of Arnold's mixed emotions. He trusts her not to mock him, nor to dispute the importance of his desire to draw her into the pattern of his thoughts. Although he knows he must compromise, Arnold is still hoping that once Rose *really* understands how he feels, she will change. She will, in Arnold's words, "learn to be a little bit more like me in bed, because that's the only way we're different to any great degree. And if she was as much into sex as me, we'd have a darn near perfect marriage."

Rose smiles and looks expectantly at Arnold. Is he finished talking? All right. Now she will tell her side of the story.

"I was brought up in a very traditional household, and Arnold was, too. It's almost comical, the way the lives of our parents are so much alike. My mother is a housewife and cooks and cleans for Dad, and she doesn't do too much else. Arnold's mother . . . well . . . when his father says jump, she jumps. Neither Arnold nor I wants to live that way. But it's okay for our parents, because they do seem very happy together. It's not as if the men are tyrants and the women get stepped on all the time. It's just the old-fashioned way, and it worked fine for their generation. Arnold and I both have business careers, we both make money and we share decisions equally.

"We have both agreed that we'll start a family in about a year. Then I'll quit work for a while. I'm not going to work while I have little kids. In a way, I expect things will start to follow the parental role more closely when that happens. I mean, we'll get more traditional. I'm not the dedicated housewife now, but when I have a baby crawling around on the floor, that floor is going to be spotless.

"I can see it coming already. I will follow somewhat in my mother's footsteps. But I'm looking forward to that time because I see it as just a stage in my life, not something I'll do forever. I'll go back to work when the children — we want two, about two or three years apart — are about four or five years old. Arnold agrees with that. I have the options, and that makes me feel very free.

"Now, to the sex problem. We keep talking about it, searching for a way to work it out so we'll both be happy. In the first year or two of our marriage, I didn't want to talk about it. I thought, 'I won't acknowledge this, and it will work itself out.' That's not happening. We have got to keep at it. We're both trying. It's not as if Arnold doesn't excite me in bed — he does — but I'm more into hugging and kissing than intercourse. He likes the hugging and kissing, too, but he just wants intercourse more often than I do. But there's nothing we can't solve if we want to. We'll get together on this thing."

This is Rose and Arnold's first real encounter with mutual dissatis-faction in their marriage, although the issue of possible sexual incompatibility has been there from the very beginning, nagging at the edges of their relationship. At first it was something to be denied, wished away, pushed aside as the-problem-with-no-name. In time, they thought, it would solve itself. Now, after several years of marriage, both husband and wife are slowly coming to the realization that they must abandon the fantasy that they will feel and act as one person about sexual desire — and, by implication, about everything else.

It's not an easy task. First, Arnold says, "She's not very much into sex, but that will change. . . ." and later, "I guess I'll learn to live with it. . . ." His ambivalence keeps him bouncing from hope to placid acceptance. Says Rose, "We have to keep at it. There's nothing we can't solve if we want to." She is still reluctant to loosen her grip on the desire to melt into Arnold. Instead of accepting her individuality, Rose tries to restructure herself until she and Arnold merge into one being. Rose still believes such a merger is not only possible but necessary. All it takes, in her view, is hard work. She thinks the simple desire to be "one," if it is strong enough, will create its own reality.

Like other couples in the Compromise stage of marriage, Rose and Arnold are silently mourning the death of their dreams. Conflict still holds terror for them, so they try to avoid it, telling themselves and one another that differences in character, personality and sexual desire can and should be crushed in favor of presenting a united front. Eventually they will become more relaxed about accepting one another's difference. In the stage of Compromise, with the help of an understanding spouse, we start accepting reality.

Until that happens, however, there is often much confusion between true compromise and an avoidance of individuality. When people refuse to give up some long-cherished romantic goal or insist on changing the other person to get exactly what they want, the stage of Compromise can become a dangerous time.

The disappointment of having to abandon childhood desires may lead to alienation and divorce for people who refuse, or who are unable, to grow as individuals. Stage two forces most of us to come to grips with at least the concept of husband and wife maintaining their individual likes and dislikes. The fantasy of being one person within a perfect union must now be abandoned — perhaps with regret but not with rancor. This can be done in much the same way that Arnold and Rose are approaching the problem: by admitting their failings, expressing sympathy for one another's unfulfilled desires and showing a willingness to try to accommodate the other person as much as possible. It's easier to let go of an impossible dream if you know your partner understands the loss and has tried his best for you.

Now Rose and Arnold must gradually stop trying to grope toward a solution and start accepting the reality that they may seldom agree on having intercourse in precisely the same way, at the same time. They are already taking their first steps in that direction, with Arnold's good-natured promise that although he's disappointed about his sex life with Rose, he can "learn to live with it."

Acceptance of such basic truths of differences within the marriage is not a signal that you are unloved or too incompatible to have a fine union. But for many young couples it is seen that way. They think differences in viewpoint, attitudes or desires indicate serious trouble. So they try to wish the trouble away by pretending that every problem has a solution, when in reality some "problems" are simply manifestations of individuality. If you accept them, they gradually become less threatening and assume their proper status as part of one's personality.

There are, of course, certain traits that you simply *cannot* accept, ignore, modify or tolerate. If Rose was really frigid instead of being less motivated toward frequent intercourse, Arnold would probably want a divorce. And that would be justified; nobody says you must spend a lifetime with a person who cannot meet your most basic needs. But one intimidating part of the Compromise stage of marriage is that most people at this point cannot yet tell the difference between acceptable and unacceptable traits in their spouses. They know they are bothered, and they usually know what's bothering them, but they don't know how important it is or what to do about it.

The fantasy of stage one is over, and each partner can no longer deny that he really doesn't like certain things about his mate. It is terrifying. Now what? The first strong impulse of this stage is to find a way to erase those "certain things." That impulse could lead to a lifetime of nagging or argument unless people quickly realize that change can't be forced. You must discriminate between what you can influence (persuading a spouse to stop smoking, for example) and what you cannot (don't ask her to give up a medical career for you). The natural thing to do is to try and find ways both people can change some traits, habits and goals by bending toward one another in compromise.

This silent struggle to find a middle ground for certain aspects of marriage is time-consuming and exhausting. At the beginning of this process, both spouses may become sharply aware of mistakes — real or imagined — and they feel like clumsy adolescents, wanting to please the parent but not knowing how and then suddenly getting fed up with even trying. In his book *Seasons Of A Man's Life,* Dr. Daniel Levinson says this is also a hallmark feeling of early middle age, when a person becomes more aware of his capacity for two opposite powers: destruction and creativity. "To construct anything," he says, "something else must be de-structured and restructured." In this stage, the couple is trying to dismantle the unreachable dream of perfect union and replace it with workable reality. At times it is a woeful task, because nobody wants to say good-bye to the fantasies of young love.

It is also a day by day struggle. People move forward with a few successful compromises, then slide back into temporary confusion. Arnold and Rose, for example, are forging a good marriage with honest efforts to accept one another's differences, but they are still battling their own wishes for a magic solution that will restore them to perfection. This leads to some compromises that are unnecessary or even trivial. One of these took place at the very end of our interview, when Rose showed how she was sacrificing her own feelings to placate Arnold by submitting to such personal questions.

Arnold was eager to talk. He couldn't seem to slay the two-headed dragon of his emotions, even after nearly three hours of earnest conversation had passed and I had long since put down my pen because Arnold wasn't saying anything new. All that time, Rose was quiet. When I finally started to leave, she offered her hand in a grateful good-bye.

"Honey, you didn't get to say much," Arnold said to her.

"Oh, that's okay. You did fine for the both of us."

"Well, don't you want to talk about your thoughts a little bit more? I really dominated the interview."

"Good."

"Good? Why is that good?"

"Because I prefer it that way. You were the one who wanted to do it."

Arnold looked puzzled. He glanced at me quickly, found no answers in my expression and turned again to Rose.

"Didn't you want to do it, too? You *said* you did. When I told you we had been contacted to do an interview for a book like this, you said it was all right with you."

"It *was* all right. But you were the one who was really hot to do it."

"Then you didn't want to?"

"Not that much."

"Why didn't you say so?"

"Uh . . . we . . . ummm . . . you seemed so eager to do it and all . . . and I didn't care that much."

"But you didn't *have* to," Arnold said, his voice rising with frustration and guilt. "So why did you say yes?"

"Because," Rose replied, "I just thought it would make you happy if I went along on this with you."

Florence And Jon

Sometimes it takes a crisis to force compromise. Then the change usually comes abruptly. This is the third pattern of this stage, and it fits the way Florence and Jon are working through this phase of their relationship.

Florence and I agree to meet for a long lunch and an interview at a hilltop patio restaurant just outside San Francisco. I am glad to have a pretty view and a waiter who seems not to care if we dally all day. Florence is a dreamy, slow-voiced woman. This is going to take some time.

The waiter, clad in jeans and flip-flops, comes to the table and slides two cups of creamy, cold soup onto our plates. I gulp mine, but Florence doesn't seem to notice the food. When I finish and the waiter has removed my cup, she looks up and says, "It's more fun to sit here quietly, isn't it, and just let the wind play with your hair." I am not sure if Florence means this or is just putting off my questions.

A gust ruffles her short black curls. She laughs and pats her swollen abdomen, and I plunge into the interview by asking how long it will be before the baby comes. "Oh, four months at the most," she answers, trying to sound nonchalant. Then she finishes her soup quickly. By the time the coffee comes, this twenty-nine-year-old woman is talking intently about the joys of her marriage . . . and the fears she is beginning to feel about this lifelong commitment.

"We have been married about five years. I think we have a very different sort of marriage, even for California. Almost everything we do is separate. Our careers are very different; I'm an artist, and he specializes in inventing computer programs. We don't really understand or particularly like what the other person does for a living. Our money is also completely separate.

"We are strong individuals, both of us, and I like it that way. I think Jon *used* to like it, but when he started seeing it meant that I wasn't going to cave in to him on everything, he started wishing I wasn't so darned independent.

"Now with this" — she pats her protruding stomach again — "we might be in for a big change. I mean, we have planned this baby, we both want it, and it's very exciting and all that. But I'm not sure anymore that we can go on the way we have been, with us both being so . . . well . . . separate in what we do with our time. I think being a parent will have some impact, even if we have a full-time nanny as we plan to. You know, things happen. Kids get sick, they want their mothers . . . I just don't know. Do you know what's going to happen? Can you tell me what's coming next?"

I have some general insight on the impact of children on a marriage, and I share it briefly with Florence. She leans forward and listens intently, squinting at me behind her mirrored sunglasses. Now and then she murmurs, "Yeah, I figure there will be tough times," or, "Oh, I *am* looking forward to nursing; it does sound great."

But I want Florence to talk, not me. When I coax her, there is another long silence. She is afraid her lifestyle will sound odd to me. Why? Because it is so different, she insists. Then, when she launches into her story, Florence agrees with me that her life is not very different after all. She refers to it that way because she likes the idea of being a pioneer. Florence's life with Jon is somewhat experimental, but it is immature rather than weird. Somehow they must both know this because they seem to be propelling themselves into maturity via parenthood.

Florence grew up in a big family in Idaho, where every child was expected to contribute to the household: doing the dishes, mowing lawns, taking care of baby brothers or sisters. Florence did all that and loved it. It made her feel grown-up, she says, and it was never too much to handle. Her mom and dad really appreciated her contribution, and when she performed well they repaid Florence with affection. There were always Sunday dinners filled with laughter and good food, quiet evenings on the front porch chatting with neighbors who dropped by, and simple but pleasant outings with her mom to the grocery store or the hairdresser.

Florence says each of her five brothers and sisters was encouraged to become independent. "Daddy always lectured us, 'Stand on your own two feet,'" says Florence. "My mother had a sister who was rather subservient, a wishy-washy woman, and Daddy thought very little of her. My mother also made fun of Aunt Rachel, saying, 'I hope none of you take after her and grow up leaning on other people for every little thing!' In fact, just the opposite happened. All the children in the family grew up stubborn and very free-willed."

At an early age, Florence started putting money in her own bank account. "One of my very first goals in life was to be on my own," says Florence. "Being financially independent has been a strong goal. And it has continued through marriage."

She met Jon at a college dance. He had been an engineering student but was on probation when they met. He was almost kicked out of school for sleeping through his final exams, then shocking the professor with muttered threats when she complained about it. Florence thought Jon was a cute bad boy in suspenders and shoulder-length hair. He came to her table and asked her girlfriend to dance. Florence wanted Jon to ask *her,* but he didn't seem interested. She got mad, pursued him, and he was amused.

They dated on and off for several months, and then Jon disappeared for almost a year. This was during Florence's junior year as an art major at the University of California. When Jon reappeared, Florence was a senior and he was a junior at the age of twenty-six. His education had been interrupted by frequent bouts of restlessness. The latest was a year Jon spent tinkering with computers in a small Los Angeles company. The company went broke. Jon decided to finish his degree, then go out and start a business of his own as a computer consultant. He was going to hit it big, he told Florence.

At first, when Jon telephoned Florence and asked for a date after a year of silence, she almost didn't remember who he was. Then the memory of her first attraction to him washed over her, and she said yes, fine, come on over.

He had changed. His hair was neatly cut. He was wearing a suit. Jon told Florence he was growing up. They started dating, and when she graduated and got a good job in a graphics designing firm, they married.

For the first year of their marriage, Florence supported Jon. She didn't mind. To her, it was a replay of old family expectations: You help others when you can, and then they help you. When Jon graduated and almost immediately began making a lot of money in the computer business, he quickly paid her back by assuming most of the payments on a small house she had bought for them. But she insisted they keep separate bank accounts.

"This is how we work it," Florence explains. "We each make our own money. We put in a certain percentage of our paychecks to pay for the basics, like heat and water. We both own the house, fifty-fifty. Aside from that, we each pay for our own food, our own clothes, our medicine, all that stuff. We go dutch treat when it comes to eating out or going to the movies. When we go on vacation, Jon treats because he makes so much more money than I do. We like expensive vacations. We go skiing. Last year we took a tall ship cruise to Greece, and we're thinking about a tour of Europe when the baby is about six months old and we feel secure about leaving it with a nanny for a few weeks.

"So far, the money thing has worked out fairly well. But it could run into trouble. I can't figure out how we're going to split the costs of raising a child. And a big problem is that I'm just beginning to get tired. Being pregnant is more physically demanding than I thought. I want to quit work or maybe go on half-time for a while. My feet are swelling. Jon says it's time to re-think how we're living. He's going to support me and the baby for a while, but I don't want to give up any independence."

Florence sighs with confusion. "Jon is right," she says finally. "I believe I got pregnant at least partly because I feel that we need a new way of looking at our lifestyle. I wanted to be so self-sufficient, but you can't work with swollen legs. Things are looking different now."

Several days later, Florence invites me to visit her and Jon at home. I arrive at a small ranch-style dwelling in a pleasant neighborhood, where quite a few lawns are dotted with wagons and tiny bicycles. I smile to myself, thinking that for a woman who insists on being different, Florence has chosen a rather traditional home in a family-style neighborhood.

The outside of Florence and Jon's home looks ordinary enough, but the inside is a shock. There is no furniture, except for a wobbly chrome and glass dinette and a pool table in the living room. Florence and Jon sleep on a king-size mattress on the floor in the bedroom. Their clothing is sorted in neat piles nearby, because there is no dresser.

Florence explains that they don't need furniture because they are *never* home. They just didn't get around to furnishing the place. The kitchen cupboards are bare. "We eat all our meals out," she says. "We have a maid for the laundry and to keep the floors clean and whatever else needs doing."

Florence asks me, "What do you think of the house?"

I shrug, trying to look neutral.

"We're not going to be able to live like this after the baby is born, right?"

I do not answer. I don't have to. Florence already feels the stirrings of change within her, and she will have to make her own compromises. She seems to know it, too. Already, she wonders aloud, "Is it freedom and independence I'm after . . . or am I acting selfish? I'm going to be a mother soon. I wouldn't have a baby unless I was willing to settle down, right?"

A marriage characterized by denial of commitment is cold and unsatisfying, and Florence now feels the need to recreate the family warmth she enjoyed as a child. By choosing pregnancy, she is telling herself and the world that she's willing to become emotionally anchored with Jon. To do that, she must realize that there is little reward in raising a family headed by a man and a woman who are so terrified of forming bonds and making compromises that they cannot agree to pool some resources or spend time creating a home together. "I'm beginning to see we can't have a baby and call ourselves independent to such a degree that we're unwilling even to invest in some furniture and make a home out of this place," she says.

"When we first got married, everything was very simple. We had a lot in common — skiing, sailing, a desire to be successful in business — and we both wanted a marriage partner who wouldn't tie us down. We had, and still have, a wonderful sex life. I figured that things would just go on that way, with us each being very strong individuals but enjoying one another. There would be no nagging, no holding one another down, no feelings that marriage is a drag. Having sex with other people, however, is definitely not part of this. We are both faithful. Otherwise, we wouldn't stay married. We may have a lifestyle that is different in the sense of being tremendously heavy in the independence department, but we both believe in loyalty and I personally think outside sex would destroy our relationship. So now when I think of it," she adds wistfully, "we're not so very different from other couples after all."

Florence and I have been talking for an hour when Jon comes home with the little cartons of Chinese food that will be our dinner. He is a handsome thirty-two-year-old with thick black hair and a dramatic smile. After dinner, he and I wander outside to sit on the steps, watch the sunset and conduct our part of the interview.

"I'm thrilled about the baby, but what if I'm not ready to be a father?" he worries, "Frankly, I'm very scared."

He didn't have a good family life, Jon says. His father was always putting him down. When he was a youth, Jon did crazy things: shoplifting, driving around in souped-up cars, breaking his nose in a gang fight. There were more than a few harrowing brushes with the law. Once he was tossed into a New Jersey jail overnight. His frenzied screams roused a guard and saved him from gang rape.

Jon's mother was always whining and exhausted from poverty and alcoholism. She was unable to control her bold, overactive son. His father's way of handling a crisis was to hit Jon hard; never mind where the blow landed or how much blood it drew. Once when he was seventeen, Jon hit him back. He knocked out one his father's front teeth. They didn't have much to do with each other after that.

Jon says Florence helped straighten him out. He had lived with plenty of women by the time he met her at the age of twenty-six, and he didn't much care for the idea of being tied down to any of them. They grabbed hold of him, like leeches, taking all they could and not giving much in return except complaints that sounded painfully like his mother's wishes to keep him at home, under control, in an emotional prison. Florence was different. She didn't want his money. She wasn't going to tie him down. How wonderful it was, says Jon, that Florence could combine independence with a marriage merger. She was warm, loving and unconditionally accepting. He couldn't help but want to love her back and keep her with him for life.

Now there is another life involved — the baby. Yes, he is proud of becoming a father. But he's not sure what compromises will be required. How much involvement will it mean? Will he be good enough, rich enough, patient enough? Will it turn out to be a mistake? Jon is bursting with questions for which only time can provide the answers.

While Jon and I are talking, Florence slips through the half-opened screen door and joins us. The need to compromise is coming fast, she says. Many times she is annoyed by Jon's actions or attitudes, but she lets it go because there isn't time to get into a fight. She doesn't want to hassle him. So, many feelings that should have been discussed still remain unsaid. Maybe that's why their marriage has been seemingly frozen in time, with a childlike emphasis on satisfactions of the moment, such as vacations, and little movement toward real emotional involvement. But just in the past month or so, Florence adds, Jon has shown a willingness to change. Now she is less afraid to open up to him and show that she, too, is a little frightened about the future. Their attempts at compromise are very basic, but they are there.

Says Florence, "When I say 'compromise,' I really mean 'change' and 'grow up.' I can see it coming on us. It's like we are both maturing fast. I mean, ZOOM. I have been the initiator of this maturity. I think I am doing it through the pregnancy. It's a signal that it's time for us to quit playing games.

"I'm willing to stop pretending that independence is God. In order to be independent, you don't have to be such a separate entity in marriage that you put on a front about staying apart. It's okay to start giving up time and money for the other person. Some people are too clinging, and we've been too independent. There is a middle ground someplace. We have to find it. That will be our compromise.

"Don't think I don't know how hard this is going to be." Florence lets her voice simmer into a husky whisper. "But I think it's worth the effort. I will go on wanting to be my own person, and so will Jon. But we can be two separate people and still be together a lot stronger than we have been. It will require some rearranging of priorities. This is the end of our extended childhood. I already see a lot of things in Jon that I don't like, and I don't pretend that I can change those things. But I think *he* can change them. And there is some indication that he will, because I think he's getting bored with being so self-centered. The baby promises rewards of a different kind. This is it. I know it. This is our chance to be adults."

Jon listens, his lips open slightly with surprise and with the thrill of being unexpectedly happy with Florence's revelations. His thin face is beaming. I can't tell if it is the reflection of the rose-colored sunset on his flesh, or embarrassment because I am there, or joy. No matter. He reaches over to grasp Florence's hand.

"She understands more than I thought," he says, unintentionally mimicking Florence's whisper. Then he turns to her. "Boy, you really read my mind." They hug briefly. There is silence. Then Jon pulls away a little and tries to fill the moment with some final thoughts.

"I'm not scared now. Well, maybe I'm scared a little. We have a lot o do. But even if I'm not totally ready, I sure am willing. I want a amily — I want Florence and the baby — more than I want a life with no strings attached. She's right; this is our time to mature. In terms of years, we're more than due for it."

Florence says to me, "We're going shopping for furniture this weekend. Want to come along?"

Being Forced Into Action

Perhaps the most productive aspect of this wobbly second stage of marriage is that it forces people into action. When a man or woman hits the wall of doubt circling the second to seventh years of marriage, there is no choice but break through it or get divorced. For decades, these years have been the time when most American marriages dissolve.

"Divorce at this point is often a suicidal gesture," says marriage and family counselor Dr. Lloyd Mendelson. "The dynamics are similar. The suicidal person says, 'I can't go on like this any more.' So instead of changing, he ends it all. The divorcing person 'kills' the marriage. It's a sweeping gesture."

Change at the stage of Compromise is necessary because it is fruitless to talk about problems unless the talk is quickly followed by action. A striking characteristic of almost all the people I interviewed was that young couples do a great deal of discussing, pawing at problems like a puppy worries a bone. It is better to emulate those who are older and wiser, who speak less and *do* more. Talking things over becomes a bore for the mature couple unless it is followed by action that puts the problem to rest. I like the advice of the fictional

Yoda, the elfin Jedi teacher in one of the *Star Wars* movies, who tells his young student, "Try not. Do. Or do not. There is no try."

Couples who get stuck in the Compromise stage are always trying. When they substitute *do* for *try,* they grow rapidly and the marriage matures.

Each of the stories in this chapter illustrates a different method of adjusting to the realities of modern married life. Larry and Millicent, made emotionally strong by secure childhoods, are able to abandon their fantasies and solve life's problems swiftly, as a team. It is taking Arnold and Rose a little longer, but they are beginning to see the rewards inherent in asserting individuality while at the same time making compromises to strengthen the marriage bond. And Florence and Jon are forcing themselves into maturity by having a baby, almost creating a crisis they can use to catapult themselves into the warmth and security they crave but have been afraid to approach.

As partners in a marriage learn to trust one another, it gets easier to give up dreams of what should be and to find real contentment with what is. In the stage of Compromise, defenses come down and people become more willing to take an honest look at their spouses and themselves.

At this stage, one can also take delight in knowing that your Prince or Princess has the proverbial feet of clay . . . so you don't have to be perfect, either. And it is important to discover that the knowledge of faults in your beloved will not destroy you. Inside there is a strength that sings, "I am strong, yet flexible. I can change. I can bend without breaking."

This is a lesson that can be learned in almost no other way except by successfully accomplishing the passage through the Compromise stage of marriage. It is an exciting preview to the deeper challenges and joys of the coming Reality Struggles.

6

Stage Three: REALITY STRUGGLES
(Years Five to Ten)

"My husband is so good with the children. He is really an outstanding and unusually loving father, so I don't mind his sloppiness." — *a young housewife.*

Reality Struggles is a rewarding but difficult and dangerous stage. Most of the early fantasies are gone, and people are facing the facts — good and bad — about married life.

The rewards come from binding yourself so closely to another person that intimacy rarely available in any other way is achieved. What makes these years difficult and dangerous is that many components make up the stage of Reality Struggles, and divorce may seem easier than working through all of them.

Married people must cope with two kinds of reality in this stage. One kind exists in your mind; what is real is that which is important to the husband and wife involved. The other kind of reality is the concrete, specific assets or liabilities of your marriage: how much money is available, for example, or how many children a couple has. These realities are there for all the world to see.

From years five to ten in marriage, the struggle to cope with the reality that exists in two people's minds involves:

(1) Deciding what is important in a life together, and thus "real" in an emotional sense, to both partners;

(2) Confronting what you consider to be your partner's bad traits and choosing to accept them;

(3) Minimizing his or her bad traits in favor of the good traits found in the spouse;

(4) Maximizing the good traits and achieving permanent idealization of these attributes.

All four tasks must be accomplished at this stage in order to cement the relationship. "It's not an easy job," says Dr. Lloyd Mendelson. "There's a lot going on at this stage. The difficulties and confusions often make people think that divorce is very appealing."

Coping with realities that exist outside of your mind — things that are obvious to everyone and can objectively be called facts — is the other, complementary task of this stage. The trick here is to find ways to entwine two separate lives. Two of the most traditional methods people use are having children and creating financial interdependence. Yet anything that brings a couple closer and makes them more necessary to one another will accomplish the goal. People bind themselves together by going into the same business, by sharing hobbies that are important to both, or by putting in long hours together building a summer home. One couple bought a pair of magnificent sheep dogs that command a great deal of time and affection from both husband and wife. This couple has no children and maintains separate finances. But, said the thirty-year-old wife, "Snoopy and Potts (the dogs) are so much a part of our lives that, I swear, I have dismissed the idea of leaving Adrian plenty of times during a bad fight because if we split up, I know we'd get into a hassle about who gets to have custody of those animals. The dogs are very important to us both. They would make it much harder for me to leave this marriage."

Ridiculous? Such a reason for staying together may seem foolish to many people, but for this couple it works. They have bound themselves — and found intimacy — in the best way available to them for now.

Idealizing Certain Qualities

A crucial task of this stage, idealization of a partner's best qualities, is largely a subconscious process. People realize from time to time that it is taking place, however, and several interviewees openly referred to it. A twenty-eight-year-old housewife, married five years, told me, "My husband is so good with the children. He is really an outstanding and unusually loving father, so I don't mind his sloppiness." Said a thirty-year-old engineer of his wife, "She is extremely loyal. I could count on her to stand by me no matter what I did: murder, rape, you name it. So that good thing about her lets me overlook the fact that I know she gets into crazy moods and maybe is even manic-depressive at times."

People who accomplish such idealization of good traits seem to be able to tolerate many other peculiarities about their mates they might consider "bad." Extreme pleasure derived from good traits apparently serves as a balm for marital wounds.

The other ways people fuse themselves together in stage three of marriage, having children and pooling money, are fully conscious acts. But most people tend to do these things because they are part of the social context of their lives, not because they are deliberately looking for ways to head off divorce. However, the effect is the same. When there are children and bank accounts in common, both partners have more inducement to work out problems and stay married.

Having Children

By the time people have been married for five to ten years, the question of children has entered their relationship one way or another. They may be dealing with one or more youngsters, may be trying to have them, or may be deciding *not* to have children. Just talking about the concept of parenthood brings a couple closer. If they become a mother and father, they are drawn together by this joint endeavor; if they remain childless, they are bonded by the soul-searching it takes to make that decision. Couples also have something in common if they want children but can't have them. No matter how the question is resolved, the discussions that inevitably revolve around children at this stage in marriage serve as a bonding agent as long as both spouses agree on the outcome. When they disagree, that means trouble.

"I want a baby very, very badly," a thirty-seven-year-old dentist told me. "My wife says children make her nervous, and she won't even consider the idea. This throws a big monkey wrench into the marriage. I hadn't counted on this because I always thought she'd mellow, she'd change her mind when she got older and want to become a mother.

"This is getting to be too much for me to handle. It's a very basic disagreement over how to live. I'm thinking of divorce."

Of all the ties that keep two people together, probably none is stronger than the presence of a child who is loved by both. In the past, children were an inevitable part of married life, barring accidents of nature that made conception impossible. Children are one strong reason why divorce was not prevalent in American society until fairly recently. As the women's movement gained force in this country, however, having babies become a *choice* among many middle- and upper-class people. Between 1976 and 1982, the number of women aged thirty-five to thirty-nine who were childless rose from eleven percent to fourteen percent. Presumably, this means that the last chance for motherhood was being voluntarily bypassed for most of these women.

Voluntary childlessness reached a peak about 1975. Those were also prime years for divorce in America. Since then there has been a gradual reawakening of interest in having children, possibly because career women now feel more secure about managing both motherhood and a job. There is a minor baby boom going on in America today, and it may be no coincidence that divorce rates are leveling off. According to a 1984 *Reader's Digest*/Gallup Survey, the number of divorces in America in 1982 was 1.2 million, the first decline in twenty years. Divorces continued to drop in 1983. It looks like a new trend is developing for more stable marriages.

One seemingly permanent trend is that many women are postponing motherhood, probably so they can establish careers first. In 1960, only twenty-four percent of married women between the ages of twenty and twenty-four did not have children. By 1982, forty-three percent of the married women in that category were childless.

One reason for the delay is because children are still seen as the great un-equalizers in marriage, since it is usually the wife who must abandon her outside goals in order to remain at home and care for offspring during their years of extreme dependency. Even career women with full-time nannies carry most of the responsibility for hiring and firing the help, leaving the job when help is not available, or stepping in during emergencies when a child insists on parental intervention. And although women have made great strides in inviting (and in some cases forcing) men to share parenthood's burdens as well as its joys, it is still the wife who, in most households, diapers, feeds and nurtures a baby and whose physical presence dominates a child's life.

But despite the extra burdens placed on women — and despite the fact that they are having babies later — for the most part they *do* have them.

Dr. Carlfred Broderick, director of a training center for marriage counselors at the University of Southern California, notes that people who have children know they are giving up a lot of freedom, money and energy but gladly make the tradeoff for the various joys of parenting and because they are aware, on some level, that children are a strong inducement for growth within marriage.

"In my view, children are the most powerful motivators a couple have to grow up themselves," says Dr. Broderick. "Having a family forces us to sacrifice, to learn to put another person's needs before our own, to expand our investment in life and in the future."

In the same *Reader's Digest* survey mentioned earlier, twenty-eight percent of the 1,549 adults polled said raising children was the best thing about their marriage. When asked to name the most pleasant aspects of being married, having children came in right after "mutual love and respect" (forty-seven percent) and "faithfulness and trust" (forty percent).

Joining Forces Via Money

The pooling of financial resources is a major investment in marriage. Money is a factor in any relationship and the way it is made and used often provides clues to the distribution of power in the family.

For most of the people I interviewed, money was still a male-dominated topic. The husbands generally made more money than their wives and felt they were entitled to more of a say in how it was spent and invested. But in the marriages I would call "happy," the men consulted their wives about major purchases and investments and there was much joint decision-making. The men did not use their greater earning power to control their wives; they were eager to share resources and to invest the money wisely to buy security for the family. And both partners, especially the women, seemed willing to sacrifice some autonomy in money decisions in order to foster intimacy, trust and a greater sense that shared finances meant interdependence.

"Money was a tremendous issue when we first got married because neither one of us was making very much of it," a thirty-nine-year-old woman told me. "I appointed myself guardian of the family treasury. I was very nervous about even going out for a movie and a meal because I wanted Neil and me to save, save, save.

"Then Neil finished his medical internship and started making a very good income. We had our first child and I let go of a full-time position in an advertising agency and took on some part-time work. As you can imagine, Neil made much more than me.

"Gradually I felt more secure, especially when I saw that Neil was careful about saving and investing. It evolved into a system whereby we both simply put whatever we have into a joint account and we both draw whatever we need out of the account. Neil buys the stocks and bonds and things like that, and I trust his judgment. I buy household items and the children's things but have also made some major purchases, like a car, without Neil. There is consulting — we ask one another's opinions at times — but we don't ask *permission* to spend.

"I see all this as a minor loss of freedom for both of us in exchange for an unspoken agreement that we trust each other because we don't keep tabs on what the other person is spending. It's like we're both saying to the other, 'Here, whatever I have is yours, too, and I have absolute faith you'll use it wisely.' "

In traditional marriages some inequality seems to be built in, because even working wives often abdicate important money decisions in favor of letting their husbands exercise control over family finances. But again, in good marriages husbands do not abuse the privilege and trust develops. Thus, sharing money becomes an important mechanism in stabilizing the marriage, clarifying roles, and keeping people together during difficult periods.

All married couples who share finances seem to fight over money occasionally, no matter how well-oiled their management methods. Learning who makes what and who spends what is a long, complicated process. It can never evolve without trial and error or continue working flawlessly. But people who depend on one another because money is tied up together are usually careful about letting these fights get out of hand. There is too much danger of damage to the marriage in a money fight, so these fights tend to end fast. Each partner tries to find a way to accommodate the other and return to the comfort of smooth money management.

People who don't pool their financial resources may have less conflict, but they also have much less of a stake in preserving the marriage. So when arguments erupt over other matters, it is easy to allow these arguments to escalate into pitched battles about the tender topic of money and perhaps end the relationship.

Having too little money may be a major problem for many married couples, but when couples who are living together without being married are polled, they also put money problems high on the list of bad things about the relationship. Staying single, therefore, does not put an end to bickering about money woes if you want to become deeply involved with another person.

While the sharing of money and children do not guarantee permanence in marriage, they do provide powerful reasons to work out problems and to keep the relationship intact. And admiring specific traits in a spouse, which I referred to earlier as "permanent idealization," is one way to lubricate the process of commiting one's self to another person enough to want to have children and share money in the first place. Thus the necessary tasks of stage three complement one another and make it possible to face some of the problems that usually erupt after people have been married from five to ten years.

Dependency May Cause Fears

Because children, money and other concerns make for deepening intimacy and more awareness of mutual dependency in this stage, people often feel vulnerable. Both men and women may be frightened. Much of the excitement and passion of the early years is gone, and the couple has to find new ways of relating.

Each partner seeks to assert his or her right to be an individual and at the same time wants the other person to take care of him. It is an internal conflict which often comes out in the form of a power struggle — perhaps as a struggle over the very things that unite the couple, with fights over who gets to invest the money or who decides on the children's education.

In this sense, the stage of Reality Struggles is a replay of what may have happened during each partner's adolescence. The growing boy or girl wants to break away from parents and is thwarted by the reality of his deep dependence on them. There is a great deal of testing, defiant behavior and demands for freedom coming from the adolescent as he or she tries to arrive at a comfortable halfway point between autonomy and cooperation. Much of the time the young person is angry at his parents because he sees them as too powerful, and he is afraid of his own desires to remain under their care. The youngster wants to get his own way, but he still wants mom and dad to meet all his needs. Parents resent this double standard and resist. A power struggle then takes place.

Imagine a fifteen-year-old boy, his hair dyed purple and yellow, with three heavy earrings dangling from one pierced and swollen lobe. This is his uniform — his public statement that he is different from his parents and that they no longer control his actions. The youngster may swagger home late, but he does come home. He wants to proclaim, "I'm me, and I'm free!" Yet he is drawn again and again to the warmth and security of his familiar hearth and the comforting people who may say they're annoyed with him, but who always come through in a pinch. The various and sometimes silly proclamations of independence, the resulting parental irritation and the testing and stretching of family ties may go on for years.

Eventually most well-adjusted children arrive at some comfortable compromise with their parents: They remain under mom and dad's care and continue to grow at the same time. This process is repeated during stage three of marriage, but not without some of the same anger and frustration that marked the adolescent years.

"In this stage you are still struggling to find your own definition of what is real, of what is true," says mental health therapist Frances Nagata. "You are back to coping with how mad you are at your partner for not meeting your expectations, for not being the fantasy you wished for. Just the way you got mad at your parents when you first decided, at adolescence, that they were only human after all.

"This stage is right after you have tried the compromises and find that they take a lot more work than you thought. If you are going to get stuck in a stage, these struggles with reality is where most people stick. I have seen couples flounder here for ten years, twenty years . . . maybe forever. For these people who cannot find reality, anger is what keeps them together. But they have terrible marriages.

"And a lot of anger comes simply because we have few role models for good marriage, so it is more difficult to know what is real. Other generations had their parents to use as role models, but things have changed more in this generation than in any other. So I believe the stages are more pronounced now than ever before. When you hit this third stage and reality isn't what you want to deal with, you are furious."

Ms. Nagata says that resenting the need to accept reality, whether it is good or bad, is a natural reaction for any adult in early mid-life. People in Reality Struggles are usually from twenty-seven to thirty-five years old. For them, the protection and mindless fun of childhood is gone. At this point they must cope with their own children and all the problems and daily decisions of parenthood. Careers also get serious; big money is made and lost. And last of all, failings of a spouse are now undeniable. All this must be faced and accepted.

"No wonder people don't want to do that," says Ms. Nagata. "It means telling it like it is, which is a painful act for most of us. But if you cannot do that rather quickly, you are in danger of getting stuck."

Being Stuck In A Stage

People get stuck in Reality Struggles, or in any other stage, partly because they lack the self-esteem necessary to say, "I can handle this." Dr. M. Scott Peck, a psychiatrist and author, says in his book *The Road Less Traveled* that one must be willing to undergo personal discomfort and psychic pain in order to perceive reality and act upon it.

"Mental health is an ongoing process of dedication to reality at all costs," he says. "The life of wisdom must be a life of contemplation combined with action."

People who cannot confront reality because it may be painful are not able to see marital problems clearly and take steps to overcome them. Instead, they may prefer to engage their partners in endless fights over small matters as a diversionary tactic. These people keep busy quarreling about decorating, in-laws, housework or the many other mundane matters that weave themselves into the fabric of daily married life, rather than facing reality and sharing life goals. This keeps them from having to face the real issues of marriage.

Psychiatric social worker Mildred Kagan says the same fear and insecurity that keeps people from facing reality in stage three of marriage might sometimes have a temporary beneficial effect: It holds the marriage together long enough to give the couple time to overcome their reluctance, face reality and continue maturing.

"The change that has to come now is to know who you are and who you're married to," she says. "In the early years people seem to be engaged in a power struggle to see who can control, dominate and change the other. It certainly was that way for my husband and me. I love a quote from Fritjof Capra's book, *The Turning Point*. He says, 'All struggle in nature takes place within a wider context of cooperation.' That's worth remembering in marital work.

"The capacity to surrender without capitulation is worth striving for," according to Kagan. "This is difficult for most couples to conceive . . . but it's the lesson that *has* to be learned in this stage. Surrender does not mean being taken advantage of. It can mean that you are building on what you learned about various ways to compromise, and facing the reality of the situation at hand, and putting the two together so the marriage can work.

"I think of the long, arduous task that my husband Irv and I undertook when we decided to build an extra room onto our house. Irv wanted a place to grow plants and I wanted a room for dancing. We locked horns over territorial rights, design, space arrangements, almost everything.

"In typical obstinate fashion, we struggled on. But we had learned how to handle each other after ten years, and how to think in terms of what was possible instead of what we each insisted on. The dilemma finally was resolved with surrender on both parts: my giving up a hot tub I hoped could be incorporated and Irv cutting down on extra space he wanted.

"The result is a lovely room we call our play room. Irv plans to grow cactus and orchids (a neat metaphor for his androgynous nature), and I have ample room for dancing and exercise, which is part of my carrying with me the pleasure I had as a child taking lessons in free-style dancing."

Ms. Kagan's example shows how each stage builds on the one before it and carries within it the seeds of the next. A person who has experienced the joy of Fantasy Time and understands Compromise will be equipped to handle Reality Struggles.

A woman I call Anita illustrates the painful floundering that occurs when married people don't trust themselves — or their partners — enough to allow the growth of intimacy by going through the stages.

Anita's Story

I met Anita, thirty-three, on a late evening flight from New York City to Atlanta. She would disembark there, switch planes and go on to her hometown of Dallas, Texas. She was fascinated by the subject of my book and asked to be interviewed. When the plane touched down at Hartsfield International Airport two hours later, I had a substantial outline of the life of a woman whose marriage was almost destroyed because she had lived in the past, believing she could not trust others. As a result, she wanted her mate to prove his love by arranging life for her. It was the same demand she had once made on her parents.

Anita is a petite, pixie-faced woman with long red hair tied back in an appealing ponytail. She has a six-year-old son and travels regularly throughout the northeast as a sales representative for a large computer company.

Although the first eight years of her marriage were very hard, Anita told me, the past two years have been wonderful. She attributes the change to giving up an incorrect view of reality and replacing it with a sounder way of looking at the world. To do this, she spent four years in psychoanalysis.

"My childhood was a struggle to get my parents to love me," she says bluntly. "I was very spoiled because they let me have my own way on practically everything. But deep down, even when I was very little, I knew *that* wasn't love. They simply did not care enough to take the time to make rules and enforce them. Everything that concerned me was too much trouble for them. So Mom and Dad pretty much left me alone, and I was terrified because I was drifting with no solid idea of what was wrong and what was right. What that means, I found out later, was that I had no way of pinpointing reality.

"I would always be trying to get my mother and father to do things for me, I guess because I wanted some proof of love. As a child I was very demanding, always nagging for a toy or a candy bar . . . and I always got it. There were no limits. My mother would say to my father, 'Oh, just give it to her and she'll shut up.'

"The other thing my parents did was let me down all the time. They promised to take me to the movies the day I came home with straight A's on my report card, but they forgot about it. I was all dressed up, anticipating an evening out with my mom and dad, and then they came in with a babysitter and left me and went out to dinner by themselves. That was when I was about nine or ten years old. I told the babysitter I had a headache and went to bed. I was so hurt and humiliated.

"They also forgot my birthdays pretty often. And they lied to me. My father let me have a dog, but the dog wet the floor a lot, so Dad said he wanted to get rid of the dog for that reason. I begged him to give me a week in order to paper-train the dog, and he said okay. But when I came home from school the next day the dog was gone. My father took it to the pound. He just made the promise of a week's time to get me off his back.

"Deception, broken promises, being ignored. That's pretty much the way I grew up," Anita adds sorrowfully. "After a while I didn't expect much so it didn't hurt so bad. But I had learned not to trust my parents, and I looked at everyone that way.

"When I got married I didn't trust my husband either, although he was a very stable person who always kept his word. And that's why I needed professional help to make the marriage work: I had to see that the reality of my childhood was not the reality of my adulthood. I had to be able to tell the difference so I could relate to my husband according to the new reality he brought into my life.

"That is very, very difficult. Once you learn a life script as a child,

you tend to carry it with you unless you force yourself to break away
from it. For me, it took four hard years of intensive analysis. But it
certainly was worth the time and money."

Says Dr. Peck, "No act is more unnatural, and hence more human,
than the act of entering psychotherapy. For by this act we deliberately
lay ourselves open to the deepest challenge from another human
being and even pay the other for the service of scrutiny and discern-
ment. . . . Entering psychotherapy is an act of the greatest courage."

Perhaps Anita, despite her depressing childhood, was blessed with
more courage and emotional strength than many people. Her marriage to Timothy, a wealthy real estate developer, took place just a
month after they both graduated from the University of Wisconsin.
At the time, Anita was twenty-three and Timothy was twenty-four.
Almost immediately, Anita attempted to recreate the scenario she
had learned as a child.

"I insisted that Tim do everything for me just to prove his love.
And it was terrible, because no matter how much he did, it was never
enough. We both had jobs, but Tim did all the housework, too. I was
a sales manager in a department store, and he was learning real estate
in a big company. He figured I was tired after a long day on the job so
he didn't mind the extra burden at first. But as time went on, he
started grumbling that it was unfair. From that he went on to decide
that I was a big baby who was spoiled and who threw a fit if things
didn't go her way.

"He was right. But it was easier for him to give in than to hassle
with me about the housework and everything else. In that sense, he
was playing the role my parents had played."

The marriage crept along on an emotional tightrope for four years.
During that time, Anita told me, there was no growth for either
partner and no stages were negotiated.

Compromise was impossible because Anita was afraid of losing
power over Timothy. She wanted the marriage to stay in the first stage
of fantasy, and for a while Timothy agreed by default. When Anita
became pregnant near the end of their fourth year together, however,
making compromises and then quickly entering the stage of Reality

Struggles became inevitable.

"We had planned the baby, but all along I suspected I might not be able to handle motherhood," Anita recalls. "I made the most of the pregnancy, ordering Tim around like a slave, and he was so happy about the baby and so inexperienced in marriage that he was glad to give in to my whims. So I got through the nine months all right.

"Then, bam, the baby was born and the roof fell in on my fantasies. Tim refused to get up for the night feedings. He had to go to work, of course, and I was on maternity leave. Also, I wanted him to run errands, take me out at night, handle the visits to the pediatrician . . . and he just balked. He was exhausted and fed up with all my demands.

"At the same time I was very anxious, without knowing why. I knew things were bad but I couldn't figure out how they managed to get that way. I had a lot of sleepless nights, heart palpitations, sweating palms — all for what seemed to be no specific reason at the time.

"Tim and I fought constantly. I resented having to do housework and baby care, things I had never done before. He hated my endless complaining. Finally he said I was a terrible wife and mother and he was going to leave me and fight for custody of the baby.

"I got so scared and confused that I went into analysis. I begged Tim to give me a chance at it, to see if I could change. He gave me six months. I remember thinking, 'Oh, this is like the time my dad gave me a week to paper-train the dog. Tim will promise, then betray me.' But unlike my father, Tim kept his word. That alone was enough to shock me into realizing I had been operating under a false reality.

"I hated myself for not trusting, but I didn't know how to become a better person. In analysis I was able to see the childhood roots for my demands and how unrealistic they were for an adult, especially an adult woman who was married to a man who *could* be trusted.

"Little by little I learned to trust Tim, and so I didn't need to have daily 'proof' of his loyalty and affection. I started easing off on the demands and doing things for myself and for the baby. The more I did, the easier it became to develop a new pattern of behavior. Tim responded with praise and he started acting loving toward me again.

"I learned that accepting responsibility for myself did not mean Tim would have no reason to stay with me. I wasn't afraid to face up to the baby's needs, and I started maturing into a responsible woman who could carry her half of the marriage.

"There is no way to tell you about the pain I went through during those years of analysis. Oh, the tears! The bitterness I had to swallow in facing the fact that my own parents didn't love me, and then *accepting* the fact and going on with life. The way I had to force myself to handle responsibility, with everything from finding a babysitter to doing the laundry to leaving work on time in order not to be late for dinner out with Tim.

"But there is also no way to describe how much it was worth all that," Anita adds with a beaming smile. "If you don't know how to face reality on your own, you must have help. It's the crazy people who *don't* go to a psychiatrist. If you need it, without that kind of help to find reality, you can't have a good marriage at all."

What Is Reality?

Before a person can acknowledge and work with reality, he has to know what it is. Freud often defined anxiety in terms of reality. *Realistic anxiety,* he said, is rational and connected to a person's perception of external danger. Perhaps this sort of fear is tightly bound to our ancient fight-or-flight reflex. When prehistoric man was startled by a tiger leaping into his path, it was helpful to be afraid because the fear released chemicals that gave wings to his plodding feet or strength to the exhausted muscles holding his club. Thus realistic anxiety, as Freud saw it, is an inborn response that helps a person cope with immediate danger.

When there is no danger and a person still feels afraid, that person is experiencing what Freud called *neurotic anxiety.* It first develops from a mistrust of people, since people are a child's first reality. Neurotic anxiety also can be eased by people. My favorite example of this is Freud's story of the child who was put to bed by his aunt in a dark room. The aunt went into the next room and the child called out, "Do speak to me, Auntie! I'm frightened!"

"Why, what good would that do?" asked the aunt. "You can't see me."

To this the child replied, "If someone speaks, it gets lighter."

The child's perception of reality — light versus dark in his room — was altered by the voice of another, trusted person. Maybe the same thing happens in marriage. What we think of our spouse may be what another legendary analyst, Jung, called the *psychic reality.* This may be defined as the reality we accept, whether others see it that way or not. This may explain why a fat woman is seen as "pleasingly plump" by her adoring husband, or why a lazy man is merely relaxed as far as his wife is concerned. When we shake our heads at a friend's choice of an improbable mate and wonder, "What does she see in him?" it may be the virtues of a psychic reality that are lost to our eyes. But the friend has this reality firmly fixed in her mind. And for the sake of her relationship, her private notion of reality is all that matters.

During Reality Struggles we drift further and further away from the beloved fantasy of a perfect mate. We have to cope with our partner's failings, but we can preserve some of the glow of young love by highlighting good points that bring pleasure. We focus our concentration on these points, and this process becomes permanent idealization, one of the tasks mentioned earlier as being essential to this stage of marriage.

Such selected virtues form the basis of a new fantasy that will serve as permanent glue to bind us happily to husband or wife. We may be forced to abandon much fantasy. But humans need pleasure almost as much as they need daily bread, and to get it people create pleasure in marriage by constructing elaborate supports around the best traits they can find in their partners. There is great reluctance to look past these supports or to allow others to damage them in any way.

An example of the permanent idealization of pleasurable traits is found in William, an Atlanta journalist who has been married to Cynthia for seven years. William has not only selected Cynthia's best traits to admire, but he has also skillfully set up a series of emotional defenses against parental criticism of his wife. William is twenty-nine. Cynthia, who is part owner of a bookstore, is thirty-four.

William's parents disapproved of this marriage from the very beginning and say they will not speak to their son until he divorces Cynthia. After seven happy years with a loving wife, however, William says divorce will never happen.

"My parents really don't like Cynthia," William tells me sadly. "They simply can't accept her because she is 'different,' and they see that as a threat. They hate the idea that she's older than me, and they say she seduced me into marrying too young.

"Cynthia is a very sensitive person, and she will leave the book-shop in her partner's hands and go off for long periods of time to be alone and just think. She has gone to foreign countries, and some-times she stays for weeks. My parents don't see how I can put up with that. But I see those separations as healthy. They keep our marriage young and remove both me and Cynthia from the petty annoyances of daily life together. We're really happy to see one another when she gets back.

"But my mom and dad always saw me as marrying a rather conventional woman, and Cynthia is anything but conventional. She is a strict vegetarian. They are shocked because she sometimes wears strange clothing. She looks beautiful in an Indian sari, but they think that's a wacky thing to wear. Cynthia can't have children — it's a medical problem — and, of course, to Mom and Dad that's a big black mark against her.

"Also, my wife is rather energetic. She will do things like dump all the silverware out on the floor, as a joke. Cynthia's high spirits sometimes get me annoyed, but she always manages to make me laugh about it. We laugh a lot. Cynthia is never a bore.

"She once went with me to a bank where we were applying for a loan, and she really cut up in front of the loan officer. He thought she was charming, but I was afraid he'd think she was out of her tree. I figured we wouldn't get the money. When we came out of the bank I was seething. I said, 'You could have ruined the whole deal. Why don't you act normal?' She danced around and said sometimes 'normal' is another word for 'dull,' and she imitated the stuffy loan officer, and pretty soon she had me really laughing hard at the whole thing.

"Cynthia just refuses to take life so seriously, and she has put a lot of fun into my existence because of it. I am a very quiet guy. Cynthia brightens me up."

William and Cynthia went through the first several stages of marriage quickly, he says. Fantasy Time ended when they began to quarrel about money after only several months of marriage. Compromise was mainly a series of negotiations, during which Cynthia curbed her desire for expensive clothing so that William had enough money to invest in some blue-chip stocks, providing security for them both.

Because each of them has selected many pleasurable realities about the other to cherish, "Marriage for us after seven years is a flower garden," says William. He sees his wife's bad points but willingly accepts them, since in his view her pleasurable traits more than compensate for the annoyances. He has even managed to idealize the annoyances, too: Cynthia's boisterousness, for example, is translated into fun for William. Even though he remains loyal to his parents and says he will never stop trying to re-establish communication with them, William will not allow parental hostility to penetrate his useful fantasies about his wife.

Cynthia and William have no children, and both remain financially independent even though they do own some stocks together. Are they less bound together, therefore, than couples who do share children and money?

Perhaps. But their idealization of one another's good traits appears to compensate. The ways people find to lock themselves together as securely as possible are as varied and as individual as the couples themselves. For example, a wife may enlarge her husband's realistic abilities as a provider, and because this good trait is important to her, she can refer to it in glowing terms and use it to counterbalance his sloppy manners or clumsy lovemaking. A husband who appreciates his wife's calmness under stress will dwell on this distinction; it helps him dismiss her habitual tardiness. When people idealize their spouse's best traits, it becomes their private reality and they will tolerate no criticism on these points from others.

Freud noted that all healthy people find some way of creating a private emotional fantasyland which serves as a barrier against outside attacks on their love objects. The barrier prevents others from robbing individuals of the pleasure and stability they get from idealizing their mate's best traits and clinging to them as compensation for discovering that the mate is not a perfect person. If Cynthia cannot be perfect — as William knows — she can be very good. She fills William's emotional needs, and he prefers to see her in a positive light.

Reality Testing

This is the process of judging whether things are real or not. When married people construct a fantasy, especially the fantasy that allows them to idealize their mate, they do not "test" those feelings. They are more than content to leave them alone.

Divorce most often occurs when there are too few good traits in a mate around which to build a joyful fantasy. Also, in some cases one or both partners are too eager to hang on to old dreams of perfection. They are not willing to abandon hopes of getting all their needs satisfied by a mate, so they decide to ditch the flawed wife or husband they have and prowl around for someone else. In the fifth to tenth year of marriage, when reality struggles are most often at fever pitch, the threat of divorce peaks.

According to numbers compiled by the National Center for Health Statistics, the median time in the United States before divorce in 1981 was seven years. In 1980, the median was 6.8 years, and in 1970 it was 6.7 years. Thus, people are making their marriages last just a little bit longer these days than they did ten years ago, at the height of America's divorce mania. But the statistics still suggest that roughly half the married American population cannot face the stages of

Compromise and Reality Struggles in the mature, creative manner necessary to build a rewarding lifelong union with the first person they marry. As psychiatric social worker Millie Kagan asserts, "Many of the people who divorce don't have any particular gripe about their husbands or wives. They don't want to go on with the marriage stages because they want to stay stuck in emotional adolescence instead."

Dr. Lloyd Mendelson agrees, saying deep-seated emotional needs draw people to their mates in the first place, so these people have obviously pulled the correct subconscious switch or made the proper chemical connection. Says Dr. Mendelson, "I don't think we often make mistakes when we get married. People have a great ability to pick the right partner the first time. They just don't understand the stages. Because of that they can't grow or allow the partner to grow. So they get disillusioned and translate that into divorce."

Nigel And Diana

Diana says she'll fight hard to make sure divorce does not happen to her, although she has always seen it as a definite possibility. If there is peace for her on this earth — and she says *if* with a wry, mocking upturn in her soft voice — she has found it with Nigel. After ten years of marriage, she'd be a fool to toss it away now, she says.

The story of Nigel and Diana illustrates two points about the stage of Reality Struggles. First, it shows how mature people, even if they are somewhat troubled as is Diana, can accomplish permanent idealization and allow their partners to do the same. Second, this story pinpoints the additional and usually lifelong difficulties experienced by a couple who do not have children and shared finances to bind them together. While Nigel and Diana say they are happily married, they do not feel totally secure.

When I come to their suburban Boston home for an interview, Diana is sitting cross-legged on the thick living room rug, her spine rigid, her elbows digging into her knees, her blue eyes wide with tension. Her body is draped in a baggy T-shirt and jogging pants. She is having trouble relaxing.

With every new question, Diana jerks her head up and her short platinum curls bounce like coiled wire. "I am ordinarily tense, so it's not the interview itself that makes me jumpy," she reassures. "It's just hard to hear myself telling the truth out loud, because it reminds me that although I'm thrilled with Nigel as a husband, we aren't really very entwined with each other."

Diana is now forty-five years old. She was thirty-five when she got tired of "knocking around," as she puts it. She was weary of the strain of an unsatisfying career and scarred with the broken remnants of several intense love relationships. She had been postponing marriage because she was waiting for a hot-shot, a great guy, a famous writer or an opera singer, or a wildly successful photographer, or *something*. But the great guys she knew always had a fatal flaw: They did not want to marry her. She was getting lonely. Nigel was nobody special, really, but he offered good sex, tenderness and a chance at love. She took it.

"I let it go. The dream, I mean. I wanted to get married to someone who had everything to give . . . and who would give it all to *me*. I'm not getting everything I want out of Nigel, but I think the reality of the situation is that he hasn't got it to give. Because he's handsome and has this marvelous Australian accent, I thought he was educated and had some class. Well, it didn't quite turn out to be that way. I have two graduate degrees, and Nigel is a pilot who only went to flight school. I like to learn, to be intellectual, and he's not my intellectual equal.

"At the very beginning of our marriage I resented finding out that Nigel's education and mental curiosity didn't match my own. It ended my fantasy, and I took it hard. But it didn't take long, maybe a year, to hit on the idea that Nigel didn't have to supply all kinds of intellectual stimulation for me. I go out with girlfriends and have a fine time discussing classic literature or debating the hidden meaning in a work of art. Nigel is a comfort to me when I need it. He gives me security that comes from having a best friend. So it's not important anymore to find Mr. Perfect. Listen, I wasn't a kid when I got married. I had to face up to reality pretty fast.

"We went through hot love, then trying to work things out, and now the sort of scary acceptance of what things really are, what *we* really are. Nigel is a good, loving man. He is not the spectacular fellow I always wanted to marry, but he is good for me. I'm nobody special. I'm okay, I'm fine, but I thought I'd be on the cover of *Time* magazine one day." Diana chuckles, amused at the sound of her own words. "I guess that isn't going to happen."

She had been hoping for a shot at glory ever since childhood but not really working very hard to achieve it. Diana was not a happy child. As the middle girl in a family of three aggressive, upward-striving female children, she found herself constantly elbowing for room in their cramped nest, always open-mouthed with protest or anger or some other pressing emotion.

Sometimes the emotions were so strong and swooped down on her so fast that she couldn't sort them out. She became a bundle of nerves and contradictions. She hated one sister and loved the other. She wanted her mom near her one moment and couldn't stand her the next. She thought her dad was tops on Sunday; on Monday, he was a jerk.

On, off, on . . . Diana's emotions flicked back and forth like a crazy light switch. She was proud of being a Jew, and at the same time she was terribly afraid of the world's bigotry. She flaunted her big breasts as a bright beacon of sexuality and secretly was ashamed of every swift sexual encounter. When she was twenty-one she told herself that Boston was a nuthouse, and in a sweeping gesture of utter contradiction she sought sanity in the rush and swirl of Manhattan.

It wasn't there. Diana started traveling, her degrees in literature wrapped around her like protective cloaks. She wound up teaching English in a small midwestern town and fell in love with another woman's husband. He liked the way she came on to him: intensely sexual, willing to experiment, restless with longing for something she couldn't define but was eager to share.

"Was it the experience I was after?" she asks herself now. "Was it simply the fun of the moment? Or was it only an extension of my lust for information, my love of knowing what's available?"

The romance fizzled and Diana went to Europe. She taught school there and made love to strange, sweating men whose names she could barely pronounce. She rarely had an orgasm. She kept searching.

Diana came back to the states because she wasn't having much fun anymore. She was nearing her mid-thirties, still single, still restless, still not sure what she liked or disliked in life. She had failed to write a great book, and it was time to admit that she really didn't want to work that hard. Fame would not trot out to meet her, and she simply couldn't find the energy to dash madly after it. She still argued with her parents almost every time they got together. She still hated one sister. No man excited her. Teaching literature was only a way to make a living, and a rotten way, she thought. On her thirty-fourth birthday, Diana stockpiled a lethal dose of sleeping pills and made out a will.

"I came very close. . . ." Diana lowers her eyes and stares at the muted pattern on the rug. She uncurls her legs, stretches and lies flat on her back, staring up at the ceiling. I stretch out beside her.

"What made you stop? I mean . . . how come you didn't? . . ."

"I don't know. It was really a low point. One thing is, I called up a friend and started crying and allowed her to talk me into staying at her apartment until I felt better. So that shows I really didn't want to end it all. I still think of suicide as my right. It's my ultimate escape to nothingness. But now I have Nigel to think of. I wouldn't do that to him. I don't fool myself into thinking I'll ever be a person without problems, but I have matured a lot through marriage. I am closer to seeing what is real.

"Nigel is real. He keeps me here. No, change that to I keep *myself* here, and it's at least partly because of him, because I am able to love him and accept his love."

It has not been an easy marriage. Nigel was recovering from a divorce when he met Diana and wanted custody of his four-year-old son. Diana said no. "I told him I could certainly understand his wanting the child, but that I wasn't cut out to be a mother so he had to make that choice for himself."

It turned out that the boy wanted to stay with his mom, so the choice was made for Nigel. He and Diana were married after a year-long courtship. Now he sees his child at least twice a week. Diana praises Nigel for being such a good father, but she makes herself scarce when his son, now fourteen, is around. Nigel understands. "She needs her space, her territory," he says. "That is the reality I have to cope with."

Nigel loves his job as a pilot. It gives him time off to play tennis, a release from the boredom of being deskbound and a fine uniform to complement his sturdy, muscular frame. And the money is good. He doesn't mind sharing money with Diana; it was she who insisted on separate bank accounts, separate incomes and separate financial plans for security in their old age. She wants that kind of freedom, he knows, but she also wants to be secure. It is another contradiction, another set of competing emotions.

That's okay, says Nigel. He solves the problem by keeping his money separate from hers but offering to pay for vacations and entertainment, because he makes more money than Diana. Diana approves of this arrangement. By now Nigel understands and accepts Diana for what she is — good and bad — and he has even learned to enjoy both parts of her.

It wasn't always that way. After the early flame of romance quickly sputtered, Diana became disappointed because Nigel wasn't as "classy" as his accent and his uniform had implied. He was a working man who just *looked* aristocratic. When she told him that, it made him mad. He screamed at her, accusing her of being a snob, and slammed his fist through the wall in frustration.

"I was trying hard to make compromises, and Nigel's temper really scared me," says Diana. "I had to come to grips with the fact that my husband has a terrible, raging temper. He has never hit me or even made the slightest move or intimation in that direction. But he slams things and puts his fist through walls. I never saw rage like that. It terrified me, especially since I'm used to winning battles with words, not with screams and muscle."

Scenes like that don't happen often anymore, says Diana. She and Nigel fight, but now the fights are attempts to struggle together to find solutions to realistic problems rather than a flailing separate battle for control.

"Now nobody needs to win," she says. "Winning in marriage isn't real, because that implies one spouse has 'lost.' I have abandoned my fantasy that it is good to have win-power over another person. I still think I'm the dominant person in the relationship, simply because I am the one who is more loved. Nigel needs me more than I need him, or at least more than I'm willing to admit to myself that I need him. I don't show love a lot. I come to Nigel to be cuddled, I come for sex, but I pull away fast, and I don't always respond when he asks me for the same kind of warmth.

"I'm working at being more loving. It is very exciting to be able to look at yourself quite objectively with the help of a spouse and see your own faults, then actually strive to overcome a fault and experience success at it. You can actually measure your own changes, because if you are honest with your husband or wife, they will tell you and you can also see them get happier as the fault is corrected. It must be the way a child feels so thrilled when he grows an inch and can see it by a mark on the doorframe."

She stops, rolls over on her side to face me, and grins broadly. "The best part of marriage right now, in my opinion, is that I clearly see the realities in myself and in Nigel and in our relationship. It isn't all a bed of roses, but I am past hoping for that. Nigel and I know exactly where we stand, exactly what to expect from the other person.

"Now and then I become aware that some fantasies linger on, when I think I'd like to get out from under our problems and find someone who is better suited to me than Nigel. You might say I slip into longing once again to find a perfect mate before it's too late and I'm old. I guess I'll always have a little of that longing in me to escape and avoid reality."

When we meet a few weeks later, Nigel, forty-seven, has no such ambivalence. He says, "I know that I am looking at my wife's good and bad points with rather clear eyes and making a very conscious decision to love her and to stick with the marriage for now."

Nigel says he can handle the garbled messages he sometimes gets from Diana. For example, Diana says she is independent but she gripes about Nigel playing mixed doubles tennis. There are a lot of attractive single women out on the courts, she says. Her jealousy, with its deep undertones of insecurity and mistrust, fouls the air.

"Why is she so insecure?" Nigel asks, phrasing it more like a sad statement than as a question. He doesn't really need to know the answer. "I *will* play," he says firmly, "because I enjoy tennis and I know I'm not out there to meet another woman. Diana's insecurities are not my problem. If she really starts to hassle about it, I suppose I shall have to make a choice between asserting my right to play mixed doubles against saying it's not worth the bother to upset her. I'd go back to just playing singles with other men.

"I don't have to understand all the reasons why Diana does something, or even why I do something. If the situation is that a problem needs to be corrected, I'll simply do it and have it over with."

Nigel says his first marriage was very "old-fashioned." His wife stayed home and raised a child; Nigel worked hard and brought back the bacon. He tells me it was an unsatisfying, one-dimensional relationship.

"I had been brought up that way," he says. "When I was younger it was my automatic behavior, to act as if the man made all the decisions and the woman obeyed and stayed at home. Then my wife had an affair with another man. We both realized then how unhappy she had been. The affair made her more confident. She realized she was her own person. She could do things on her own and she didn't have to rely on me.

"She married that other guy. And I learned a good lesson. When Diana came along I was really attracted to her rather fierce independence. It was exciting; it still is. Diana is ever so much more interesting than a woman who keeps mum because she thinks it's only the man's place to speak about important things."

Nigel says Diana gives him a wider, more sweeping view of the world; he says he got "intellectual awareness" from her. In return

Nigel gives Diana the capacity to have fun. He likes people, good wine, a lusty night out with laughing friends. With Nigel around, Diana smiles a lot more.

Their sex is good. Both Diana and Nigel say they believe in being monogamous. An affair would surely smash the relationship. "I trust her," Nigel says simply, "and I want to be able to keep that feeling of trust."

Says Diana, "At the beginning I asked if he wanted an open marriage and he had a fit. He said *no,* of course not! Now, I know I couldn't do that either. I couldn't tolerate the loss of trust, the integrity loss. It would mean our words weren't good. It would make us into liars."

Nigel says trust in a marriage is tremendously important. His trust of Diana is now taking root in a form that cannot be shaken, and such trust is the best thing anyone could want from a marriage, Nigel says. Once Diana told her girlfriend a secret that Nigel had confided to her, and he was heartbroken because she had betrayed his trust. Diana was sorry, too. She hadn't realized the information was something Nigel didn't want to share with anyone else. Diana's pain was sincere, Nigel says; he knows she'll never do that again. And he also knows she won't "fool around" with another man.

"I can tell what's real from what's not real," he says with a self-assured smile. "As I have said, I know Diana's good points and her bad. She is trustworthy. That is real."

Diana's strong need for "territory," as she calls it, is also real. It is a sometimes disturbing characteristic that Nigel has learned to overlook. She is too picky about her friends, whereas Nigel will quickly embrace other people and invite them out for a night on the town. Diana guards her privacy and her home. She doesn't like people popping in on her. She is not at ease with children. When Nigel's adolescent son comes for a visit, Diana often goes to her bedroom and softly locks the door or slips out to see a movie.

"I used to resent that," says Nigel. "My desire to have her gush over the lad and drop everything else when he was around so she could be an instant parent was based on my own chauvinistic ideas of how women should be with children. Now I know better. Diana's space cannot be violated. She simply doesn't like children. That's okay with me now. I have accepted her personality. She is a working person with her own schedule, and I don't have the right to dump the boy on her against her will. He is *my* boy, *my* responsibility. Why drag Diana into it if she's not willing?

"I don't want a life built on sacrifice, and neither does Diana. We are in love and loyal. But we don't sacrifice much for each other. And I don't think we are devoted to one another come hell or high water. We're devoted to ourselves.

"We want to stay together as long as possible, and there is no reason why that won't be forever. But there are some things that could tear us apart. I would not give up an exciting job to stay with Diana if she refused to relocate with me. And as I said, if one or the other really had a meaningful affair with someone else, I don't know if the marriage would stand through that.

"But I'm not worried about such problems now. I will face them when and if the time ever comes. Although I do sense that a new period of our lives together might be around the corner, right now the reality is good, so why make up things to think about that are glum? This is about as good a marriage as we can have, considering that we don't share children or money, and I'm happy to settle for it."

Marriage Is Imperfect

Psychoanalyst Dr. H. Lee Hall says realistic people will not be totally, blindly happy in marriage. That's because marriage is just as imperfect as other things in life. Our mistakes have been in idealizing this particular social institution and surrounding it with a shimmering halo of perfection.

The same bold, pragmatic Americans who conquered the wilderness, pioneered space technology and mastered the fist-thumping rules of big business are often fools when it comes to marriage. We have wanted to keep that area of our lives "clean," untainted by the strains of the rest of the world and unscarred by reality. That childish desire has cost us dearly in divorce when inevitable truths slam into our consciousness.

"Reality will come because it *must* come," says Dr. Hall, "and we as a society, and as individuals, are to blame if we are not prepared for it. Quite simply, reality does mean seeing the good and the bad in your partner almost as well as other, more objective, people see it and coping with it on a mature basis.

"At this point, the stage of reality, the mature couples begin final acceptance of one another just as they are. Of course, they have managed to construct those protective fantasies around their partner's good traits.

"By and large, people who divorce from five to ten years into the marriage, most often during the well-publicized 'seven year itch,' are still preoccupied with the fantasy of a perfect lover. Being madly in love was lots of fun, and they want to do it over and over. They don't realize how shallow an emotion that is. Maybe they'll get divorced, hang a bunch of gold chains around their necks and find somebody to make them feel good again.

"With reality acceptance comes a terrible loss of self-esteem at first. You know your fantasy is gone, and you think, 'How awful! I blew it!' That's why people — men especially — think they have to do something drastic to make themselves feel better. They might buy younger-looking clothes, a snazzy sports car, perhaps take up marathon running. Or they might find a younger lover — and if they divorce their wives for her, the same pattern will probably repeat itself. It's a nasty joke.

"People who come through this stage have gone far enough in the separation process to be able to be individuals. And by now there is a tremendous reserve of affection, shared memories, goods owned in common, maybe children, even some guilt to keep them together. There is nothing wrong with that. In terms of preserving the union, it works."

The advantages of Reality Struggles are inherent in the tasks of this stage: children are often added to one's life; security is heightened if finances are shared; and one's partner becomes capable of objectively pointing out some faults so they can be corrected if desired. At the apex of this stage of marriage, each partner has a reasonably clear view of himself and his spouse. There is much excitement in being able to successfully arrive at this stage.

Of course, troubles are not over. Now that a person has the information about who his spouse really is, decisions must be made in the next stage as to what to *do* with that information.

But for now, a major step has been taken toward growth. People have arrived at the bold truth that no one can change the world for them. No one can "complete" you...except you. One's marriage partner is just another person. He is special, yes, but the magical powers and wild expectations are almost gone. A person who has negotiated the stage of Reality Struggles knows there is only one ultimate problem-solver in life.

It is you.

7

Stage Four: DECISIONS
(Years Ten to Fifteen)

"I am in a stage of my life and my career where the buck stops with me. I am the adult, the responsible party." — a forty-year-old nurse, married fifteen years.

Psychiatrist Roger L. Gould, in his book *Transformations*, tells a story that describes the core message of this stage. He says a profound sadness hit him and his wife Renee at the very moment they fulfilled a long-held dream and moved into a home of their own. On the first night in their new house they slept poorly, and on the second night they were close to tears. Later Dr. Gould figured out what happened.

"We felt sadness the second night in our dream house because something had died," he said. "What died was a protective illusion connecting us to childhood and our parents."

The decision to buy a house was something only a grown-up could do. When that decision became concrete and the Goulds were really *in* the house, it became painfully obvious that they had severed another bond of security with their parents. They were much closer to being on their own in the world.

This event in the Goulds' life symbolizes the stage of Decisions. It is a time when couples must learn to make very important and often permanent decisions both as a team *and* as individuals acting in the best interests of that team.

People make decisions all through marriage, of course, but after ten to fifteen years together the press of time makes life choices seem critical. Also, as people realize they can cope on their own, they have yet another choice: to stay in the marriage or leave. Staying may mean accepting more responsibilities than one had bargained for, but after investing together so heavily in children, shared money, aging parents, mortgages or other joint ventures, leaving is harder than ever before. In the stage of Decisions, married people feel both the exhilaration of important decision-making and the crush of responsibility that comes with those decisions.

"When I was younger, the decisions I made weren't really critical, it seemed, because if things went wrong there was plenty of time to take a different path," a forty-year-old nurse told me. She has been married fifteen years. "Now time is not on my side so much. Also, I am in a stage of my life and my career where the buck stops with me. I am the adult, the responsible party. So I feel a lot of pressure to make a right decision all the time, and not having room for mistakes is very stressful."

It is exciting to realize you have the power to make and enforce decisions. But that power sets you apart as an adult who must face the consequences of each independent act. You bought a house and now you have to live in it, pay for it and face trouble alone if the roof collapses. You can no longer run crying for help from mom and dad. That knowledge is terrifying.

Up to about the tenth year of marriage, people often float in a womb of self-doubt about career choices, relationships with parents and peers and ways of building a foundation for lifelong marital compatibility. So they rely on another significant individual — most often the mate — either to make decisions for them or at least to approve or veto those decisions. The wife or husband provides the same sort of safety net against bad decisions as did parents in earlier times. If things go wrong, there is someone else to share the blame and to try to help correct the problem. This makes decision-making a less lonely process and takes the sting out of failure.

When a couple has been married from ten to fifteen years, however, life has usually become so complicated that a spouse is no longer the automatic decision-making partner and blame-sharer. He or she is usually too busy.

"I used to be able to sit down with Artie and have these long discussions over should I go in and ask for a raise, and how could I do it without getting my boss mad and risking the job. And Artie would sort of help me with a plan of attack," a thirty-five-year-old office manager tells me.

"But now we just don't have the time for so many talks like that. We've been married twelve years. We have two children. Artie is really wrapped up in his own job. It's not that we don't talk, but I don't feel like I can lay a problem at his feet and he can spend hours dissecting it with me and coming up with an answer. There are a lot of distractions. It's the housework, the children, the telephone ringing... everyday stuff like that.

"And even more to the point, I can't say I'm comfortable with asking Artie to take over my decisions like that anymore. He has plenty of little nagging problems of his own. I should be able to make up my own mind. I'm old enough."

Self-Reliance Is Scary

Advancing age becomes a serious factor in the decision-making process. People married for ten to fifteen years are usually from thirty-three to thirty-eight years old. Many of the men and women I interviewed were in their early or mid-forties at this stage, either because they married late or were on their second marriages. The source of identity for people from about thirty-five to forty-five years old is gradually moving from outside to inside — from others to themselves. It is no longer appropriate to rely on even a beloved spouse to stamp YES or NO on decisions.

This growing self-reliance, and the ghost of fear it often brings, is another hallmark of the stage of Decisions. Having come through Reality Struggles by arriving at a reasonably objective view of one's partner and anchoring the relationship with shared money, children or other commitments, it is now time to follow up these broad choices with specific, daily decisions. Only now the decisions seem more important because middle age is swiftly approaching. Like the Goulds sitting sadly in their dream house, people know they are finally cut off from parental support. In addition, there is fear of too little time to take corrective measures if choices happen to be wrong.

Each decision, no matter how large or small, takes energy. It is a tormented moment in time suspended between need and action. In the high-intensity years of early middle age, there is often too little opportunity to mull over options. Thus, some decisions take on the shape and intensity of a crisis when something must be *done*. In the Decisions stage of marriage, such moments seem to fly at couples relentlessly.

Levinson describes important moments of decision as "marker events." He says those are the decisions that stick. People learn from them, and they produce permanent changes in attitude and behavior.

Examples of what I perceive as marker events are the choice to have a child or to forego parenthood; moving to a strange city; changing careers; or even accepting or rejecting an extramarital affair. No matter what people do, the choice is bound to have a major and lasting impact — and each one of us knows it.

It takes guts to make a decision that changes the course of one's life and the lives of others in the family. At this point, a couple can't afford to make too many mistakes. Others depend on that performance, and mistakes are likely to be far-reaching, permanent and costly. People can step forward and bravely accomplish a difficult task, only to become engulfed in old anxieties shortly after all the new behavioral mechanisms are in place. You bought the house...but can you really handle that mortgage? The baby is here...do you really want it? Instead of retiring to Florida, mom and dad heeded your wishes and bought a condominium down the street; now, can you give them the emotional support you promised?

It is common to have anxieties and doubts about one's abilities to follow through after important decisions are made. But it seems those woes are pushed on us in double time during the stage of Decisions. This may be the period in our lives when we most need to be alone with ourselves and with our mates, to nourish the growth of maturity. Yet it is difficult to travel through this time without disruptions and unwelcome surprises. An aged parent demands attention; a friend cracks up; our seventeen-year-old daughter gets pregnant. The forceful winds of outside events topple plans and jumble the orderly courses we had set for our lives.

This is happening to a couple I call Donald and Molly. Just when they thought they had figured out some direction for their marriage and their three children, unexpected responsibilities popped up to shake their faith in having control over life. But this couple isn't breaking under the strain. Instead, they are using the Decisions stage to gain new strength as individuals. This gives Donald and Molly not only occasional relief but specific methods of working through — or at least tolerating — each new and constantly erupting crisis.

Donald And Molly

When I press the buzzer to their New York apartment, Donald immediately yanks open the door and stands there grinning. His blue short-sleeved shirt is plastered against his chest by a combination of sweat and soapy dishwater. A towel hangs from one shoulder. He quickly wipes his hands and grasps me warmly, pulling me inside while he apologizes for the steamy mess visible just beyond the half-opened kitchen door.

Donald offers a chair and a cup of coffee. Then he takes the towel and rubs the top of his balding head, making sparse brown hairs point madly in several directions. He is a short, stocky man with soft brown eyes and work-knotted hands. He tucks the towel under his arm, notices his wet shirt and grimaces. "Wait here," he demands jovially. "I'll go change. Make yourself at home, okay?"

It is not hard to do. Four-year-old Suzanne approaches shyly with a plate of cookies and beams when I take two — one for me and one for her. She stuffs the cookie into her mouth and snuggles beside me on the sofa.

We are on the ground floor of a Kew Gardens residential development, about an hour from the bustle of Manhattan. This is a densely-packed neighborhood, but it has some of the look and feel of suburban living. The streets are lined with small shops, and there is grass and trees around each apartment structure. I can hear the laughter of children playing outside on rusty swings.

With his cramped household and busy work schedule. Donald fits into the barely controlled chaos that permeates the atmosphere. To me it is both comforting and unnerving, perhaps because it is such a familiar pattern of family life in the tenth to fifteenth years of marriage.

Donald is thirty-six. So is his wife, Molly. They have been married twelve years.

Molly bursts into the room, gasping because she's late. She did double time on the last mile of her jog, she explains, so she wouldn't keep me waiting too long. The dog, which ran with her, pants with exhaustion. The small, flop-eared mutt barks sharply at me a few times, then obeys Molly's command to shut up and lie down.

As Donald reappears wearing a clean shirt, Molly promptly announces, "Oh, I'm so sweaty!" and insists on rushing to the bedroom to change into a clean jogging suit. Their eleven-year-old twin boys pop into the room, demanding milk and cookies. Molly hears their request from the other room and calls out, "Tell them to fix their own snack!"

"But I have the kitchen almost cleaned up," Donald protests. "They'll make a mess!"

"No,we won't," the boys promise, almost in unison. They scamper away, delighted to have free rein.

"Yes, they will," Donald mumbles. He notices Suzanne and carries her, wailing, to bed. She leaves a trail of cookie crumbs, which the dog immediately tries to erase with its slobbering tongue. When Donald returns, he shoves the dog away and vacuums up the crumbs with a hand-held machine. Then he sinks into a chair beside me and says, "This is what life is like all the time around here. Noise. Confusion. Crumbs on the floor. A lot of nitty-gritty, everyday stuff. There isn't a moment's peace. I feel like God made me part human and part vacuum cleaner."

He is only half-joking.

Donald is a junior engineer with a large New York chemical company, and Molly works part-time in a department store close to home. This is Donald's first marriage, while Molly had been married for three years and divorced for two years when they met. The twins were born less than a year after Donald and Molly were married. Since both Donald and Molly are staunch Catholics, they did not want to use artificial means of birth control, but they also didn't want any more children. After Suzanne was born, they reluctantly abandoned the rule of the church and Donald had a vasectomy.

Molly had a year-old daughter, Deborah, by her first marriage. Long ago, before she met and married Donald, Molly had agreed to let the child live with her ex-husband because, as she puts it, "I was too young and too scared to think I could take care of her on my own."

Molly's parents hated her for that, she says. They couldn't speak about it for weeks. She had asked them to help her raise the child — she wanted to move back home with mom and dad, she says — but they backed off, saying they were too old to have a baby around all the time.

Now Deborah has returned to Molly's care. The girl is sullen and insecure, and her disrespectful mannerisms have thrown everybody off-balance. Donald and Molly are constantly trying to figure out how to discipline Deborah and show love to her at the same time. The younger children don't know whether to embrace their half-sister or merely to creep out of her way. The only people who seem unperturbed by Deborah are Molly's parents, who are shielded from all the confusion because they live in a nearby nursing home and share none of the responsibility for this new turn of events.

"Still, I hope they'll be excited because Deborah is back," says Molly. "Somehow if Mom and Dad think it's a good thing, that will make the adjustment easier. I'm glad Deborah is living with me, but she is a handful. She can't understand why I gave her up, even though I've tried explaining it to her a hundred times. And I saw her almost every week while she was growing up, so it's not as if we ever lost contact with one another.

"And she won't accept Donald. She resents him trying to be her father. Also, she is very bossy with the boys, and sometimes she's downright mean to poor little Suzanne.

"Even so, if my parents are happy about her coming to live with us, I see it as a very good sign. I know they can't help us a bit to handle Deborah, but emotionally I feel better if my parents approve. I guess I still judge the impact of things as to how they'll please Mom and Dad. Maybe I still hope they'll take the burden off me if it doesn't work out."

Deborah is almost fifteen years old. Six months ago her father took a job on an oil rig in Saudi Arabia and sent the girl to live with Molly and Donald. Deborah is at the movies this night. When Molly comes back into the room and the interview begins, she and Donald both immediately pinpoint the girl's arrival as a crisis that pushed them into the Decisions stage.

"It's been especially hard because we had to adjust to a whole new way of life," says Donald. "I hadn't bargained for this extra child. It added to my responsibilities and sharpened my perception that at this point in my life, the decisions I make are probably permanent, so they had better be *right*.

"And that's a very frightening thing. Suddenly I was supporting a fairly large family, stretching myself to the limit, and having to deal with another person in the house who was hostile to me from the word go. Deborah is in the pits of the teen-age years. I started asking myself, 'Do you really want to take her on?' I decided yes, both for Molly's sake and because I felt it was the right thing for me to do. I'll tell you frankly that there are moments when I have regretted that. It's hard enough to manage three children and monitor your own changes in the relationship with your wife. Then a new person appears and brings up questions like teen-age sex and the possibility of drug use and school performance. Molly and I have a lot of new things to learn, fast.

"It seems like every time I turn around, there is a new situation to confront," Donald says with a sigh. "The boys need expensive dental work and braces. Suzanne wets the bed almost every night. The dog runs away. Molly gets mad because I leave my dirty socks on the floor. Deborah talks on the phone for hours and annoys the hell out of me because I have to make some job-related calls and she won't give me a break.

"So all this is going on in the house. On top of it all, Molly's parents are getting very demanding. I think Molly spends too much time at their nursing home when she is needed right here. Also, my father died last year and my mother is very lonely, so I try to give her attention. Believe me, it's hard to cope with that kind of grief from your parent. It hurts me to see what Mother is going through.

"Sometimes I get to the point where I'm taking more than I can stand, and I feel like I want to get out of the situation. I'm not getting any younger, and while I don't mind doing my share, every now and then I feel like I should just get out of the whole mess."

Donald stops for a moment. He slides back on the sofa, looks at Molly, shrugs and smiles.

"Of course, I won't get out. The marriage is important to me, and I love my children. I just get quiet and grumpy sometimes. I would like less confusion around here."

Donald and Molly are feeling the pressures of what I call the "Sandwich Years." Like the meat between two slices of bread, they are crushed from below by the demands of their children and from above by the needs of aging parents. There is little time for self-examination or for nurturing the marriage relationship. Responsibilities seem overwhelming.

Almost always, married people at this stage think life has trapped them into shouldering more work than they had bargained for. Even when there are no children, the accumulated details of ten or fifteen years of married life weigh heavily on both males and females. They are alarmed by the flood of everyday decisions they must make and by the knowledge that making such decisions fixes them firmly as family leaders. Despite continuing fantasies such as Molly's — that mom and dad can still bail them out of trouble — people in the Decisions stage know there is no longer any strong person older or smarter who will take the blame if things go wrong. People I interviewed who were at this point in marriage often echoed Donald's words, "I'm taking more than I can stand. . . . I should just get out of the whole mess."

Donald is soft-spoken and earnest. "When I get to feeling over-whelmed, I don't actually leave," he says. "I get silent. The one little thing the priest says before you get married is, 'Don't go to bed angry. Always make up before you go to bed.' Obviously, the priest has never been married. When I get so exhausted from all the demands, all the decision-making, I just turn off and get silent and give Molly the cold shoulder if she has been after me and it's just more than I can stand. It takes me a day at least, and maybe more, before I can sit down to talk to her. I need the time to let my hands quit shaking, or whatever."

Molly is sitting cross-legged on the floor, petting the dog. She nods her head in recognition. "That is difficult for me because I can't stand the silence," she says. "I want the problem over with and forgotten right away."

"But our problems aren't the type to go away fast," Donald protests. "It's the kids, or your parents, or my mother. It's not having enough time, it's money. . . . "

Molly adds, "We learned that making compromises is just the start of it, just the beginning of dealing with the complexities of adulthood."

"Yeah, and nobody works harder at being adult, being serious, than we do," says Donald. "This marriage is *it*. Divorce is not an option for us. Not only because of the church, but because of our feelings for one another and our own sense that it would just be running away from a situation that, after all, we created. You can't have children, take life by the horns, and then decide halfway that you'd rather not go through with it and just dump everybody.

"Also, we have been through an annulment, which is the church's official recognition that your previous marriage doesn't exist. To Catholics, that is very important. It's very difficult, very emotional. Molly had to go through about fifty-two essay questions, I think, and dig up five people who would serve as witnesses for her. Once you've been through it, you realize the extreme seriousness of marriage and divorce. What the annulment does is make it clear to both people what a marriage is. So there's no excuse the second time. It makes you very much aware what a commitment is and what's involved, so when you go into it a second time, you should have your head on straight. Our eyes are very open. We know what's required of us, and we're both prepared to follow through. But it is hard. At about this time in life, the resentments do start piling up."

Those resentments, for Donald and Molly, now seem to be centering around the sudden appearance of a difficult teen-ager in their lives. Perhaps this couple would have sailed more easily through their mid-thirties if it hadn't been for Deborah's intrusion. Yes, they are over-busy with work and childcare, but they appear to have made their decisions about jobs and parenthood as a couple.

Such agreement on very basic decisions is essential for progressing to this stage and getting through it successfully. While a major goal at this time is to learn decision-making skills on one's own, couples must see eye to eye on the essential stuff of married life, such as having children or sharing money. These tasks should have been completed in the previous stage of Reality Struggles, and if so, this is when they pay off. If married people never agreed on those goals, they will have serious friction now, because they finally realize their basic value systems are different. If that is true, they have only two choices: modify the value systems or get divorced. Either way, a joint decision must be made.

Agreement on every issue is impossible, however, even in the most compatible unions. Donald is a cooperative and supportive husband, but the strain of his responsibilities sometimes outweighs the joys, and he is tempted to blame his exhaustion on Molly. She knows that and says she doesn't hold it against him.

"He is a wonderful husband," says Molly. She smiles up at Donald from her seat on the rug. She is very short and slender with dainty features. With her long blonde ponytail and her petite jogging outfit, Molly doesn't look like a middle-aged mother and wife, but that is how she describes herself.

"I'm not into a career," she tells me. "Being home with the children and having time for my parents and my friends is the real fun in life. I have a sales job twice a week, but I like it mostly because it gives me a chance to dress up and meet friends for lunch. My real outside interests are in sculpture and pottery, which I do as a hobby.

"I wouldn't like a demanding career because it might cut off my chances to do these other things," Molly explains. "I do most of the chores around here because Donald works full time and my job is part time. But Donald is very, very good about driving the boys places, or arranging for little Sue's nursery school and stuff like that. That's a burden which he lifts from my shoulders. I feel like I have it easier in the marriage, because my time is mostly my own and I can quit the job if I like. Donald doesn't have that option. So I try to bring in some money, and he tries to take over some chores. That way, it evens out.

"The money is something we are completely together on. We each give what we have and take what we need. Nothing is separate. I think people who keep separate accounts might be really saying, 'I don't fully trust this person I'm married to, so maybe I should keep a hedge against divorce.' Besides, I don't see how it's possible to keep money separate when there are children involved. It's not my place to look at other lifestyles and criticize. But I honestly couldn't figure out how to separate our funds even if I wanted to. It seems like that would be a great source of trouble in a marriage. We are in this together, for life. Everything is thrown into one pot, money included. If we don't both agree on something, we can talk about it."

Molly is still partly in the stage of Reality Struggles, idealizing

Donald's good points and hoping she can smooth over their troubles with talk. Donald is confronting Decisions, largely because he feels that he must struggle harder to maintain control of his life since the appearance of Molly's rebellious daughter.

"I have to ask myself, with each new little family crisis, 'Is this worth fighting for?'" says Donald. "It's a very exhausting process. Do I want to fight so that family decisions will go my way? Do I even want to keep chugging along to make this marriage turn out great?

"We had the intention of blending this into one family, but we sometimes conflict on how to make that happen. For example, I'm kind of hard on the kids when it comes to study habits. Stereos going on in the evening when they should be studying, camping out on the telephone when that's a distraction from study time, I come home and I have to police that. And it's an irritation for Molly, because she'd just as soon let the kids — especially Deborah — have a good time. So it's not only the decisions that have to be made, it's following through with them that's hard.

"Sometimes the decision comes easy, but then we have to remember the other person might have been tempted to be dishonest about agreeing. What I mean is that we might decide to limit Deborah's telephone time, and then I will come home to find that Molly let the girl talk on and on. So it means my wife is not abiding by the decision, and that makes me mad because it was *our* decision and I just assume we'll both stick by it.

"So I'll confront her on this, and she'll say she changed her mind, or she never was in agreement in the first place, or it's too hard to enforce the decision. I get terribly frustrated because I thought we had made some progress and we didn't. I think, 'We didn't accomplish a thing.' Those are the times I must remember that many decisions simply have to be made between me and myself, not me and Molly. She's not going to help me with a lot of these decisions. A person gets married and spends time trying to be a unit with his wife. Then, after all that trouble, it dawns on him that the real trick is to have the strength to make individual decisions and enforce them himself.

"And that's when I feel like I'm sliding over into a real adjustment, when we both have to realize that on some issues we're not going to win the other person over to how we feel, *ever*. I do slide around a lot. Maybe, in that respect, I'm a failure."

Molly tries to laugh, but Donald's bluntness is scaring her. She looks sad. Then she reaches over and pats his hand, squeezes it and turns to me.

"He is definitely not a failure. This *marriage* is definitely not a failure. We have been doing some griping, but can I put in a few words about the good times we have? Being together as a family is the greatest joy I have ever known, and I know Donald feels it, too. Otherwise, he wouldn't be here."

"That's true," he says with a smile.

"Okay. Well, we really care for each other," Molly goes on. "We have the same values, principles, beliefs in religion — all the important ingredients are there. We share the same goals in life, and we're not disappointed in one another after all this time, no matter how frustrated we might get once in a while.

"When we met, we were both looking for a relationship with God as individuals and looking for a Christian partner, too. And we found it, and the religion is a big factor in helping us through the rough spots. We are on common ground. If you really love someone, you are willing to give up something you want or something of yourself for the other person. That's a decision, too, you know.

"Donald is having a rougher time than me over Deborah because she is my child by another marriage, and she sort of got plopped into his lap, and she is not making a good attempt to accept him like he is trying to accept her."

"True," says Donald. "I have to remember I'm the adult and I have to go the extra mile, but I wish Deborah would try also."

"So it's rough on him," Molly goes on. "But you know what I think helps most? It's something Donald and I did last week, almost like a mental exercise. . . . "

"Oh, our fantasy vacation!" Donald cries happily.

"Yes," says Molly. She smiles broadly at him, and for a moment their eyes are locked and the electricity of love between them is so strong it almost hums in the air. They are embracing without even touching one another — one of those moments of true marital intimacy.

Molly turns to me. Her cheeks are flushed. "Listen!" she says with excitement. "Here's what we did. See, we never get a weekend where we can go out without worrying about kids. It's frustrating, because we would like to have a weekend every now and then where we don't have them and we could do something or just not do anything at all.

"So what we did one night was to just talk about how we feel, without having to make any decisions on those feelings. How would we feel if we could get rid of the kids? Really picture it, you know. And we said a lot of things that we had been keeping inside ourselves and not sharing.

"We said sometimes we just wish the kids would disappear. That it would be beautiful to be alone together with no problems, no interruptions. That we both sometimes just feel like slapping Deborah, or screaming 'Shut up!' at the boys, even if they're not being bad. We just want some quiet. I even told Donald I fantasized the dog would get run over by a car so there would be one less thing to clean up after.

"Having heard each other say it was refreshing. It was the best 'vacation' in the world! First of all, we heard the other one feel like we feel and it allowed us afterward, having admitted this, to go back to the fact that the kids are ours. And is that something we got trapped into, or did we accept it? We like to think we got what we asked for and not what we got stuck with. You can't love your children if you feel like you're stuck.

"It was a good exercise. It was so nice thinking about it. . . . "Molly's voice trails off, and she looks to Donald for help.

"Maybe it was a little ugly," he says. "But it really helped resolve what was becoming a crisis for me. I was scared because I was coming close to making another decision, to saying, 'It's me or Deborah. Either she goes or I do.'

"It really hurt Molly that I felt that way. But the honesty we shared was like a soothing balm on the wounds. It gave me great strength to go on, to try again, to stick to my original decision to accept this child and make her part of our family and make it turn out okay for all of us. It is so much better now that I know Molly is having trouble with her, too. I'm not alone, and I won't be put down for my feelings.

"This sort of open, honest exchange about what we thought were 'taboo' feelings has had another marvelous effect," says Donald. "As angry or frustrated or pissed at me as Molly might get, now I really know I can expect that she'll always bounce back afterwards and tell me she does love me and I'm still important to her. We have stretched that to the limit, it seems. It is the ultimate in trust. I expect that response after everything we've been through. Because we can share honesty while we're making decisions jointly or separately, our relationship will survive."

Playing Mental Games

Donald is probably right. He has cleared away the cobwebs of marital fantasies in earlier stages and replaced them with a mature view of his particular world, as he shares it with Molly. He knows they can face and make important, often permanent decisions. But he also knows they can still get happily lost in fantasyland when they need an escape. It is a marvelous technique to ease some of the burdens of this stage of marriage; together they play mental games to get relief from grown-up responsibilities. Their fantasizing allows them to temporarily abandon their chosen roles as provider, parent and leader. It's a mental vacation, free from decisions.

The fantasies are especially helpful for Donald, who otherwise might be paralyzed by fear because he sees his everyday decisions as last chances to make good. He is comfortable in the role of father and reliable husband, but now and then he wants Molly to share the side of him that is more playful, less burdened by responsibility and just out for a good time. As long as Molly accepts and encourages his fantasies — as long as she shares the need and desire for this type of intimacy — Donald can come back refreshed and slip again into his "daddy role."

Molly has less stress in her life right now. She has more time for relief-giving hobbies and less ambivalence about being a parent to Deborah. Maybe that is why she is sometimes one stage behind Donald. She is still engrossed in selecting his best traits to idealize and has settled strongly on his performance as father and provider for the family. Molly sees her decisions as part of a cooperative effort involving Donald and their children. Donald has advanced to the concept of making decisions on his own.

A kind and cooperative spouse, of course, doesn't gallop out and make unilateral decisions that deeply affect the course of the relationship. I don't know any stable spouses who bought or sold a house without including their partner in the plans, or who announced, "Surprise! We're moving to another city."

I have, however, talked to people who felt victimized when their partners overstepped the bounds of propriety and cooperation by trying to shove their own ideas down a wife or husband's throat. One partner made a decision on something that deeply affected them both without discussing it first. The victimized people almost always were already divorced or plunging quickly in that direction when I spoke to them.

One thirty-eight-year-old woman said her husband bought her a white Cadillac because he wanted her to be seen in a car that would match his white sports model. The husband did this even though he had heard his wife say, several times, that she would enjoy picking out her own automobile and wanted a small one in red or black. She told me such arrogant decision-making on her husband's part was typical of the way he attempted to dominate their relationship, under the guise of being generous and giving.

A divorced husband confided that his wife decided on her own to have children by not taking her birth control pills. This was after they had both agreed not to have children for at least a year. She announced her pregnancy with, "I have a sweet surprise for you, dear. . . ."

"I still am not sure if she really believed she had the right to make that decision alone," her husband said, "or if she thought I was dumb enough to accept such an act of domination and disrespect."

The decisions we must make on our own are those that will determine the course of our lives as individuals: career choices, solving parental problems and deciding on methods of confronting and solving problems in personal philosophy. Donald's decision to accept Deborah, for example, was something he did on his own. He had Molly in mind when he made that decision, but he knows the difference between taking his wife's needs into consideration and allowing her demands to override his own judgment.

All of us are constantly walking the tightrope between exercising autonomy in the decision-making process and showing the cooperation necessary to make a marriage function. Sometimes those lines become hopelessly blurred. Nobody I talked to was sure, all of the time, how much of a decision was affected by the spouse and how much was an independent thought or act. The best one can do in the stage of Decisions is to cooperate when possible and act alone when necessary.

Lester's Story

One critical objective of the Decisions stage is to overcome the fear that a wrong step can lead to disaster. Such fear can leave a person dangling in torment between the need to decide and the fear of deciding. It can strangle a marriage.

When we meet for an interview, Lester looks like a strangling man. He has come straight from the airport to my home office, and the first thing he does is stick two fingers between his shirt collar and his neck and yank hard. The force of his movement loosens his tie and pops a button, which Lester picks off the rug with an apologetic smile.

He is sweating. He asks for some iced tea, looks around my office and settles onto a small blue and white sofa. Then he takes off his jacket. He sees that I am wearing sneakers, points to his shiny black business loafers and asks if I'd mind if he slips them off. He yanks at them quickly and with a grateful sigh.

Right now, life is hard for Lester. He is a lawyer with a big Wall Street firm. At the age of forty-six, he has already made enough money to retire, but he likes the profession and there is no reason to slow down now. In fact, he says, he wants to work harder so he can bury himself in paperwork and avoid going home as much as possible. His fourteen-year marriage to Toby is on the rocks. He can't decide whether to file for divorce. That's why, when he learned he'd be coming to Atlanta to see a client, he agreed to come a day earlier and be interviewed. Maybe if he talks things out, he'll be able to make a decision.

This is Lester's second marriage. He describes his first wife as a "nag." He was in law school when they got married, and she supported him through the lean years.

"I appreciated that and did everything I could to make her comfortable," he says. "Then she got crazy. All she did was nag me for things. She thought I could make a lot more money in a much shorter time than was possible, and she pursued a lifestyle that would put a billionaire into debt. I just had to get out of that relationship."

He stayed single for three years after the divorce. Then Toby came along. "She was loving, attentive, sensationally sexy, beautiful . . . a fantasy come true. I was older and wiser and didn't expect the answer to every question out of marriage, like I did with my first wife. But I definitely knew I wanted Toby. We lived together for two years before I asked her to make a final commitment. I thought things were pretty solid."

Lester looks down at his hands, clasped limply on his lap, and his whole body seems to sag with sorrow. He has a thin, sensitive face and very straight black hair, cut short and neatly parted to one side. There are distinct traces of gray at his temples, and his moustache is also graying delicately. He is a slim but sturdy-looking man who appears very prosperous in his brown suit. But now, talking about his failing marriage, he seems weak with doubt and almost listless. He hears the need to make a decision not as a rational voice but as a high-pitched, demanding scream. It is wearing him down.

"I got through other difficult times of marriage all right," he says. "I seemed to be able to cope with the realization that Toby wasn't perfect. About four or five years into the marriage, I started seeing some big things I didn't much notice before. They annoyed me, but I could take it.

"She was messy, and it got on my nerves. She was terribly disorganized, too. Toby is a very talented chef with a good position at a really fancy New York restaurant, but her boss is always calling the house, reminding her that she left a burner going or something. But I guess she's so good at what she does that people put up with her sloppiness. At the beginning, I thought it was cute when she forgot things and all, but when the house was a mess and people were coming over any minute and I'd done my share of the work two hours ago . . . well . . . it wasn't so cute anymore.

"That wasn't so bad, in comparison to what came next. I noticed I was a more affectionate partner than Toby. I was taking her hand more often than she was taking mine. It started to gnaw at me: 'Could it be that I need her more than she needs me?'

"Yes, to a certain extent that was true. I could even come to grips with it. I just figured out what I liked best about Toby and made a very determined effort to disregard what I didn't like. I thought, 'She is staying married to me and she seems happy, so everything must be okay, right? So what if she is less physically affectionate than me?'

"Then Toby hit me with a bomb. She said she wanted to have a child. Now, that wasn't the way it was supposed to turn out. We'd already made the decision to remain childless. It was one of the first things we discussed when we talked about getting married. I had said I wasn't cut out to be a parent. Toby told me that was okay. She would have preferred a child, but she said it didn't make all that much difference to her. She assured me she wouldn't feel cheated or resentful. I remember her saying, 'You'll be enough for me. I'll be happy just with you.'"

The memories are hurting Lester. He stops talking and asks for more iced tea. When I leave the office to get the tea, I watch Lester for a moment or two from the hall. He rises from the couch to stare out of the window, and his shoulders drop like the flowers of late summer. I can feel the hard point of his grief.

Lester gulps the tea, then sinks back against the sofa cushion and goes on. "So we stay married for nearly fifteen years, happily childless, or so I thought. But Toby, being twelve years younger than me, was apparently just biding her time. When she got to be thirty-three last year, I guess she felt her biological time clock was running out. Toby said she'd changed her mind and wanted a child. And she was adamant.

"I thought I could handle it by taking time off from my practice and showing Toby how wonderful life could be for us if we weren't burdened with a baby. I had been working hard since I was fifteen. In college, I worked. In law school, I worked. I wanted *fun*. And I never had fun until I met Toby. Also, I was forty-five years old, feeling like I was approaching real mid-life fatigue. I wanted a long rest. And I figured, 'If I can't talk Toby out of having a baby, okay, at least we'll have one last fling.'

"So we went away for almost a year. It took some pretty fancy arranging at my law firm to do that, but I'm a senior partner and everybody understands burnout, so they just helped me work it out. Toby quit her job and said she'd start up again after the vacation.

"Well, it wasn't so hot. We had a great time at first, going around the country in a van and seeing things like the Grand Canyon and Baxter State Park in Maine. But little by little, Toby got restless. She would say, 'Let's go home and get serious,' and she said she missed the neighborhood, the house, her friends. She got pregnant as soon as we got back.

"The first child miscarried." Lester stops here. His voice cracks, then screeches upward in a nervous chuckle. "I took this as a sign from God that He or She agreed with me and there would be no baby. But Toby was determined. She wasn't going to back down on having that baby. She insisted on trying again. I really can't say exactly why, but something in me told me to go along with Toby. Now she is three months pregnant."

With the droning patience of sadness, Lester counts off the reasons why he does not want a child. He is too old. He will not be a good father. He likes an unencumbered life. Kids make him nervous. And at thirty-four years old, Toby is no spring chicken; she could have a deformed baby or have serious trouble or even die.

"Now I'm really wondering if the marriage is worth fighting for. The essential question I have to decide is, can I be happy with this new turn of events? You have to have the hope that things will work out. But what is so scary is not the hard work involved, but the suspicion that even if you work at it, things won't get better.

"I am very frightened. But more than that, I am weary. I have to make a decision: stay married and have a child with Toby and give up the kind of life I'd planned for myself, or get divorced and try to find a woman who can share that kind of childless life. I can't seem to come to a satisfactory way of saying one thing or another. I'm too exhausted to try and make a decision."

Lester correctly senses the wide chasm he must now leap in order to join Toby in maturing into parenthood. He is confronting what I call the *decision exchange*. When a major lifestyle change becomes inevitable, a person must decide which way to turn depending on the exchanges he wishes to make. Lester's choice revolves around exchanging the joy of youth — which in his mind is represented by childlessness — for the mellow richness of a deeper relationship with Toby and with a child.

For Lester, the exchange is difficult because he has managed to skirt the issue for so many years. At an age when most men have built upon earlier life stages and successfully emerged as nurturing individuals, Lester still wants to be nurtured himself. Later in our conversation he admits, "I like center stage, and a baby would steal my thunder." At one point he swallows hard and tells me, "I can't get enough attention. I loved it when Toby would make a fuss over me. When the baby comes she will make a fuss over the baby, not me."

Stunted by immaturity and paralyzed by the fear of making a decision, Lester writhes in emotional torment. The problem must be resolved one way or another, he says gloomily. I ask him how he thinks it will turn out. He puckers his lips and blows out a long, exhausted sigh.

"Feeling tired, as I do, I'm apt to be simply carried along by Toby's determination. I don't think I want to face another divorce. And I really care for her, so it's not simply a legal question. It's as if a force bigger than myself has come along and is pushing me into a role I'm ill-equipped to play but will have to master if I want any chance at happiness. The role of father and husband. *Mature* husband. I don't have the spunk to do it, but I don't have what it takes to fight it either. The decision will go to Toby almost by default. I think if I go on feeling this way, I will have lost the option to make my own thoughts count on the matter, because my emotions are so jumbled now that I can't be sensible about this thing.

"I feel unhappy and cold. I'm not active in the marriage right now. I'm resigned to it. I don't think I can overcome the frustrations and the hostilities I feel toward Toby for getting me into this. And I can't get myself out.

"We won't ever be the same again, I know that. The days of wine and roses . . . they're gone. We can't act like two little kids on a lark anymore. I will have to accept a more traditional kind of marriage for a man my age. I just pray that I can go on to this different life and scrape out whatever joy will come along in a new relationship with Toby. Of course, I hope I can be a good father. I am not the type to leave a child. I take responsibilities very seriously, once they're there. I just hope I can find the strength."

When I recount Lester's story to Dr. Lloyd Mendelson, he says Lester is in the process of an "emotional divorce." At each new stage in marriage, he claims, people "divorce" their spouses and then "remarry" them, undergoing a continual process of rejection and acceptance. As a growing snake sheds its confining skin and then proceeds to fill out its new coating, the married person progresses through the painful growth patterns that point the way to ultimate partnership. For people who have delayed growth too long, like Lester, making an important and irreversible life decision can carry a gut-curling bite. But, says Dr. Mendelson, even if people accept basic responsibilities at a more appropriate stage, such as having children, it takes most of us half a lifetime before the decision-making process reaches its peak.

"You are in your forties before you break with your parents," he says. "It takes that long before you can allow mom and dad to be real, struggling people. Until you can see your parents objectively, you can't dialogue with your spouse in a way that makes both joint and individual decision-making really comfortable. Once your parents have been placed in proper perspective, you can see your spouse in perspective, too, without the fantasies attached. Then you can sort of step up and assume the mantle of adulthood in a full manner. In most cases, that very much includes being a parent yourself."

Lester's "guess" that he'll go along with Toby's wishes and become a parent is a thinly disguised wish of his own. He may not want to progress to the next stage, but to fail now and abandon the marriage and its potential for growth would cost him too dearly in self-esteem. Lester's real decision is not whether to have a child, or even whether to stay in the marriage. It is far more painful than that. It is a choice between seemingly intolerable concepts: divorce and failure, which would crush his self-esteem, or maturity, which snatches away his fantasies forever. Somehow he knows he will grow old no matter what he does. So Lester is allowing himself the illusion of coasting along with Toby's decision in favor of maturity.

"You get stuck, or slide far back, if you can't take on the responsibilities that come with each new stage," says Dr. Mendelson. "When people say they're tired and they seem to be going into the stage with a great deal of depression, that is really a sign of some growth. They are, at least, accepting the realities instead of turning away and sticking their heads in the sand with a divorce. Going on with a stage while you're depressed about it is a very important way of preserving your self-esteem. At least you can say, 'Well, this was very hard to do, but I did it and it's not so bad after all.'

"Kids fall off a bike and cry, but it's well known that mom should put them right back on. Why? Because the fall is a blow to self-esteem, and to correct it at once and keep esteem intact is essential to growth. If you start feeling so frustrated, or so weary of marriage that you can't stick with it, you 'fall off' and never get back on. You get stuck, possibly with repeating marriage and divorce over and over again. That is hell on your image of yourself as a successful person, no matter what kind of hot-shot you are in business or your profession.

"In severe cases, I've seen people who were so inept at decision-making they couldn't carry on a relationship with the opposite sex for more than a few months. With people like Lester, they might drag themselves into the next stage, but at least they get there. They grow. And it gives them reason to be proud. We can't live well, we can't look in the mirror and be content, without that sort of pride."

Lester's pain in the stage of Decisions may be extreme, but it doesn't seem to be that unusual. Growing up sometimes hurts very badly, especially for people who equate it with growing old. Lester is a good example of how people push themselves to and through this stage on their own, because they are so out of step with their partner's progress that fast decisions have to be made unilaterally in order to catch up.

A Happy Ending

Exactly a year after my interview with Lester, I rip open a gold-trimmed envelope and read an invitation to his and Toby's sixteenth anniversary party. Since I plan to be in New York, I arrive at their house on the appointed day, bursting with curiosity.

Lester rushes to greet me in the hallway and insists that I follow him upstairs to the nursery to see his infant son. He bounces up the stairs. There is no trace of the lethargy and sadness Lester displayed during our interview. Obviously, he is at peace with his decision to accept fatherhood.

"Accept it? I *love* it!" Lester cries happily. He bends over an ornate brass crib and tenderly lifts up his child. The baby's small head wobbles, and his mouth opens into a wide, contented yawn. Lester cradles him expertly, as if taking care of a baby is something he has been doing all his life. His gaze is riveted on the child.

Lester and I are momentarily alone. I cannot resist the opportunity to ask Lester how he resolved his dilemma so successfully and emerged victorious from the Decisions stage.

"In earlier years of marriage people are making compromises with each other," says Lester. "I think I learned that (in the stage of Decisions) I had to make compromises with *myself*. I had to look at my own values, and what I saw wasn't pleasant: a babyish, selfish man denying a child to his wife and to himself because he was so insecure that he didn't want anyone to share the woman's attention.

"I felt very alone, as I told you. But then I realized, 'If you divorce Toby, you'll *really* be alone.' I didn't want to go back to singles bars or have an affair.

"I finally wrote down my alternatives on a piece of paper. They were to get divorced and give up a wonderful shared history with a woman who had a lot of good points; to slog along being depressed and grumpy and probably have Toby get miserable enough to divorce *me*; or to face up to the reality that I could find a lot of positives in a new life as a father and a more mature husband. The first two alternatives seemed pretty grim. I took the third.

"Of course, I wasn't able to accomplish this change overnight. I was in the habit of being selfish, and it was just as hard a habit to break as biting my nails or smoking three packs a day. I set the goal for myself of doing two little unselfish things for Toby each day. One day I might get her a cup of tea in the morning and do the dishes at night. Another day I'd give up a golf game to drive her to the doctor for her check-up and then take her to lunch. Since she was pregnant, she was especialy grateful for every little bit of help. And the more I gave, the more she opened up and gave back to me, and the good feelings started snowballing, and . . . well . . . by the time the baby was born I could see there was a real payoff in making a conscious decision to be unselfish.

"Maybe it sounds corny, that sort of forced unselfishness," Lester chuckles. "But it works. Now I have *this*."

He looks at the baby with a wide, sunbeam smile. Says Lester, "Sticking around for him was the best decision I ever made."

8

Stage Five: SEPARATION
(Years Twelve to Seventeen)

"I think I need a little time alone to swallow the facts about my marriage. . . . I simply want to get some breathing space." — a forty-year-old woman, married for the second time.

In its most dramatic form, the stage of Separation means that couples either settle down or split.

This is perhaps the most troublesome but also the most constructive and intensely absorbing stage of marriage. People must now fully merge into the partnership and come to grips with a final acceptance of what married life is like for each person . . . not what it might have been or what he or she wishes it could be. Such acceptance unlocks personal potential and frees each partner from trying to assert control over the other's emotions.

At the same time, after about twelve to seventeen years of marriage, people want to carve out their own definitions of life and of their places within it. They can't really change the emotional makeup of their partners, but they *can* change themselves. People who want to feel independent, mature and self-reliant within a marriage have to break away now from the last traces of destructive emotional dependence on their spouses. Says Jung, "...it takes half a lifetime to arrive at this stage."

It hurts to separate, and a hallmark of this stage is often a deep and long-lasting depression. People are giving up final hope for perfection in their mates and coming to grips with the realization that they have very little control over their loved ones.

The stage of Separation is marked by anger, too. It is almost impossible not to get mad at a husband or wife for being unable to change to your complete satisfaction. And one also is angry at all the hard work that seems to lie ahead — the work of changing yourself, all alone, because the spouse can't help.

Actually, by the time depression and anger bubble into a person's consciousness, most of the internal work is already done. Dr. M. Scott Peck says depression means growth has already taken place, and "since giving up or loss of the old self is an integral part of the process of mental and spiritual growth, depression is a normal and basically healthy phenomenon." Anger is also a good sign at this stage. It proves that both partners are intensely interested in the relationship.

People who are active in their marriages continually clash and turn away from one another, come back again and do well for a time, then clash once more. This circular process may be repeated over and over as each partner gets frustrated with trying to resolve a problem and temporarily gives up. These battles may or may not help people figure out better ways of relating to one another in any stage, but they do keep both partners excited and involved. As long as they are searching for solutions, it is obvious that they care enough to continue the relationship and get back together.

The only time fighting becomes a dead-end is when one or both people stop caring about a resolution. A forty-seven-year-old technician told me, "I knew for sure my marriage would end in divorce because I heard myself telling the marriage counselor that I really didn't care how things turned out. There was nothing my wife could do to keep me involved. I wasn't mad at her. I was simply not interested."

In *Gone With The Wind*, Scarlett O'Hara could tear at Rhett Butler continually and he could be hateful in return, yet they always reunited for one more try because they were irresistibly drawn to one another. The marriage ended only when Rhett told Scarlett, "Frankly, my dear, I don't give a damn!"

The Second Time Around

Losing interest in what happens to a marriage — or to a mate — can be merely a sign of fatigue if those feelings pass quickly. But when lack of involvement drags on and on, it may signal an end to the relationship. Often people who detach and divorce in this way during the stage of Separation think they have seen the end of this unpleasant time in their lives. But they marry again, go quickly through the other stages with a new spouse and promptly find themselves struggling with Separation the second time around. This time, however, if they are depressed and angry instead of just being uncaring about the outcome of this stage, they can stick with their second mate and forge a lasting bond. Many of the divorced people to whom I spoke said there seems to be no escape from recapitulating the stages with each new spouse.

"I just seemed to pick up with Jason where I left off with my first husband," laughed a forty-year-old public relations writer. "I got married for the first time when I was twenty-one. Leo was an alcoholic. He was drinking heavily even in our early years together, and he was just a kid himself, only twenty-three when we married. Good thing his father was rich, so Leo and I didn't have money worries, even though he couldn't hold on to a job for very long.

"He wasn't a sloppy drunk or loud or abusive. And, oh yes, we were both 'enlightened' about the problem; we called it a 'disease' and acted very sophisticated. I can't remember all the AA meetings I attended with Leo and all the very touchy counseling sessions. It must have been a million.

"Eventually I got the feeling he was never going to change. He would just go through life being very sorry to have caused me so much trouble, very contrite and little-boy charming but never a responsible man. I got bored with it. I wanted to have a real life; I wanted a husband who was grown-up. I wanted children. After almost exactly twelve years, I had had it. Really, Leo just bored me. I simply didn't care anymore. So we got divorced.

"Now, here comes the part about Jason. He is everything Leo wasn't: mature, reliable and an excellent wage-earner, and we have a lovely little girl. We have been married six years. But I'm at the point where I felt like I was with Leo when he and I broke up. I want to get away from Jason. But this time it's not that I don't care what happens. I am really frustrated because I'm feeling too dependent on my husband and I want to feel as if I can be my own person. I don't want to get divorced again, and I don't think we will.

"I think I need a little time alone to swallow the facts about my marriage. Jason is a neat guy, but he can't be my everything, and there is a lot going on that I don't like in this marriage. Sometimes I feel like being married is a prison. He won't pick up his own damn socks! There are socks on the floor every single day — black socks with lint on them. He comes home from work and pulls off his shoes and socks and just leaves them wherever he happens to be.

"Now, why am I so furious about those socks? Really, I could kill him over the socks. It doesn't make sense to me — Why don't I just pick them up, or leave them there? — but the socks eat away at me.

"So I want to be alone for a time to figure that out, to ask myself why I am so damned furious about such a little thing. I am sophisticated enough to know that it has a deeper meaning. I think this is just my time to break away in order to accept Jason, socks and all, and make peace within myself. I did that with Leo, and we got divorced. I guess I have to do it again with Jason. But I don't think it means divorce this time. I simply want to get some breathing space."

Two Types Of Separation

When the strain of this stage becomes too intense, one or both partners will initiate the separation. There are two types of separation: physical, where one partner leaves home, and emotional, where the couple still lives under one roof but remains estranged, aloof and seemingly unattached to one another. If the marriage is sound, neither type of separation will sever its bonds, but either can stretch them painfully. There may be many fights. Bickering, sometimes over the smallest of issues, seems constant. There also may be long periods of simmering discontent during which marriage partners hardly speak to one another.

"That's what happened to us," a stylish, dark-haired office manager told me. "This went on when Phil and I were both forty-three years old and had been married nearly eighteen years. I'm fifty now. But I remember it like it was yesterday, because it was clearly the turning point of our relationship.

"We had two adolescent girls. We had the feeling that we had to get away from each other for a while or we'd bust, but neither one of us wanted to be the one who walked out on the kids. So we stayed in the house and put on a front for them, but inside we were seething at each other.

"For about a year, we had both been paying more attention to our respective careers than to one another. It was a way of avoiding working out problems together. I had a lot of dinner dates with other men. It was on business and nothing ever got going in the way of an affair. I sometimes flirted with someone I found attractive, but that's all. I was too scared to do anything else. Besides, I really didn't want to hurt Phil past the point of no return.

"I was pretending to ignore him, and he got madder and madder, but neither one of us could swallow our pride and say, 'Let's talk this out.' Finally he retaliated by having an affair with his secretary. It was fast. He broke it off because he felt so guilty and then he told me about it.

"I hit the roof, but I did it very quietly. I was sarcastic. I just said, 'Fine. You want other women? Be my guest; I won't hold you back.' I didn't tell him to get out, and I didn't get out. I just gave him the cold shoulder. We still lived together, we still took care of the girls together, we still pooled our paychecks and all that. But there was a terrible distance between us. Sometimes, if he came into the kitchen and I was scrambling some eggs, I'd just take the pan off the burner and walk out. I became very guarded in everything I said to him. I wasn't unfriendly, but I was distant, polite, sort of formal. It was a period of just leaving each other alone.

"There were plenty of dinnertimes when the only sound was the clinking of silverware. We just didn't want to talk, because then we would have to discuss what was going on and we just weren't ready. It was okay to sleep in the same bed, but we each got in on our respective sides, and we were very careful not to let our flesh touch. I remember that what I missed most was curling up against him naked. We had always slept that way. There was a certain spot where my fanny touched him and felt so warm, and now it was cold. My buttocks actually ached in that spot. I was thinking, 'This is really a pain in the ass!'

"This went on for nearly a month. As I look back on it now, it was the loneliest time in my life. And the strain was incredible. Maybe it would have been better to be apart physically. But still, during that period, we both got a chance to readjust our thinking for the first time in over seventeen years of marriage. I can't tell you exactly how it happened, but we got a breather that somehow enabled us to say to ourselves, 'Okay, now you can see what kind of a person you are married to. How come you are still together?' Of course, the answer was, 'Because you want to be. You want to go on, you want to grow old with him, you want this marriage.'

"I think maybe I was the one who finally started talking. I don't know; maybe it was him. Anyway, it was surprisingly easy to communicate again because I guess we just got to a point where we'd had enough of a rest. During that month we both completed the change from emotional kids to real grown-ups. So when we got back together, the quality of the relationship had changed. We were on an equal footing, somehow, and neither one of us was trying to live his life through the other."

The emotional distancing of separation gives people a rare opportunity to be alone with themselves. It is an inner voyage of discovery. Says Dr. Clark Moustakas, a psychologist, "Some kinds of self-discovery emerge only through self-reflection, self-confrontation and meditation, and in no other way. The personal relationship is just what must be abandoned in some of life's critical moments."

People do see Separation as a critical moment. Sometimes they feel suspended in a half-life between marriage and the threat of divorce. In this stage of marriage, a person is often desperately aware of the need to make life-altering changes. It is not a happy time. One must find answers to some ultimate questions: Can I be satisfied with this marriage? Is it better instead to try for life alone or with someone else?

Since for the most part I was interviewing people engaged in successful marriages, the answer usually was, "I can be satisfied." But arriving at that answer wasn't easy. Couples in the Separation stage enter reluctantly, fight off the fear and muddle through. Only later — when they emerge in the stage of Together Again — do they realize that permanent adjustments have been made.

"It's a little sad," says one man. "As a result of our pain during this time, the marriage is infinitely more rewarding, infinitely more stable. I really like myself, so I can really like my wife. But now I realize I'll never be a kid again."

Marilyn And Mel

The Separation stage readies people for the reconstruction of their marriages into mellower, more workable unions. It also forces emotionally dependent spouses to allow their partners and themselves room for growth. These things rarely happen, however, without the perception of going through a crisis.

A couple I will call Marilyn and Mel, both forty years old and married seventeen years, had to face several crises — financial and sexual — before they could give up the ways they were manipulating one another, break with severe emotional dependence, and progress to an honest relationship.

I hadn't seen this couple for almost five years. Mel and Marilyn were my good friends when we all lived in Washington, D.C. After my husband and I moved to Atlanta, we heard that Mel and Marilyn were zooming up the financial ladder. They bought a three-story brick house in Georgetown and completely remodeled it. They sent their son to a nearby private school. When their little girl became old enough, nothing would do but an exclusive Georgetown private kindergarten. Mel was pulling in big money as a government consultant at the time, and Marilyn was a senior lab technician who assisted in research for a private drug company.

Mel and Marilyn were born and raised in Virginia. They came together in grade school and never really dated anyone else. When I met them almost twenty years ago, Mel and Marilyn had already blended so completely into one another's lives that everyone assumed they belonged together forever.

Mel is a soft-spoken, earnest man with an irresistible smile and a charming mop of brown curls. Marilyn has an athletic figure, sleek shoulder-length brown hair and an energetic charm that brightens rooms like the sudden snap of a light bulb. I had always viewed them as the ideal pair: smart, good-looking, wealthy, sane and very much in love. I was convinced that nothing had changed.

"Ah, but it *has* changed," Mel begins. "We had always been together, even as children, and as I saw it the world consisted of two people: Marilyn and me. Nothing and nobody could intrude. Oh, we continued to be very close to our parents — You remember how wonderful they are, don't you? — but what I'm saying is that it never dawned on either one of us that we'd want any type of relationship except what we already had. Who could improve on perfection?

"We built a little cocoon of home and hearth and family. It was wonderful. But we didn't grow . . . as individuals, as a couple or as a family. Even having kids didn't change us much. We saw the two children merely as extensions of ourselves."

Marilyn interrupts Mel here. "Maybe it would have stayed that way if we didn't get into the financial problems," she says.

"Yes, that was part of it," Mel agrees. "About five years ago the government started closing the purse strings for consultants and pulling them tight. No contracts were being given, and, of course, it wiped me out. I was forced to take a glorified sales job that required travel."

"It was awful for both of us," Marilyn sighs. "I was still making good money, but you can't do all this on one salary, even if it's a very good salary." She sweeps her hand around the room and I notice the tufted couches, the thick Oriental rugs, the luxurious shimmer of hand-cut marble in the foyer.

"It was painful for me to have to leave for a few days every week," says Mel. "I hated saying good-bye to Marilyn and the kids. I hated the hotels and the restaurant food. I hated airports and taxis. I was miserable. So I had an affair."

Instantly I stop peering around the house and focus my full attention on Mel. "It really hurt both me and Marilyn," he says softly. "The bubble burst right then."

Mel's bubble was his remarkable ability, like the legendary Don Quixote, to hang on to the impossible dream: a deep-rooted belief that Marilyn was a perfect partner, almost literally born and raised to be his mate. The two even seemed to share their original families. Mel's younger sister was best friends with Marilyn's sister. Their fathers worked together in a small accounting firm. Their mothers telephoned one another almost daily, chatting about the children and exchanging recipes, and later they traded information on the availability of part-time jobs.

Mel says he can't remember a picnic or a Sunday outing or even a school play without Marilyn's presence. And to Marilyn it seemed as if Mel had always been the center of her universe. It was the most natural thing in the world to grow up assuming she would one day be his wife. There was no doubt about it.

"We graduated from high school and then went on to college together. During the senior year, our parents started talking about how the wedding would be. A couple of weeks after we got our diplomas, we got married," says Marilyn. "There was absolutely no fuss and no real decisions to make. No nervousness or cold feet or anything like that. It was as if it was simply meant to be, as if we were following some preordained plan to entwine our lives from beginning to end."

Without realizing it, they went through the normal stages of marriage. The honeymoon feelings lasted a long time. There were periods of discontent and some marital discord, but Mel and Marilyn continued to cling to one another, avoiding much growth as a couple. Then came the money crunch, and fear plunged between them like a knife.

"Marilyn was already a successful technician when I lost my contracts," Mel explains. "But when I needed her most to contribute some money, she quit her post and took on the mothering role with a vengeance. She was scared, and she sort of curled up by the home fire."

"And he resented that," Marilyn says.

"Yes, I did. I know now it made her feel needed, important in the relationship, but it was totally impractical. At that point, I wanted her to be more of a partner than a little wifey. I was a thirty-eight-year-old man with two young children, and the world was cracking all around me. We had an expensive house, tuition for private schools and mountains of debt. The responsibilities were overwhelming. I felt out of control of my life. I wondered, 'What the hell am I doing here?' "

Marilyn leans forward slightly in her chair, glances at Mel and picks up the thread of his thoughts. "I asked myself the same question," she says, "because I was in a panic. I knew he wanted to split. I could feel it. He wanted out. We never had let go of the fantasies of being one person, so I couldn't believe that Mel could possibly think of leaving. We couldn't exist apart!

"We had never talked about it," she goes on, "and I guess it was because I really couldn't face up to what might be happening. I felt extremely vulnerable at that point. I had two youngsters, I was home with them and I hadn't kept up with advances in research medicine, so I was letting my career slip away. I was a terribly insecure person then. We're talking about just a year ago or less. I tried ploys to keep

Mel dependent on me. I bent over backwards to be the perfect wife and mother so I could send him on a guilt trip."

Mel is studying his fingernails. He brings them to his lips one by one and softly gnaws at the cuticles. Then he suddenly realizes what he is doing, flushes pink and stops. He murmurs that he never got close to walking out on Marilyn, but it wasn't because of his devotion to her. It was the kids. The children provided emotional cement. He was separated from Marilyn at that point not by physical distance but by his own slow horror at discovering, at last, that they were *different*. She was compulsive, perfectionistic, intellectual.

And how does Mel describe himself? "Me? I'm disorganized, content not to be intellectual . . . definitely a lazy bum."

What about the affair?

"It was over in about six months," says Mel. "She was a very lovely woman I had met on the plane during my travels, and it just so happened that our business plans often took us on the same flights and to the same cities and even to the same hotels. It was tailor-made for an affair, and I just sort of slid into it. I didn't feel happy about what I was doing, though, and if Marilyn wanted me to be guilty . . . well . . . it must have worked. I told her about the whole thing after it was all over."

"Talk about alienation," Marilyn chuckles sadly. "That was really it for me. I felt worlds apart from Mel. I just couldn't face it. Not alone, anyway. So I went into therapy. I saw a really good psychiatrist and built up my self-confidence again, and I got to the point where I could project a feeling to Mel of, 'Goodbye, if you don't love me. I won't fall apart.'"

"I never wanted a good-bye," he reminds her.

"I know."

"I was scared, too."

"I also know that."

"Marilyn's therapy worked," says Mel. "It was good for her self-esteem. And because she acted so much more secure about herself, I started examining myself, too. I came away with a whole new realization of what I wanted in life. So now I am settling on the notion that what I want was what I had all along. I had tasted an alternative lifestyle with the affair, and I realize that wasn't what I wanted."

Mel is now pacing the room. The only sound is the soft scuffing of his sneakers.

"The best thing that happened — the thing that is starting to bring us together again — was learning to like *ourselves*," says Mel. "It was when we stopped being whimpering and sniveling and dependent."

Armed with the new coating of her therapy, Marilyn went back to school. She earned another, more specialized degree. Sometimes in the evenings, she would go out to bars with her female friends instead of rushing home to Mel. She felt a gratifying upsurge in individual interests; now she could indulge a long-buried passion for ballet dancing.

Mel snickered that dancing lessons at Marilyn's age were "silly." She ignored him. "I was realizing there were differences in us and that they did matter. He can't share everything with me. I had to accept that. We are becoming two distinct people, standing alone and apart from one another, possibly for the first time since very early childhood."

They both agree that the subject of divorce never arose. "I have fantasies. I will allow myself to have them," says Mel. "But they're only fantasies. I would never leave her."

Marilyn smiles. "Me neither," she says. Then she turns to me. "We don't need too much in the way of fantasy here. We can let each other breathe. We can talk about anything, and that's one reason why I cherish Mel. Oh, he annoys me sometimes. I don't mean to say there aren't times when I feel like smacking him. And I still do get depressed.

"But there is one thing that has always closed off the possibility of chucking it all. I see Mel as a very special man. He is willing to communicate and let his feelings show. And that's so much more important than the other bullshit of liking all the same activities and having exactly the same interests in life. Maybe we can't do ballet together, but we sure can communicate."

"Without fear," Mel interjects. "That's an essential point. It keeps me committed beyond all taboos."

We have been talking a long time. Mel drifts outside to finish a small project on his car. I join Marilyn in the kitchen, perching on a three-legged stool while she prepares food for the evening meal. The children are sleeping at a friend's home tonight. I ask Marilyn what Mel might have meant by saying he was "committed beyond all taboos." She stops abruptly and flashes a resigned, knowing smile.

"I *knew* you'd catch that," she says. "I was just wondering when."

"What do you mean?"

"The taboo is having an open affair."

"You mean he is having another affair?"

"No. I had one, too."

It was part of being separated, she explains. Her misery over Mel's transgression heated into despair and then raging fury. She wanted to punish him for what he had done. She wanted revenge.

Marilyn met her lover in ballet class. The attraction was immediate. She went to bed with him the first night, and after she overcame her initial awe ("I had never been with anyone but Mel, and I didn't think I could do it with anyone else") she felt stirring of affection for this new man in her life. After they had been dating on the sly for about two months, she told Mel about it.

"What was his reaction?"

"It was odd, I think. He seemed to accept it as his just desert. He said that I was an individual, I could do as I saw fit, and he didn't have to be the only one who could satisfy all my needs. It was obvious that he certainly couldn't share ballet with me. Somebody else had to do that.

"Mel knew he was still the center of my love. But he really went into a funk, a terrible silent depression, because I was not hiding my sexual transgression or feeling sorry about it. He broke the same rules, but he was overcome by guilt. I wasn't. He accepted my behavior nevertheless, and that's what he meant by sticking by me beyond all taboos."

I climb down from the stool and lean against the kitchen counter. When I look at Marilyn, she guesses what is on my mind.

"Yes," she says. "The affair is over. It never really presented a threat to Mel . . . and none to our relationship. It is becoming part of our shared history. But I am being honest about it, and so is Mel, when we say it crushed full trust that we were two people just made for each other. Obviously, he could find another woman, and I could find another man. Boy, that can strike a blow to your ego!"

For a while Mel wallowed in his depression, punishing himself for his own affair by refusing to tell Marilyn to cut the ties with her lover. He lacked the self-esteem to demand that Marilyn stop this unacceptable behavior. As a result she felt less loved.

Marilyn knew she was overstepping the bounds of marriage. But until Mel could gain the strength necessary to assert himself, Marilyn could go on thinking the affair was just a harmless act of individuality. It was just two weeks ago, says Marilyn, that Mel demanded that the affair end, and Marilyn said good-bye to her lover. While Marilyn was openly having an affair, this couple remained in a gray, confusing state of marriage without fidelity or basic rules of conduct. This was their separation. In such a situation, neither partner had any real responsibilities or rights. They are still not sure these rights can be reclaimed; that's why Mel and Marilyn aren't quite finished with Separation.

What Are My Rights?

One of the major issues in the Separation stage is figuring out what one's rights are and how to assert them. What does it mean to be an individual at this stage of marriage? Just how far can you and your spouse go in being independent? When should you put your foot down and call a halt to activities that make you too uncomfortable, such as an affair? Now that you have stopped clinging, where is the comfortable halfway point between dependence and autonomy?

These difficult and troublesome questions rise like steam from the depths of childhood, for the Separation stage is the final, shuddering climax of the mother-child relationship. The Separation stage may be the married person's equivalent of the last years of being a teen-ager. Some teens find it impossible to grow up unless they get out. They leave home for the Army, an early marriage or they simply run away. They need physical distance in order to accomplish an emotional break. Twenty or thirty years later, in the Separation stage of marriage, they may need to pack their bags and replay the same old scene . . . this time, with the mother-substitute, or mate. This becomes a physical separation.

In physical separation, it is usually still the man who walks out. If young children are involved, it is probably the only way to keep the whole family from panicking. But this arrangement also may signal a fast start on a new life for the man, while his wife is still stuck in the same surroundings she has probably come to resent: a messy kitchen, piles of laundry, terrified and wailing kids. In most cases, it is still true that when a man leaves home he often leaves home-connected responsibilities. His wife assumes the double burden of coping with all the chores, plus her own misery over the separation.

One thirty-five-year-old woman, who realized this would happen, told me *she* decided to leave. She was unhappy because during the stage of Separation, when she was trying to modify her lifestyle, her husband balked at helping her make the transition from housewife to career woman. They had been married for sixteen years, she said, and "he wasn't the earth and the sun to me anymore, and I needed room to grow." When he blocked her growth, she squeezed his hand good-bye and left him standing silently at the kitchen door with their only child, a ten-year-old girl.

Instead of checking into cheap hotels or trying to find a furnished apartment, this woman slept in the guest rooms or on the couches of sympathetic friends. At first she wouldn't tell her husband where she was. Then she relented and gave him her itinerary. He politely said thank you.

"I could actually hear the change in him over the telephone," she recalls. "He didn't act as if I'd better give him the information or else. He was realizing, 'Hey, she's a person.'"

She moved frequently so she wouldn't intrude too long on any one friend, and she kept in touch with her child by visiting her at school every day during the lunch break.

"It was a time of terrible disruption for all of us," says the woman. "I'm sorry I had to go through it and put my family through it. But I just couldn't stay in that house one more minute. It was exactly the same feeling I had when I was seventeen. I felt so *trapped*. And I knew if my husband left, I'd really be in the same position I was trying to restructure the marriage in order to escape, with him out enjoying a career and me stuck inside the home.

"I wanted to see if I could go it on my own, to tell myself that I was an individual and not a dependent person. Of course, I stayed with friends, and while you might not call that being completely independent, they were a source of great comfort because I was a nervous wreck. But still I proved I had the guts to walk out. And I needed the time away from Carl to think about why I felt so trapped and how I could modify my life without getting a divorce.

"The separation lasted about two weeks. I was exhausted from all that moving around, so I came home. But my purpose had been served. Once Carl saw that I was serious about forcing some sort of change in our lives, he sat down with me to discuss it. It took a lot of trial and error, but eventually it worked. It was an adjustment, and it meant not an end for us but a new beginning."

"Sticky, Gooey Closeness"

Writer and researcher Nancy Friday, in her book *My Mother, My Self*, says the first part of marriage is an attempt to repeat the clinging relationship, or symbiosis, we had as infants hanging on to mother. We yearn for the same "sticky, gooey closeness" that marked our first love relationship with an all-powerful, protecting figure. Since it is almost impossible to get so close to another person without wanting to break away sooner or later, early childhood symbiosis must end, and so must the symbiosis of marriage.

It is difficult to pull away from mother — and later from your marriage partner — without some anger and guilt. Few children can assert their independence calmly. And the only kinds of marriages that can avoid a stormy period of separation are those where both partners enter the relationship as fully-formed, mature, independent people — and fight hard to stay that way. It doesn't happen often. Says Friday, "An almost superhuman conscious effort is demanded if we are to maintain our individuality in marriage."

Living apart for a while may reassure married people that they are still individuals with a continuing ability to accept or reject life situations. This knowledge removes the resentment of feeling helplessly stuck in a marriage, unable to resolve problems even if you have been trying to talk about them. It is wonderful to talk things out in a marriage, but many people talk their relationships to death. Being apart and silent for a time gives people a chance to figure out how to *do* the things they talked about.

British researcher Jonathan Gathorne-Hardy, who wrote *Marriage, Love, Sex & Divorce*, says some couples separate for a while just to make life exciting. This happens most frequently in the fourth or fifth year of marriage, right after the man and woman foolishly feel nothing new is going to happen in their lives together.

"And so we see the couple of four years becoming desperately fearful of the flatness, the sameness, the jog-trot of married life, desperately trying to disturb the emotional ties which are gradually forming among the smoothness and serenity of their lives, desperately trying to revive the sensation and passion and love again."

These early separations are not productive, and they are not part of the Separation stage. A separation may come at any point in marriage, and serve a variety of functions, without erupting into the fully-formed stage of Separation which occurs from twelve to seventeen years in a first marriage, and possibly much earlier when people are married for the second or third time. But splitting for a while to remedy boredom at any time in the marriage is probably a cover-up for two lazy and immature people who prefer not to deal with the responsibilities of togetherness in daily life. They think the excitement of the separation will make their sexual juices flow again.

But separation, emotional or physical, doesn't work that way. You have to devote the time alone to hard thinking about yourself and your marriage. Nothing will really change if you just break up for a while to alter the pattern of a boring life. If and when they do reunite, such couples slip into the same structure and emotional form that shaped their marriage in the first place. They are soon overtaken by boredom again.

Perceptive grown-ups don't confuse boredom with familiarity. Most mature adults like a certain predictable quality to their lives. The sameness of the days is balanced by the ever-increasing excitement of deepening intimacy. Gathorne-Hardy says people who expect bell-ringing romance all the time, and who separate in any stage as a way of trying to get it back, don't know what a marriage is supposed to be and are cutting themselves off from deeper satisfactions.

"Marriage begins with romantic love," he writes, "but the day-to-day, year-to-year grind of that condition, the endless proximity, the strain of children, the need for security, require quite different qualities and feelings from the supposedly intense fires which started the whole thing off: tolerance, compromise, often self-sacrifice, humor, loyalty, kindness, stability. Emotionally it demands something that although sexual is far closer to affection and fondness, to friendship, than to passionate love."

Sondra's Story

Sondra says she would like a real friendship with her husband. That's what she wants out of this period of separation. For seventeen years, Barry has been her mentor. Now it's time she grew up. She wants to be on equal footing with him. And she says he's scared, because he doesn't understand or yet accept her desire for a reevaluation of their marriage.

Sondra kicks the grass with the tip of her Nike running shoe and stops to squint up at the sun. There is still time to run one more mile before she heads back for a shower and a midday business meeting.

We start off together, puffing lightly, and I can tell from the frown on her shining dark face that she is still thinking about this adjustment and how to make it come out all right.

Sondra is a tall, willowy thirty-nine-year-old who was born in the misty farm country of North Carolina. Her father owns a small plot of fertile land in the shadows of the Blue Ridge Mountains. Sondra was born at a time when it was not common or fashionable to be upwardly mobile, and also black.

But Sondra's mother had great plans. She supplemented the family farm earnings by working as a housemaid for the rich white people who vacationed in the mountains.

"Mother was a favorite with them because she was neat and light-skinned, and people weren't afraid of her like they were of some of the very dark women, because the whites associated dark with being dirty," Sondra recalls. "Mother made quite a nice salary, and she put it in the bank so she could send me and my two sisters to college. And she accomplished that."

Sondra became a nurse-administrator. In 1970 she took a job as a manager of a fine private nursing home for elderly Jewish patients. There she met Barry, a physician specializing in geriatrics and the owner of the home.

At once, Sondra liked the sincerity that beamed from Barry's blue eyes. She liked the way he ran the nursing home: with pride, with care, and with obvious affection and respect for his patients. It was a model nursing facility, and Barry, to Sondra, was a model man. He "adopted" her. Many evenings, when they worked side by side in the offices on the top floor of the home, he encouraged her to expand her career, to learn, to forget her self-imposed label as a black woman and to think of herself instead as a human being with unlimited potential. Barry is nearly ten years older than Sondra, and to her he seemed very wise. Under his guidance, her self-confidence blossomed.

Sondra's admiration for Barry gradually deepened into love. No matter that he was a white man. No matter that she came from a poor farming family of Baptists, and he was a wealthy Jewish urbanite educated at fine schools. "Stretch yourself," he told her. She got up the courage to tell him of her love. Barry said he felt the same way. Sondra converted to Judaism. Two months later, they were married.

"It seems to me that we went through our marriage in a very orderly fashion, without much pain," she tells me after we finish jogging. "I was braced for some real trouble because of me being black and him being white, but I have to say I was pleasantly surprised.

"First of all, our families were supportive. Barry absolutely won my mother's heart — he is a charmer — and Dad saw my marriage to a white man as dangerous but definitely a step up. Up from poverty, I guess, and up from the stigma he still felt was attached to being black.

"Barry's mom and dad didn't seem to have any trouble accepting me at all. I don't know... maybe it's because I'm fairly light-skinned... but they were very nice to me, and now I think they don't notice what color I am because they both refer to me as their daughter, and I call them "Mom" and "Dad." Barry comes from a liberal Jewish home, and they were always sort of interested in civil rights, and with them it was a very honest thing. They just took me into the family like I believe they would have taken any woman Barry wanted to marry.

"So that was all right. And since Barry and I worked together at the home, there weren't any employment problems for me to contend with. Also, we were happy to discover that people didn't look at us twice when we came into a restaurant. I never felt like anybody stayed away from us, or refused to be friendly, because we were a mixed couple. We live in a nice house in a mostly white neighborhood, but there are a few black families around the corner. Again, no problems with neighbors. So societal pressures weren't any heavier on us than on any other couple.

"Barry has always been sort of a protector for me, a strong father figure. Not that he's *that* much older. It's not that. I think I needed somebody to tell me it was all right for a black farm girl to come to the city and be a professional woman. He did that, plus he gave me romance and also security. It was as if Barry would shield me from any harsh realities I might find, any prejudice or tough times.

"And in a way he did that and still does. We work at the home as a team, and in a sense I never had to go out and elbow my way into the job market like other black women I know. Also, I didn't have to compete for a good black man. They are very hard to find. An educated black woman today has a tough time finding a male counterpart in black society. Marrying Barry solved that problem for me.

"I was only twenty-two when we got married. I was glad to be taken under his wing. It was only since about last year that I started asking myself, 'Can you stand on your own two feet?' The answer was not clear to me. I got very, very depressed. I still feel sad sometimes.

"Part of this change in me is that our daughter, who is sixteen years old now, is going to college next year. She isn't the least bit afraid to be in a dorm with all white girls. We didn't plan that to happen. It just worked out that way. The school she's going to is in Boston, and they assigned her by computer to a dorm. When we went for a visit, I realized she would be the only black girl in that unit.

"She's lighter-skinned than me, even, but you can still tell she's the product of a black parent or grandparent along the line. But I'm bothered by these issues, not her. It's just not part of her world. She didn't even seem to notice that all of the other girls were white. And I see that she is strong and independent, and I cringe inside myself because I am her mother but I don't have her kind of courage. And it's because I am still clinging to Barry. So I wanted to just get away emotionally, put some distance between me and Barry, to prove to myself that I am a real person and not a black Barbie doll."

Sondra and Barry are living together through this separation, but Sondra has placed an emotional barrier between them so she can "think this out." Barry does not want to be interviewed on the subject. He is confused and angry. What is wrong with his wife? he asks me. What does she want? Why is she turning inside herself like this and locking him out?

Barry has marched through their marriage like a general. Sondra has been his loyal soldier. Because of his greater wealth, earning power, age, education — and maybe because of his race — Barry has always had the power in this relationship. He used it wisely. He encouraged Sondra to spread her timid wings. But now, perhaps, she has gone further than he dreamed. Secure in his implicit claim to greater authority within the relationship, he is confused and angered by this sudden challenge from Sondra. It is as if after spending a lifetime accepting his kindness, she now has blamed him for its crippling effect on her psyche.

"I know Barry feels as if I'm ungrateful. I expected him to think that way, but I'm hoping he'll see that isn't the case at all," says Sondra. She plops down on the grass at the side of the blacktop jogging path. Her pink headband is soaked with sweat. She lays back, elbows akimbo, and shuts her eyes tight.

"I really want to break out of this feeling that I'm nothing without Barry. In a funny way, it doesn't really involve him. It is certainly not a question of me not loving him any more. I do. I even told him that. He's scared that's not the case, but I have told him very firmly that I love him now more than ever, and he said, 'I just don't understand this, then. What are you doing this for?'

"And I tried to explain it to him. I said, 'I want to be my own woman, so instead of your being like my daddy or my big brother-husband, you can be my friend. I want to be equal with you in my own mind.'"

"Did he understand?" I ask.

"Not yet, no. He is very unhappy right now. I'm not thrilled with it either. But I don't want to break up. I want to break *out*."

Perhaps it has been natural for Barry to assume the role of nurturing parent to Sondra. He is a strong male, and many males like to be teachers, mentors and protectors of others, especially as they grow older. Females also enjoy this parenting role, but it is most often acted out through their children.

Young men seek mentors of their own when they first begin careers or life courses, and they often select an older man who will help them. This older man — a boss, a professor, a superior in the Army, perhaps — also teaches the growing male how to be a mentor, in turn, when he matures. This is done simply by example. But few women have female mentors who serve the same purposes, because, at least in the past, they have not had a great supply of successful older females to whom they could turn and say, "Teach me." One's own parent may serve as a vital role model in many areas of life, but it is rare to have a mother or father in your chosen field who can give objective advice. So women who want to grow are often forced to select a powerful male who will help them learn the ropes in life and in business.

Barry has been Sondra's mentor. She now sees him as unsuited for the role because it is time for her to mature into self-reliance. With her lost image of Barry as full protector, Sondra is depressed. She is unconnecting, and this realignment also probably will force Barry into a new look at the relationship.

No mentoring situation can last forever. The more powerful figure is eventually challenged as the less dominant person slowly gathers strength. That is the basis for Sondra's emotional separation from Barry. If Barry can accept her as an equal, and if he is emotionally strong enough to relinquish some of the power he has over her, he will emerge as Sondra's friend . . . for life.

Sondra says the Separation stage of marriage is costing her dearly. She feels sick a lot of the time. People who are going through this period in their lives with some awareness of the changes taking place do show obvious signs of distress. They experience loss of appetite, sleeplessness and being cranky and super-sensitive. Some people describe a sensation of being ripped apart. One wife described "a heavy pain in my chest." A male scientist told me that in the month he was estranged from his wife, he vomited after almost every meal and lost fourteen pounds. Another man had heartburn continually.

Such pain is real. Researcher Jessie Barnard studied couples who were alienated from one another at one or more crucial periods of marriage and says actual areas of the brain have been disturbed and are sending chemical signals of distress. People undergoing separation often look tired and pale because they are working hard at restructuring their marriages, and they feel the intense emotional strain.

However, this is not the same sort of agony experienced by people who are deciding to end marriage. To them, being apart is a welcome relief from tension. They are not in the Separation stage because this stage presumes a temporary realignment and then a return to the same marriage partner. Instead, divorcing people are either preparing for life alone or getting ready to enter the first stage of marriage all over again with someone else. They're free at last, and after much initial sorrow and anger, they often look and feel better than ever. They are no longer exhausted by struggling with questions about how to improve the marriage. It is over. They are relieved and can get on with a new life.

Psychiatrist Ari Kiev, who writes about forms of separation and adjustment in his book *How To Keep Love Alive,* says a healthy period of being emotionally alone is tough on both partners but intensely rewarding if you stick it out. A marriage is made stronger by any form of separating if it helps you learn to experience deeply-repressed feelings, primarily the fear of being alone.

"Separation can be an opportunity to grow and widen your own horizons, both mutually and individually," says Kiev. "This, sadly, is lost on many people because of the fear of being alone."

Says a forty-two-year-old poet, "My big mistake has always been the horrible fear of being alone. I like to think of myself as an independent woman, but that's bullshit. I just don't feel comfortable unless I've got a man with me almost every minute.

"My husband and I separated three times between our fifteenth and seventeenth year of marriage. Twice the separation was emotional and once he left home. Each time, I didn't give either one of us a chance to make any real moves toward a better relationship. Instead I rushed off to find another man. I met them in singles bars, restaurants, art shows, anywhere. It was as if I had to fill a terrible void. I never used the separations to think things over. I never gave myself the chance.

"So we divorced and I lost him. Now I'm getting older and I'm afraid. I'm not going to be so good-looking after a few more years, so I'd better learn how to hold on to one man because it isn't going to be that easy to keep finding replacements. With the man I'm seeing now, I'm trying to develop the ability to be strong and alone in the sense of making my own decisions and not clinging to him as if I would die if he didn't provide some direction for my life. I think this will help keep me from devouring a man, from insisting he be my perfect person. I have to be my own perfect person."

Sondra tells me she does not expect to emerge from this stage of marriage as a perfect person. Her goal is to wipe away the lingering hope that Barry will *make* her perfect or that he has the power to do so.

Several months after our first interview, I telephone Sondra to find out if she has successfully completed the stage of Separation.

"Not quite yet," she says after a moment or two of thought. "Barry and I have been fighting a lot, something we really didn't do until now. I think the fights mean I am asserting myself. He isn't used to that, so he objects, no matter if what I'm saying makes sense or not.

"But I feel more alive than ever. I have a sense of strength, like I'm accomplishing something very important. I don't feel like a wishy-washy person anymore. I have an identity of my own, not one that Barry carved out for me. And I'm not depressed.

"Barry doesn't relate to me in the same way as he used to. To be honest, he isn't as nice to me. I don't mean that he's nasty. He's just not as protective . . . not as concerned or fatherly. For example, he used to simply accept any mistakes in my work, and now if I make a mistake he holds me accountable. He's not coming after me to check up and see that my mistakes are caught before they cause any trouble. And he isn't so sympathetic of my feelings or my health. He *expects* more, and he gets mad if I don't deliver. He used to say, for instance, 'Oh, if you're having your period you should stay home today.' Now he says everybody has their bad days, so unless I'm really having terrible cramps, I should do what's expected of me.

"Sure, I miss being babied. It was nice. But I like this better. I respect myself. So I think that's why the depression is gone for me.

"Barry is still sort of down in the dumps, but he is also much better. For a while he was so unhappy he was barely speaking to me. Now I think he understands what this is all about. I sort of dragged him into it. He said the other day that this experience has made him feel very alone at times. Me, too. But honestly, I just don't see any other way of staying married and still breaking away enough to have some real self-respect. Maybe Barry could have done without it, but this was a very necessary stage for me."

The Capacity To Be Alone

Despite its discomforts, the stage of Separation has plentiful rewards. The capacity to accept being alone is one of this stage's greatest gifts. In Separation, one learns that it is acceptable to be alone even if you are married. This is a radical concept in our society, because we have always assumed that the marriage partnership precludes voluntary emotional isolation and that married people must always share their most intimate thoughts with one another.

We may not know it at the time, but we are alone through every stage in our lives. We are alone gasping through the birth canal. Alone, we tiptoe into school for the first time, and we endure pimples, pubic hair and hot sexual shame alone. We stumble through the stages of marriage trying to adjust to our partners, but we are alone in feeling the emotions aroused by those adjustments. Dimly, we know we face old age and death as single, quivering beings who are alone.

Still, we fight being alone. It scares us. Some people are so anxious to avoid this feeling that they endure crowds, unfaithful friends, foolish partnerships or unwanted children, all to avoid the absence of some other human being whom they fantasize can save them from dreaded solitude. Eventually, however, we all learn the inevitable truth — that being alone can be helpful at times, and it does not have to mean being lonely, not if we have found inner security and self-respect. Perhaps one sure sign of emotional maturity is a person's ability to think, act and be comfortably alone.

This quality is often a happy product of the stage of Separation. Once a person finds peace in being alone, he or she is ready to rejoin the marriage partner and start building a new and stronger foundation for life together.

Stage Six: TOGETHER AGAIN
(Years Seventeen to Twenty)

"After twenty years, this marriage is like money in the bank. Look, we have a lot invested here. Now it's time to relax and rake in the dividends." — a forty-eight-year-old man.

The living room, freshly painted and decorated with white carnations for this event, is crowded with family and friends. Mona enters first, wearing a pale yellow suit and clutching a single flower. At forty-seven, she is still slender. Her short black hair is heavily streaked with gray.

Artie walks behind her, looking very serious in a blue striped business suit. He takes Mona's hand and they repeat the same wedding vows that joined them more than twenty years ago. Later, as he is gulping a celebratory glass of champagne, Artie admits this "wedding" is much more fun than the first.

"Looking back at it, I have to say I was a dumb kid when I first got married," says Artie. "I was twenty-eight years old, but I didn't know much about how to handle myself or how to handle a relationship.

"I gave Mona plenty of grief. I always had to prove myself, to be macho. We had fights. Of course, there were good times, too, and we have three wonderful girls.

"I promised Mona that if we made it to twenty years, we'd renew our wedding vows. And I'm glad we did it, because this is a lovely ceremony and it means so much more to me now that we know everything that went into making this marriage work.

"If I had it to do over," says Artie, "and I knew what I know now. I'd still marry Mona but I wouldn't put her through the hoops like I did. God, I expected so much of her. It took a long time for me to realize she's only human, and so am I, and being married to someone doesn't mean you can just drain them dry. After twenty years, this marriage is like money in the bank. Look, we have a lot invested here. We've been through a lot of crap together, and now it's time to relax and rake in the dividends."

Artie's cousin has brought his fiddle to the celebration, and a merry tune sounds from one corner of the room. Artie looks around, spots Mona whispering to one of their grown daughters and moves quickly to his wife's side. "May I have this dance?" he asks with mock formality. Mona smiles broadly and puts her arms around her husband's neck. They dance lightly around the room.

"Don't they look like a couple of kids?" the daughter asks. "Boy, I hope I can still be in love like that after *I'm* married twenty years."

The daughter can probably have her wish, but only after she has gone through the stages of marriage as her parents did. Artie and Mona are in the stage of Together Again. Young love may be more passionate, but it can never be as rich and rewarding as this mellow time.

After about seventeen to twenty years of negotiating and renegotiating the relationship, each person now feels there is much invested in the marriage. There are good things to enjoy in the spouse, and most people no longer want to waste any more time concentrating on what might be bad.

Thus the couple married for half a lifetime rediscovers one another. They are willing to forget old hurts and heal the wounds of past fury. Together Again is a leap of faith into what is seen by many people as a new marriage with the old partner.

Although people may have taken their wedding vows twenty years ago, this is when they really say, "I do." The renewal of vows is not uncommon at this point. Finally, people know what it means to commit for life.

Author and editor Robin Morgan says people who are sensitive and aware of the progression of marriage will zoom into a new dimension at this stage. The groping of youth and the sputtering discontent characteristic of the "settling in" stages is gone. After much agony, separation is over and people feel firmly entrenched in the partnership. In her own marriage, says Morgan, consciousness of the struggle cost her dearly in "pain, dense silences and furious outbursts, craziness, depression." Now come the rewards. Morgan describes them as "challenge, elation, laughter, excitement at our capacity for change, awe at the courage of intimacy, tenderness, and sympathy and a certain savored . . . coziness."

Relaxation At Last

The stages leading up to this point are characterized by intense emotions and feelings that both partners are searching for the best possible expression of affection in daily life. It is hard work. Together Again is definitely a feeling of relaxation at last, coupled with excitement because partners are taking new interest in one another. Dr. Norman Abrams, a psychiatrist, says couples in the stage of Together Again start seeing nice traits in their spouses once more. They fondly recall the fun they have shared over the years.

"Up to this point people have stopped remembering all the good times," says Dr. Abrams. "After about seventeen to twenty years, they start looking again at the photos in the family albums. Or they might be jarred by an old movie and remember how they held hands during the whole thing in the dark theatre.

"Affairs go sour. Men tell me they don't want to fool around any more. Now they enjoy their wives. The singles bars are cold. They say that going home is comforting and reassuring. They notice the nice things their wives will do. One man said, 'I suddenly realized nobody else would make me a drink every night, exactly the way I like it.'

"The women also make an attempt to see the positives in their husbands," according to Dr. Abrams. "By this time they have grown more confident, and they are not tied down by little babies. So they know they are not in the marriage because they have to be but because they really want to be.

"Couples arrange for a romantic weekend together. They take a computer course and the two of them feel like kids starting out together. Maybe the woman who once jogged with her husband and then stopped will start exercising with him again. Or she'll putter in the yard just to be near him.

"The intensity and passion of the early years is gone, but I think that's just part of the aging process. As you get older the intensity of everything is diminished. What you have in this stage, instead, is a marvelous and very intimate friendship and comfortable, satisfying sex."

What are the psychological mechanisms that allow people to move from the flailing discontent of Decisions and Separation to the stage of Together Again?

If the husband and wife have experienced a real emotional or physical separation in the previous stage, they now know that being alone is not equivalent to personal death nor to the death of the marriage. Because they survived the loneliness and pain of being apart, they emerge as more confident people. They can handle being alone, and it is now obvious that if they stay married, it is because of devotion to the partner and not because of fear.

So the marriage is voluntary, after all. Neither partner is stuck. They are *willing* to stay.

This willingness fuels the desire to think positively. The partners remind themselves and one another of all they have in common. Both also seek new ways to relate and recapture excitement, and often they are successful. The jogging, the computer courses, the puttering in the yard, all enrich the marriage once again and create an aura of good feeling. It is as if the sapling of love, planted so long ago, has weathered storms and is now receiving additional fertilizer for new growth.

Dr. Donald L. Donohugh, writing about marriage in his book *The Middle Years,* says the revitalization of marriage after about twenty years constitutes a new relationship based on the experience of the old. He says, "Reflection will show that no matter how a marriage was begun, if it has survived to middle age, each partner has much to match the other, and each has helped to develop enough common areas of interest to neutralize most of what may make the marriage difficult at this time. There is a great deal to build on . . . marriage in middle age can be the most thoroughly satisfying aspect of our entire lives."

It is also easier now to tolerate a spouse's failures as merely his or her old habits. They do not reflect on or inhibit the relationship.

"I learned not to take everything personally," a forty-eight-year-old doctor told me. "I realized my wife wasn't messy because she wanted to hurt me. She just doesn't *see* the mess. So I decided to say to myself, 'It has nothing to do with me. She would be this way with anyone.' And once I did that, I could just live and let live. She sensed that I was accepting her, finally, for what she was. So we both relaxed a lot more. On a scale of one to ten, I stopped acting as if every little annoyance was a ten. I stopped manufacturing crises for myself."

This new relaxation does not wipe away the memory of past battles. There is always a residue of bitterness, disappointment and hurt. Scars remain. Some people say they feel an enduring sadness for all the times the partner was willing to let them go. At those times, they felt rejection. In a long marriage, there are many such rejections, but it is necessary to push past the hurt feelings and dwell instead on the many times of acceptance. If a marriage is seen in this positive light, each partner then feels that the combined weight of the happy times is stronger than that of the unhappy times.

"When you think of it that way," a forty-three-year-old management specialist told me, "it's very difficult to imagine breaking up after twenty years. You know, the longer you stay together, the harder it is to split. My husband and I share a lot of history. I can't tell you why I married him in the first place, and I can't tell you why the marriage is so good now and why we're having fun and being able to put aside the old pain. Good times build on good times more than bad times build on themselves. You tend to remember the good more than the bad, if you want to. So after all this time, I still love him."

The good feelings that come with the stage of Together Again gather their own momentum. The couple is no longer engaged in a power struggle.

According to Dr. M. Scott Peck, a person who has achieved the potential for continuing growth sees power not as the ability to coerce others but as the capacity to make conscious, informed decisions. Little by little, people who review their past experiences and make the effort to learn from them can go on to develop methods for enjoying the present and avoiding many future mistakes. When they do this, says Peck, people are "possessed by a joyful humility." They do not see themselves as the center of the world but as a well-oiled cog in the great wheel of the universe, able to give up selfishness in favor of devotion to others — specifically, to the spouse. This is a spiritual dimension that comes to us in middle age if we actively strive for it, working to obtain power over no one but ourselves. Says Peck, "Such a loss of self brings with it always a calm ecstasy, not unlike the experience of being in love."

In the stage of Together Again, one sees love itself as "calm ecstasy." Power is no longer an issue in the marriage. Fights still may occur now and then, but because each partner is more self-confident, neither has to win. In earlier stages people made compromises with one another. Here, in consciously deciding not to fight because winning is no longer important, the compromises are made with oneself.

Jake And Michelle

The peace and renewed passion of this stage are illustrated by a couple known to me as Jake and Michelle. They agreed to be interviewed, they said, to share their delight in having overcome a trauma that shook them deeply in the fifteenth year of marriage during the Separation stage and which left lifelong scars. Even though Jake and Michelle were pulled apart by what happened to them, their commitment to growth formed a bridge of love that was certainly battered but not broken.

Jake was waiting for me outside the huge factory gate of a shipyard in Connecticut, where he works as a draftsman. The sun is hard and bright on this winter day, and he holds up the palm of his hand to shield his eyes from the glare. Jake is a man of average height, and he seems a little overweight in his snug-fitting blue pea jacket. He has a pleasant face and blue eyes framed by stylish aviator glasses.

Jake sees me and steps forward timidly to ask if I am the writer who has come to interview him about his twenty-year marriage. I tell him yes, and he flashes a smile. He says I do not look intimidating. We laugh and go off for a restaurant dinner and a long talk about this forty-five-year-old man's life, which he says is now joyful.

Jake comes from a working-class family of conservative Jews. His father was a plumber and his mother is best remembered, he says, by her long hours in a perpetually overheated kitchen from which emerged roast chicken, noodle puddings, chopped liver and other ethnic culinary delights. Life was not difficult when he was a child, Jake tells me. Rules were simple and rigidly enforced, and he grew up believing that if a man did his job, remained faithful to his family and loved his God and country, life's modest rewards would not be withheld.

Jake has been a draftsman since the age of eighteen, when he graduated from high school and took his first job at the shipyard. It was to remain his life's work. The company sent him to technical school, gave him raises and pension plans and kept him happy for all of these twenty-seven years, he says. He never wanted to change jobs; never wanted to advance very far or go on to another career.

"I have always wanted to be just what I am," he tells me. "I am not a terribly ambitious guy. I don't enjoy working until I drop. I am laid back. I'm not a big reader or an intellectual person or a genius of any sort. I'm rather plain. My values in life are home and family. Once in a while I enjoy seeing a baseball game and I like fooling around with computers. I'm a computer nut, and my hobby is buying small computers and working out my own programs with them.

"Basically I'm a simple person," says Jake. "I like to think that a fellow's heart is what's important. I judge a man by the way he treats his parents, his kids, his wife. Being honest is a top priority. Holding down a good job and bringing home a paycheck. Caring about his country, having some feel for religion and the love of his fellow man. You know, all the traditional values.

"I married Michelle because she shared those values with me. We were both nineteen when we got married. Michelle and I met in high school, so we've known each other for a long time. And we have gone through everything together. You name it, we had the experience. We've had two kids, money troubles, pressure from the in-laws, and...uh...difficulty with sex. And we have come through what you might call matters of life and death."

Jake's face turns red, and he gulps from his water glass. He peers around the restaurant to make sure he is not being overheard.

"I never thought I'd be admitting these things to a stranger," he says with a nervous chuckle. "I never thought I'd do a lot of things. But I've changed a lot lately. Me and Michelle are in a wonderful period in our lives. Things have calmed down so much over the past year. We hardly fight any more. It's just a pleasure. And after what we've been through, I'd say it is also a little bit of a miracle."

Right from the start of their marriage, money problems hit Jake and Michelle the hardest. They settled in a small apartment in Hartford, and even though they were able to buy a roomy condominium after Jake got several raises when he was in his mid-twenties, they never did get the big house Michelle wanted. She decided to go to work part-time in a gift shop, and Jake says he was enthusiastic about her job.

"I liked the idea," he tells me. "It meant we would have some extra cash, and by that time we had two little boys, so we needed any money that came our way. Also, I could see Michelle was getting bored being at home all the time. Everyone needs a change of scenery. So she went to work, and it didn't seem at first as if much had changed. Boy, if I had known what was going to happen. . . . "

Jake and Michelle decided to save Michelle's earnings for a very special event: taking the family to Israel for the Bar Mitzvah of their oldest son, Adam. The decision was made when Adam was twelve years old and his brother Eli was ten. Jake and Michelle are both observant Jews, and the ceremonial welcoming of a young Jewish person into adulthood at the age of thirteen was an important ritual for them and their children. Most Jewish boys and girls observe that ceremony, after years of study, in their Temples surrounded by family and friends. Jake and Michelle wanted to hold the ceremony in Israel, as close to the holy Wailing Wall as they could get. Then they would return and have a big family party for Adam at home.

Trouble came almost the moment they started to carry out the plan.

"It meant money and lots more of it," Jake recalls. "Michelle got crazy about that. She started scrimping and saving, even to the point where she wouldn't buy meat for weeks so we'd save money on groceries. And all of a sudden her job in the gift shop wasn't good enough for her anymore. She wanted to be a hot-shot, maybe manager of the store instead of a saleswoman, to make a bigger salary.

"She also started bugging me about my salary, saying I wasn't making enough and I was a big nothing career-wise. That really cut me down. She had never indicated that I wasn't good enough for her. Now she called into question my abilities to provide for the family, and that was a blow to my manhood. This was when we had already been married for fifteen years, and I felt that she was restless and wanting to make some sort of a change in our lives. But this was a very destructive change.

"Then her father got into the act. He's a widower. Michelle's mother died of breast cancer about ten years ago. He said we were being selfish to have the Bar Mitzvah ceremony of his grandson so far away where he couldn't participate. We tried to see his side. We tried to tell him how much it would mean to Adam, too, but he just complained as if we were disowning him or committing a terrible sin in God's eyes. He got to my father and then my mother, who were both alive at the time, and they started in on us about it. Before we knew what was happening, the whole family was in a hullabaloo about Adam's Bar Mitzvah.

"This was about five years ago. As I look back on it now, it was a turning point in my life, and Michelle will probably tell you the same thing is true for her. It got so bad that we were bickering all the time about it.

"Now I realize that it wasn't just the Bar Mitzvah that was stirring things up. That just seemed to be the major issue at the time. But after fifteen years or so of marriage, we were both getting annoyed with each other. And I was especially feeling the strain of having two growing boys and not so much money coming in, with a wife who kept reminding me of that fact. I had never felt inadequate as a man and as a provider, but at that point I started feeling that way. I tell you, it can eat your heart out.

"I started getting fat and our sex life went to hell. I always eat when I'm unhappy, and I can't make love unless I *feel* loving. And at that point I wasn't having too many nice feelings about Michelle. Everything seemed so complicated, I didn't care about anything anymore: Michelle, myself, even the kids. I guess just feeling that I had an obligation to everyone and I had to see it through, that's what kept me from just running away or joining the Navy or something crazy like that. I didn't feel like talking about it to my friends, and I sure didn't have the money or patience for visits to a psychiatrist. Whew, what a terrible time!"

That was the stage of Decisions. But as Jake and Michelle moved into Separation, things were going to get a lot worse. The time for the trip to Israel grew near. One day Michelle interrupted her frantic Bar Mitzvah preparations for a visit to the doctor. She came home red-eyed and told Jake in a quivering voice that she was pregnant.

"What a shock!" he says, spreading his hands wide and then taking a reassuring sip of wine. "It was like a hard kick in my guts. I felt the same way as Michelle, that I didn't want the baby. But what to do about it . . . well . . . that was another question."

At that point Jake and Michelle had no extra money. Their sons were almost grown. They felt too old, too tired, too frazzled to go through another pregnancy and the long infancy of an unwanted child. All night and part of the next day, they weighed the pros and cons of having a baby. Judaism taught them that each life was sacred and children were to be cared for and sheltered. But didn't that also mean protecting the lives that were already there? "We knew there was no way we could afford that baby, financially or emotionally," Jake says sadly. They decided on an abortion.

"So we were together on it, at least," he says. "We had made an important decision as a team. And it was a terrible decision, one that was very painful for us both. But at least we agreed. That was very important to me.

"Michelle went to work that afternoon. See, we had been up all night and all morning talking about what we should do, and we both stayed home in order to be able to talk. She wanted to go to work even though she really looked exhausted. I couldn't go. I was wrung out, feeling really bad and so tired that I could hardly see straight. I remember that I fell asleep on the couch after Michelle left. I had a horrible dream. I dreamed a little baby girl was reaching out to me, crying 'Daddy! Daddy!' She looked just like me, and I realized it was *my* baby. I always wanted a girl."

Jake is weeping silently now. The tears roll down his cheeks, hang for a moment at the tip of his chin, then splatter softly on his empty plate. He takes his napkin, pokes it under his glasses and wipes away the wet signs of his bitter memories. After a few moments of silence, he can go on.

"The dream woke me up and I just shot out of that couch. My heart was beating so fast. My hands shook. I went to the telephone and called Michelle and said, 'Let's think this abortion over some more. Maybe we're rushing into the decision. Let's go see our rabbi and ask for some advice on this.'

"I didn't tell her about my dream just then, but I think the tone of my voice said it all. She could hear that I was very upset. She said okay. We'd talk it over again after dinner that night, when the boys were in bed.

"Well, she didn't come home for dinner. That was the first time in our married lives that she didn't show up. I was frantic. I called her father, I called my parents, I went out in the car searching the streets. I even contacted the police. You can imagine that I didn't sleep a wink that night.

"The next morning Michelle shows up. She looks as if she's been run over by a truck, all mussed up and no makeup on and this tired, pinched look on her face. I could tell she had been crying a lot. She had been through something terrible. So I ask her, as gently as I can, what has happened. And she says to me, 'I had the abortion.'"

Jake says the world caved in on him then. His period of separation started at that moment. There was screaming, bitter fights, days of not speaking to one another. Jake says he felt betrayed and deeply wounded. Eventually the shock wore off, and Jake and Michelle reached a silent, aloof truce. They went to Israel, and Adam had his Bar Mitzvah at the Wailing Wall. Two years passed. Eli was a Bar Mitzvah boy, too. This time the ceremony was held at a local Temple with a party at home.

Jake says he remembers when their long, exhausting, emotional estrangement came to an end. He and Michelle were cleaning up after Eli's Bar Mitzvah party. Michelle said she was too tired to move any more, so she'd have to do the vacuuming later. She went to the couch, curled up against a pillow and closed her eyes.

"She looked so little, so fragile," Jake says. "All of a sudden I felt very tender toward her. I don't know why I did this, but I went to the closet, got out the vacuum cleaner and without a word plugged it in and did the rug.

"Michelle opened her eyes, but she didn't say anything. She just watched me. When I finished I put the vacuum cleaner away, and I just was sort of standing there, feeling a bit confused and silly, and she reached out her hand to me and motioned for me to come and sit next to her. And I did.

"We just sat there for a while and held hands. We didn't say one word. But I was thinking to myself, 'The bad times are going to end, right now. I'm tired of feeling mean and lonely. I have to forgive and forget, and Michelle and me have to get on with our lives. We can be happy again; we can have fun. The boys aren't little anymore, and most of the pressure is off. I don't want to get old feeling like this. I want to love Michelle again.' "

The inevitability of aging may propel people like Jake into the stage of Together Again. The knowledge that time is running out makes people more determined to rekindle the quality of life.

This knowledge coincides with the relief of giving up the illusion that one must hold out for a mate who will fully complement one's personality and adhere to one's value system. As they ripen into the stage of Together Again, people no longer feel obligated to nurse old grudges, looking for relief or revenge. They learn to accept both themselves and their spouse as multi-dimensional people who are imperfect but okay. This acceptance almost immediately enables a man or women to experience a deeper intimacy with their spouse than they have ever known.

In *Passages*, Gail Sheehy notes that middle-aged couples can arrive at a state of happiness that is richer, riper and more deeply fulfilling than that of younger people.

"Studies record a dramatic climb in satisfaction with marriage in the mid-forties for those couples who have survived the passage into mid-life together," writes Sheehy. "What this finding reflects is not that our mate miraculously improves but that tolerance can become spontaneous once we stop displacing our inner contradictions on our spouse."

Outside events help the process along. The fight to acquire money and status is either won or lost by now, and people begin to seek contentment instead of the excitement of struggle. At this point most men are at peace with their careers and are slowly turning to the more intimate satisfactions of home and family. The so-called feminine part of them is allowed to emerge. Family researcher John K. Antill, who questioned 108 married couples, found that feminine traits in both males and females were one of the keys to satisfaction in marriage. When men showed these traits, defined as "nurturance, sympathy and warmth," says Antill, both husband and wife reported being happy.

Most often, men let their feminine characteristics show in middle age or later, when they no longer feel compelled to put on a show of masculinity for the sake of impressing others.

Women in mid-life either have their own outside jobs or interests or have decided that homemaking is right for them. They, too, feel free to express greater personal warmth. Worries about providing properly for children aren't as severe, or those worries are gone altogether because the children are grown and on their own. Finally, women can put aside the crippling guilt that often haunts the early child-raising years. According to sociologist Keith Melville, women especially show some initial dislocation when children leave home and then a sharp upturn in happiness.

Mature sex now becomes better than ever before. Most couples in the stage of Together Again say they have sex at least once a week — less than they once had, but as one woman told me, "When we do make love, it's so much more relaxed, so tender, so much more satisfying than when we were first starting out and nervous about it all the time."

William Kephart, an expert on marriage, says sociologists once thought marriage could be charted as starting out with high-intensity sexual feelings, then slowly declining in satisfaction. Now, he says, experts think marriage is a "U" curve. It starts out with high satisfaction, drops, levels off, then gets better and better until it reaches a high point once again.

"Our sex life had always been up and down, up and down," Jake tells me. He orders another carafe of white wine, fills my waiting glass and smiles shyly. "During the time we felt apart from one another, sex was practically zero. Then after the day I did the vacuuming, I didn't feel like I had to prove a point anymore by withholding affection from Michelle. I'm not even sure I knew what the point was, except I felt like Michelle went ahead and did something on her own that really concerned the both of us, and my dignity was offended. Once I got over that, I could reach out for her and she responded to me. I guess she was also ready to feel good again.

"Anyway, our sex is wonderful now. Better than before. I've lost a lot of weight, and Michelle praises me for that. For the first time in years she has started saying things like, 'You're handsome,' and 'Oh, you look so nice in that suit!' She wears her hair the way I like it and she puts on perfume before bedtime. So we are like young lovers, only better, because we tell each other what we like and dislike now."

It is also in this stage, says psychiatric social worker Millie Kagan, that people finally figure out how to complain effectively when things go wrong. "There is no set rule," she says. "The important thing to know is when you're bugged past endurance, and when that happens you complain. When you do complain, make sure your partner hears you. Not necessarily obeys, just *hears*. Later he or she may offer a gesture, a word, that says, 'I heard you. I'll try again.'

"That's all you can reasonably ask. That and some success in actually doing better so you don't have a replay of the offensive behavior."

Jake says Michelle never betrayed him again. They have since had many long talks about the abortion. Now he understands her panic, and she sympathizes with his pain. He says perhaps their reconciliation actually started some time before the vacuuming incident. Somewhere, he says, it was "perking inside us both, waiting to come out." When he made the gesture of vacuuming the rug to spare his exhausted wife another chore, it was the long-awaited signal that told Michelle that he had, at last, accepted her need to abort the child even if he didn't accept the act itself. At once she leapt at the opportunity to mend the marriage, and the stage of Together Again burst into full bloom.

"At this point all the fights aren't over and the problems aren't solved," says Kagan. "Maybe that will never happen. But there is an essential element of trust that was lacking before. Now you can afford to be vulnerable. This applies especially to men, who fear tenderness when they are young. They're afraid that if they expose their vulnerability, the wife will take advantage of it and use it somehow to rob them of manhood. Many men I see in my practice can't explain how they think this might happen. They're just afraid of it, without being able to make much sense of the emotion.

"But if a husband and wife get to the stage of Together Again, if they've come this far, the man is usually ready to trust that if he exposes his balls, his wife won't cut them off. No, this is not just vulgar language," explains Kagan. "Men actually use that metaphor very often, so it is important to see it that way, as this very intimate and very basic gender-related feeling.

"The wife who understands this will not crush her husband. Maybe she *has* crushed him before, perhaps many times during the course of the marriage. Complaining that a man doesn't make enough money, for example, is a way to crush him. But now she will finally be ready to accept and help protect the new tenderness she sees in him, mixed in with his masculinity. And in turn, she will trust the man not to overpower her, not to swallow her, not to kill her individuality."

The next day I meet Michelle at the same restaurant. She is a ruddy-faced woman of forty-five with gently graying brown hair. Michelle is fast-talking and energetic. She is eager to tell her story and share her delight in this pleasant stage of marriage. Briefly she recalls the jarring events that led up to this point, telling me that while Jake's rendition is basically correct, they probably never will see things from precisely the same viewpoint.

"I'm a woman, so of course it seems different to me," says Michelle. "The abortion was a terrible thing. It was the worst decision I had to make in my whole life. It was a choice . . . well . . . it was a non-choice, really, a choice between something awful and something *more* awful. As I saw it, as I still see it, there wasn't anything else I could do. But that doesn't make it right. I've decided that on the issue of abortion, there is no right or wrong. It's beyond human labels or judgment.

"The night Jake and I agreed on the abortion was probably the most traumatic night in my life. I didn't want to do it. Neither did he, but our backs were up against the wall. Then when I finally felt I had the strength to go and do what I had to do, he calls the next afternoon and it seems as if he's changing his mind. I went into a panic. He didn't *say* he was changing his mind. All he really said was, let's talk it over some more. But that was enough to throw me into a real tizzy. I felt I couldn't discuss any more about it or I'd go nuts. So I rushed out to do it before I lost my nerve.

"I knew I was doing something wrong. I knew it was unfair to Jake to agree to talk and then to go behind his back and have the abortion fast, before he could have any more say in the matter. But I felt like it was my body, essentially my responsibility and, therefore, my burden, and the person who had to stop passing the buck was me. So that was why I took matters into my own hands.

"I knew with the condition of our finances and my state of mind, there was no way I could get through a pregnancy and stay sane, much less take on the job of raising another baby. Also, remember that I was thirty-nine when all this was going on. That's pretty old to have a baby. At least I felt it was old for *my* body. I had a rough time with the two boys, and I didn't expect a pregnancy at that age to be any easier.

"I agree that I went a little nuts about that trip to Israel. Somehow in my mind it was something I owed to Adam, something that had to be done at all costs. It was very obvious to me that if we had another child at that point, of course the family would have to cancel the trip. But I was also aware that the trip was only a small part of the reason for the abortion. Maybe no part of it at all. I just didn't want another baby, and neither did Jake, and we simply had to come to the conclusion that an unwanted child is worse than an abortion. I truly believe that with every fiber in my soul. I think it is a sin to give birth to an unloved child, one you know you can't care for with all your heart.

"A mother's job is more, much more than to do the biological act of having the child. Her job really just begins when it's born. She has to provide the emotional stability, the nurturing, to make that child grow up well and to give it every chance. If she can't do that, she has no right bringing that child into the world. She can't have it and then turn it over to somebody else and say, 'Here, you do my job; you take over my responsibility.' That's a great sin. So in my mind, I committed the lesser of two evils."

Michelle is crying, her breath puffing out in little choked sobs. The waiter removes our plates and brings coffee, trying not to notice Michelle's tears. I imagine he wonders why I am here again, two nights in a row, with yet another weeping person. But Michelle's sadness flickers away quickly, and soon she is telling me that the horror of the past has been worth it, because it apparently paved the way for the comforting, intimate stage of marriage she and Jake are sharing now.

"The boys are grown. Adam is eighteen and Eli is fifteen, and most of the hard times of raising them are over. They are very good boys; we have no trouble with them at all.

"I'm the manager of the gift shop now, so my salary is okay. That means our money worries, while they're not gone completely, don't consume our lives the way they used to. So that's much better.

"But you know the nicest thing about now? It's that Jake and I don't try to push one another into little boxes anymore. What I mean is that I don't hold him to rigid standards I had set in my own mind of what a man should be and what a man should do. And he doesn't hold me to what the ideal woman should be and do. We have eased off on each other. We see the other person as a person, not as a superperson."

Jake and Michelle are on the upswing of the "U" curve of marriage. After the strain of misunderstanding and distrust that pulled them apart in the stage of Separation, they are reuniting in a marriage with new rules. The rules are unwritten and perhaps, in this case, even largely subconscious. But Michelle, at least, is aware of their basic intent: Neither partner any longer holds the other to an ideal that cannot be fulfilled.

Personality Can Now Emerge

Keith Melville calls this phenomenon the "non-scripted" marriage. Roles are now less important than personality traits. The husband and wife no longer see themselves or their partners as the living definition of *man* or *woman*. Instead, the spouse is becoming the realistic embodiment of his or her own personality and character traits . . . and almost nothing more. It is a great relief for both partners to be released from their stiff roles of ideal gender representative. To a great extent, this is what makes it possible for satisfaction to zoom upward in the stage of Together Again.

In the early stages of marriage, people are called upon by their spouses — and by the pressures of a gender-based society — to perform as men and women are supposed to act. By and large we still see men as strong, uncomplaining and aloof. Woman are seen as attractive, frail and supportive. The man should be aggressive in business, upward-striving and accomplishment-oriented. The woman is supposed to carve out her career with a gentler hand or announce her desire to remain at home. Ambivalence is seen as a sign of weakness in both sexes; a real man or a mature woman is supposed to be sure of what he or she is doing.

All these expectations, the "supposed-to" of life, gather strength as the couple progresses to the middle stages. If children become part of the marriage (as they do for many), the difficult parental years lend force to the gender-imposed roles. Partners call upon their spouses to play the part of mom or dad, judging them as good or bad depending on how well they perform that role and depending on their idealization of what a parent should be.

But in the older, riper and much less strained period of marriage, which begins with the stage of Together Again, gender roles become far less important. Males can express themselves tenderly without being worried that gentleness will be mistaken for weakness. Women can let the energetic, questing side of themselves show, because they have put aside worries about proper female attributes.

If the children have left home or are old enough to be in charge of themselves for the most part, the parent role is also greatly relaxed. Now the real person can shine through, freed at last from the "should be" of life and able to express not the expectations of others but the true self within.

It is this true self that the partner falls in love with all over again. It was present before marriage as the essential spark that drew the mates to one another in the first place. Over the years, it was dimmed by an overlay of gender-related expectations. Now it is back again, and so is the attraction these people originally held for each other. Thus, in the stage of Together Again, many couples say they are falling in love once more with the same person and "feeling like a kid again." This time, however, the feeling is far deeper than anything a young person could experience, for it is partly rooted in the shared history of seventeen to twenty years of marriage.

Change Is The Third Partner

Part of this new depth of feeling comes from a willingness to accept change as a welcome part of marriage rather than something to be feared. In the past, change has brought much pain and robbed couples of the honeymoon stage, but now people understand that change also makes it possible for them to enjoy Together Again. If a couple is willing to see change as a third partner in the marriage, since it is inevitable anyway, they can look forward to the challenges it brings. As soon as people recognize change as an essential and ever-present ingredient in marriage, they also realize that marriage has been defined in stages all along. It is usually in mid-life that such an awareness dawns on people.

"People resist change (up to this point), tending to cling to what is familiar out of their need for security," say marriage experts Roslyn and Leonard Schwartz. "Perceiving marriage as an evolving system with identifiable stages may help you flow with the coupling process rather than fight it. Who is right or wrong...becomes a moot question.... The most favorable background for interaction is one in which both partners accept the inevitability of change."

Learning to love change deepens one's feelings of affection for the marriage partner, because the partner is ever-changing. Thus, love at the stage of Together Again takes on a mystery and complexity that cannot be fathomed or even recognized by younger people. Now the changing partner is a source of great excitement rather than a threat.

The relaxation of these later years extends outward from the couple to family and friends. It is not unusual, for example, for a warring mother-in-law to be cared for in her old age by the son-in-law she criticized for so many years. She is old, and he has mellowed to the point of not holding her actions against her anymore. At this stage, both partners in a stable marriage tend to react the same way to the needs of aging parents and to the death or departure of loved ones. When a parent dies or a child leaves home for college or marriage, there is a loss. The couple grieves together. This shared emotion pushes them closer and they seek comfort and companionship in one another. At the same time, the loss of a loved one forces them to realize once more how essentially alone we all are, so each partner looks inside himself for added strength. This gives middle-aged people more inner security and peace, which they share with their partners.

People who are from forty-three to fifty years old, which usually is the age of those in the stage of Together Again, also stop holding friends to extremely high standards and accept them more readily as imperfect but still desirable human beings. Old friends become more dear because of their shared history; new friends are cherished because they are harder to find.

Couples in Together Again are also much less concerned about what others may think of them. For example, it is now perfectly acceptable to go on vacation alone or with a friend instead of with a spouse. Because they have been freed by their spouses from strict adherence to gender roles, people at this stage can also free themselves from roles imposed by society. They may still wish to do what is proper, but the definition of propriety has greatly expanded.

Sexual jealousy virtually disappears in Together Again. People trust their spouses and let go of long-held fears that any interest in a person of the opposite sex might mean the spouse is abandoning them. A person can watch his spouse interacting with others and admire the spouse for this, rather than feel threatened by it.

Jealousy over the accomplishments of a husband or wife also

diminishes. Couples in this stage take pride in their mate's adventures and are less devastated by their spouse's failures. In success or failure, both partners now can be what they are, not what their mates have wanted them to be.

An Essential Tradeoff

As good as all these things seem, however, it would be wrong to paint a totally rosy picture of this stage. Marriages may enter a period of rebirth only to fall apart shortly thereafter. More and more, older couples are divorcing, presumably because the new freedom people experience at this stage also helps them to break out of marriages that may have been too confining all along. In 1960, only four percent of couples married fifteen years or more got divorced. In 1980, that number had leapt to thirty-five percent.

Perhaps a prime psychological trigger for divorce at this stage is the inability of one or both spouses to make an essential tradeoff. They must agree to control themselves instead of trying to control each other. There is a natural anger about having to do so; it is never easy to relinquish the notion of control. The reward, which is a new relationship with the same person, must be greater than the punishment or the perceived loss of power. If it is not, trouble will erupt again.

If an angry couple does not divorce at this stage, they may simply live out their lives clinging to one another in a dismal, unfulfilling marriage. Says Levinson, "The result (of unresolved anger at this point in marriage) may be separation and divorce, but there are other outcomes as well. A period of open warfare or silent conflict may end in a kind of cold war truce in which a poor marriage is endured because of various external or internal constraints."

There are many such constraints. One or both partners may be dependent and frightened, telling themselves that family and friends will desert them if they get divorced, or that they are not attractive or appealing enough to find another partner. People rationalize their lack of stamina in seeking a clean break by worrying about what the children or the grandchildren will think, whether divorce will harm their business or social standing, or by saying they cannot afford to give up the money involved in the marriage.

Rather than taking the chance of divorcing, therefore, people in marriages of this kind may simply endure the relationship, going through the motions of being married without feeling any real affection for the partner. They maintain separate interests and activities while putting on a front of togetherness for the sake of family and friends. Women, especially, may force themselves to live out a life of denial this way, for many of them have been conditioned to think of themselves as martyrs who have no choice but to stay in a loveless marriage because they cannot survive alone.

There is another reason why some people stay together after almost all rational reasons for doing so have been stripped away: They cherish their anger and love the excitement of fighting. These people need conflict. If they can fight with a spouse — even though this is crazy behavior — it keeps them from going even crazier. In any stage, fighting helps them organize their thoughts and gives them direction and purpose in an otherwise empty life.

But by far the most overwhelming reason why marriages cannot be completed in the stage of Together Again is the unwillingness of one or both partners to welcome and work with change. The narcissist who dwells on his own needs and sees his personal universe as all-important may come to the brink of Together Again, stall there briefly, then lose his grip on marriage after years of holding it together by sheer force of will.

This is what happened to a man I will call August. His marriage failed after twenty years, just as it entered what seemed to be the stage of Together Again. August's self-centered approach to this stage of marriage held a false promise of happiness in middle life because he appeared to keep his ability to manipulate people and events, resisting all but superficial changes. But August could not make the essential tradeoff of power for relaxation. And he could not accept the reality that once a marriage begins to mature, it can never return to its original state. It must go on, simmer painfully or end.

His story is a blunt warning of what can go wrong in the stage of Together Again when a person rejects his last chance to embrace change.

August's Story

Today is August's birthday. He is fifty-one years old. Today is also the first anniversary of his divorce from Martha after twenty years of marriage, and this week marks August's entry into his second year of psychoanalysis.

In his penthouse apartment in Washington, D.C., August leans on the plump arms of a black leather sofa and softly outlines the tale of a marriage that could have made it but didn't.

A purple-tongued chow, festooned with a thick spike collar, pants at his feet. The dog seems ill at ease. August asks me if I mind having the dog in the room while we talk. Then, without waiting for an answer, he tells me, "This dog only bites on command. He's very sharp." August rubs his hand across the dog's massive head. It stares at me and growls.

With the startling clarity of a man who has invested much time and money in analysis, August is able to pinpoint his mistakes and those of his former wife. Perhaps, given his harsh and unyielding nature at the time of divorce, those mistakes were inevitable, says August.

He is a tall, slender man with a dignified sweep of sparse black hair crowning a craggy, austere-looking face. His wardrobe is impeccable, which suits the image of a politician. August holds a high-ranking post in government that he secured through long, ardent years on the campaign trail.

This is a man who is comfortable with power. He likes control. Taking command of people and shaping events is August's chosen career role. Trouble is, he says with a wry smile, he extends the love of command to his personal relationships as well. He could not give up the need to exercise power over Martha. The tradeoff of power for intimacy wasn't good enough for August. He says that is what killed his marriage.

"I always saw myself as the head of the household, even if I was away on business a lot. Martha was not a stupid person, and she did a wonderful job of raising a son and daughter practically by herself. She also handled our finances and decorated the house. She held the marriage together. That's what I expected her to do, and she did it just fine.

"I guess I could date our troubles to about the twelfth year of our marriage. The children were both in school, they were growing up fast and Martha was getting restless. I wasn't there with her for much of the time, and she'd tell me, 'August, even when you're here, you're not *here*.' It was true. My mind was a million miles away, on some Senate bill or policy meeting or something else. Household stuff seemed very tame and boring in comparison to the excitement of my public life.

"One day — I remember it clear as a bell — Martha announced she was going back to school to get an advanced degree in business. Now, that was a shock. I had no quarrel with what she wanted to do; I am not a Neanderthal. It was the way she did it that blew me away. Instead of coming to me and saying, 'Look, I'm bored, I'm dissatisfed and I want to go back to school, so how about discussing this with me,' she just went ahead and did it unilaterally. I could even accept it if she said, 'I have already made up my mind and all I need from you is some cooperation on how to run things differently from now on.' But no, it was just, 'I'm going. The house and the kids are *your* problem.' It seems as if she had felt deprived for a long time, and by dropping everything on me without warning, she was getting revenge.

"I didn't understand that until a few months ago," August sighs. "It came out of my analysis. I'm not saying that if I had understood it then that it would have made any difference. I don't know. So far I haven't wanted to change myself all that much. I simply wanted to understand . . . and I think I do.

"But at that time I felt as if my world was spinning out of control. I was confused all the time. I know change is inevitable, especially changes in husband-wife relationships as the wife wants to become more independent and pursue a career. But I had not been prepared for any change. You see, Marth was angry at me, very angry, and she never let on. Instead she just buried it, and then it exploded in one terribly irrational act.

"Somehow we got through her four years of school. We used housekeepers, babysitters, drivers, you name it. There was a lot of rushing home on my part so the children wouldn't be alone at night. Martha took a lot of night classes.

"I accepted all this partly because I was feeling terribly guilty about having denied Marth a life of her own up to that point. Also, I did think I should take more responsibility for our children and our relationship. So I tried to pitch in as best I could, and we limped along. I was mad and I complained a lot, though. I let the children know their mother was being irresponsible, and I got a kick out of it when they acted snippy toward her.

"Then she graduated. I was half very proud of her and half angry at the cost it had extracted from me and from the children. I asked her what she planned to do next. I didn't want to be taken by surprise again. She said she wanted to have some time to think it over, to look around for a good position in management. The children were in their adolescent years, still fairly dependent, especially for carpools and things like that. Martha and I agreed that she would resume her driving chores and would keep on making dinner so we'd have as much of a family life as possible. That was beginning to be more important than ever to me, because it seemed that soon the children would be grown. If I didn't spend time with them at that point, since I had missed out a lot in their early years, I'd never get to be part of their lives.

"I told all this to Martha. She seemed to understand, and we had a good year or two during which she took a nice job, but one that allowed her flexible hours and plenty of time off. It was a pretty low-key position, much to my relief. I figured she had done her thing, and now I could concentrate on my work again. I felt like I could catch my breath and keep up with things."

August shifts on the sofa and reaches up to flick on a curving black lamp that hangs above his head. At his sudden movement, the chow leaps to its feet, stiffens and bares its teeth. I shrink in my chair and ask August to please put the dog in the next room. But he ignores my request with a chuckle and a sharp word to the dog. It sits down, panting. Says August, "You're afraid of the dog, eh? Well, relax. I've got him under control."

The apartment has grown dark, and in the shadows of the lamplight this man looks sad but unbroken. There is a proud set to his jaw that seems to imply defiance. He may know what went wrong, but so far there is no indication that August was willing to modify himself very much to avert marital disaster.

"Little by little life seemed to settle back down to what it used to be in the marriage," August was saying. "I still held the reins. Oh, Martha had a job and all that, but by and large I saw her as the same pliable little lady I had married, and I gradually stopped feeling threatened. Sure, I had changed somewhat. I had done some driving for the kids, and I was home more at night. But inside it just seemed right to me to be the strong factor in the family and to dictate the way things would go. I thought Martha was comfortable that way, too. Again, she didn't complain.

"When we had been married almost twenty years, both kids went off to college. We had the house to ourselves and it was very nice, very sweet and peaceful. I was going great guns in my career. As far as I knew Martha's job was just fine. She didn't talk about it very much. We went out with friends, mostly to diplomatic parties and things connected with my position. Our sex wasn't frequent, but it was okay. I was happy.

"Then, boom! Martha drops another bomb. She announces, 'I'm going to be gone for a month on this special study tour.' I was really stunned. It was the height of the party season, and we had accepted a lot of invitations to important affairs. I got furious. I told her she promised not to hit me like that again with plans before we discussed them together. Her answer was, 'You don't really listen to me anyway. You're in your own world.'

"I told Martha if she left, I'd divorce her. Flat out like that. She said, 'I don't believe that.' We didn't have a terrible fight or anything. I simply said, 'Try me.'

"Well, she did. She left for that month, and I just couldn't get over the feeling that I'd been deserted. More than that, I was deeply humiliated. She would simply not let me participate in her plans, and she made me look like a fool in the eyes of everyone we knew. So instead of running after her, which I felt was a very demeaning thing to do, I filed for divorce."

Is August sorry now? He shrugs his thin shoulders and glances away. "I am what I am," he says softly. He reaches down to stroke the chow. "If I can't be in a relationship where I have control, I guess I'd rather not be in the relationship at all."

Martha could not communicate, and August could not change. She is locked within her silence; he is prisoner of his self-imposed gender role. Unable to reach out for intimacy and unwilling to exchange power for relaxation, Martha and August were doomed to circle around the stage of Together Again without ever being able to penetrate its warm chambers. For people who cannot complete the psychological connection necessary to cement a long-standing marriage and who are unable to tolerate opening themselves to fully trusting the mate, the stage of Together Again is an empty promise. When a marriage ripens to this point, it becomes painful to endure a lack of depth because there are now few distractions to pull your attention away and allow you to ignore dissatisfaction.

For people unable to progress, there are three possible outcomes to the stage of Together Again: Couples can float here without entering the stage, enduring an unhappy marriage quietly; they can act out their volcanic needs by fighting until they are stilled only by extreme old age or death; or, like August, they can approach the stage, refuse to exchange control for intimacy and get divorced.

The desirable outcome is the one achieved by Jake and Michelle, who found the "coziness" Robin Morgan talks about. This happens to most people who have the emotional stamina and the willingness to insist on true friendship within a marriage. It brings out the best in each human being, like a sturdy new branch on a deeply-rooted tree, and readies them for the next and final stage of marriage.

Stage Seven: NEW FREEDOM
(Years Twenty to Twenty-five and Beyond)

"Am I a different person after twenty years of marriage? Oh, yes. With my husband, I am not ashamed of taking what I need and giving when I can. With myself, I am finally secure, rid of old hang-ups, at peace." — a forty-three-year-old attorney.

At dawn, when he bolts out of bed to snap off their radio alarm, she rolls over on her back and watches him dress. He is leaner now than when they married twenty years ago. His chest hair is almost all gray, and there are also traces of gray in his wiry red moustache. She finds it attractive.

Her eyes follow him around the room as he slips into his suit and bends to tie his shoes. Then he comes to sit briefly at the edge of the bed for a good-morning kiss. She rises and they go downstairs for breakfast together. Over bagels and freshly-brewed decaf, they repeat the comfortable, almost mindless rituals she calls "touching base."

"What are you going to do today?" she will ask him.

"No big deals. Lunch with a new client. Then a closing at three. How about you?"

"A firm meeting at nine-thirty. We're talking about the Jacoby case; you know, the one where the bank manager is facing extortion charges?"

He murmurs yes, he remembers that case. He wants to hear about it at dinner. Are they eating in or out?

"Let's eat in tonight. I can make a turkey casserole."

"Fine." He rises, rubs his lips with a paper napkin and bends over her for another kiss, this one to signal his departure for the day. An hour later she, too, will be dressed and ready for work, having seen their teen-age daughter off to high school and jotted down instructions for the maid.

Weekdays always begin like this, a forty-three-year-old attorney tells me. Few things disturb the pleasant sameness of her days. After a turbulent youth, these mellow middle years are a relief.

"All the time I was in law school and for many, many years thereafter, Bart and I were just hanging in there. I think we stayed married during the bad times because of our daughter, Saralynn, and because . . . well . . . we both had this corny notion of having made a promise of 'till death us do part.' Certainly there were many good times, but over and over I would think, 'I don't need Bart to support me, so why am I putting up with all this crap?'

"Now I know why I put up with him and he put up with me. It's because there really is a pot of gold at the end of the marriage rainbow. We finally have adjusted to ourselves and to one another so completely that we can let our hair down and not be ashamed of anything. I arrange times for us to be alone and talk; our breakfasts together each morning are perfect for that, whether or not we have anything special to say to each other.

"And he asks for certain things he wants me to do in bed. He never did that before. Maybe he was ashamed or worried I wouldn't do it.

"We each have our own law practice, and while we exchange information about our respective careers, we don't rely on one another when a problem has to be solved. If Bart is interested in one of my cases, fine. If not, I don't mind. That doesn't mean he isn't interested in me. When we were younger, I'd have a fit if he wasn't all wrapped up in every word I said.

"Am I a different person after twenty years of marriage? Oh, yes. With my husband, I am not ashamed of taking what I need and giving when I can. With myself, I am finally secure, rid of old hang-ups, at peace."

Coming Full Circle: Renegotiation

People who have been married from twenty to twenty-five years or more often report such feelings of inner peace. At the same time, they are groping toward some fuzzy new beginning of a relationship that has survived much pain and is now open to fresh experiences. This stage completes the journey of marriage because it comes almost full circle back to the first, very exciting honeymoon years.

Most often the children are grown and gone, and there is finally emotional energy to spend on one another. The marriage is structured much as it was when it first began, but each has a "new" partner because the mate has matured dramatically over the years. There may be career changes, and in many cases there is movement to a new home. Often the couple is free of many annoying social responsibilities that drained strength and time in earlier years, such as carpools or "must come" corporate cocktail parties. And, as opposed to many of the previous stages, where it once was a struggle to find spare moments to spend with one another, now there is time to fill together.

How can people adjust to such changes? It is through specific discussions of how to use the time they now have and capitalize on the many opportunities that have suddenly presented themselves. I call this the process of *renegotiation*.

"You can't assume at this stage that the time you have will fill up on its own," says psychiatric social worker Maxine Rosen. "If you do make that assumption, you will tend to become more and more involved in separate activities and will lose a center or a home base for mutual interests. That home base was once provided by the children, by money problems, by parents — all the things you used to fight about. Now the reasons to fight are gone, but if you don't renegotiate the marriage at this point, the mutual bonds may be gone, too. The loss of those bonds without renegotiating new bonds are, I believe, a prime reason for many late divorces."

This is why the lawyer rises early to have breakfast with her husband — to forge a bond with him every day, to "touch base," as she puts it. With care like this, the stage of New Freedom can make marriage even more rewarding than it was in the very beginning. New Freedom is *better* than a young marriage. Couples may be childless for all practical purposes, but now friendships with grown children provide extra support for their togetherness.

Although the partner has changed, and is thus a new person, one has witnessed these changes; but when people are first married a spouse is a stranger, and his or her changes up to that point are a mystery.

Now, too, there is money for a new home, a less demanding career or even retirement. This provides an emotional cushion that wasn't present during youth.

Both people in the marriage have also learned freedom from role expectations. And, although they must now renegotiate ways to use their time and many other aspects of life together, maturity provides people with better ideas on how to do this more creatively. The couple knows each other's likes and dislikes; there is little effort wasted proposing unsuitable activities, as there was in the confused beginning of the marriage.

People generally feel an overwhelming need at this point to squeeze the best from life before it is too late. For many of the people I interviewed, it was the wife who said she felt this need most strongly.

"Suddenly one day I was unloading the dishwasher and I realized that I had two feelings about this time of marriage," says a fifty-five-year-old housewife. "I felt both joy and terror. I thought, you have *time*. You are *free*. There are no toddlers clinging to your skirt and no carpools to run. There are no teen-agers slamming the refrigerator door at 2 A.M. It's just like starting out with your husband all over again, and this time you'd better do it *right*."

To some people this intimate challenge comes at a time when it seems that many of life's other doors are beginning to swing shut. Corporate men start eyeing the new young lions in the office as potential executioners. There is a steep rise in suicide rates for American males between the ages of fifty-five and sixty; that rate probably has a great deal to do with top managers being suddenly "junked" by their companies at that age. Thus, many men start their own small companies to avoid forced retirement, or they redirect their energies toward hobbies, travel, consulting or teaching.

Females entering New Freedom may be watching their daughters push ahead in the careers they wish they had for themselves. If they do not find hobbies or volunteer work adequately rewarding, they may turn those wishes into action. Colleges are filled with over-fifty females returning for their degrees, who then march off triumphantly to start small businesses and make money for the first time in their lives.

At the same time, if a woman has had a career all along, it now seems all right to slow down and take tap dance lessons, learn to draw or indulge in a hobby which in earlier years was considered too time-consuming. All of these changes signal life decisions that call for some renegotiation in the marriage.

There is an art to recognizing all the options available during this stage, openly admitting the desire for change and including one's spouse in deciding on methods by which the change can be achieved. It is offering to compromise, but unlike compromises made in earlier stages, it is *not* asking for permission. People in New Freedom are not afraid to change without permission from a spouse. The change can be something as simple as a new hairstyle or as complex as getting a job. Or it can be emotional, such as deciding to end a disagreement even if one's spouse is still in the mood to fight. For example, a mature wife does not have to wait for her husband to be loving after a fight, thus giving his "permission" for her to be loving, too. She can initiate loving behavior on her own — a playful invitation to sex or a candlelit dinner — when *she* feels the urge to do so. If the husband responds, fine. If not, she can feel cheerful and free of anger anyway, because she has decided on her own not to be angry.

Lack of a need for permission to make any moves, big or small, comes at this stage from a mature realization that people are in control of their own feelings. The control does not emanate from one's spouse. Feelings are guided by a conscious decision-making process. You are no longer the helpless victim of wild emotions that in youth could push or pull you in various directions. Now people *choose* the directions in which their feelings will go. It is possible to say to one's self, "I may not feel like loving my husband right now because he is still pouting about our fight, but since it will be good for the marriage, I will love him now and invite him out to dinner tonight."

Attentive Listening

By controlling feelings with rational decisions, a person can rise above false pride to become an expert in renegotiation. A decision can be made to listen to what the partner has to say, as you invite him or her to participate in, but not control, your movement. Securely married people in the New Freedom stage even make appointments with one another to sit down and devote time not to discussing an issue, but simply to *listening* to what one partner has to say about it. The partner who is listening puts all other concerns out of his or her mind, working hard at hearing words and inflections and watching body language. The spouse being listened to is assured that he or she has self-worth and is not being ignored in any way.

The breakfast chatter described by the attorney is a reassuring ritual and a way to stay in touch, but it is not attentive listening. *Attentive listening* is a vital part of renegotiation. It is a strong specific signal to a spouse that his thoughts and needs are valued. It is not a promise to act on those needs if they prove unreasonable. It is merely a commitment to absorb the information.

The simple act of listening can soothe a partner's fears about the many life changes that will be initiated at this stage. For example, when a wife who suddenly finds herself liberated from child-rearing decides to go back to school to get a job, this may puzzle and threaten her husband. Or if she remains at home but radiates an air of emotional independence, he may find this change equally disconcerting.

In his book *Transformations,* Dr. Roger M. Gould says his wife started growing rapidly after their children left home, and he struggled to maintain the status quo. He couldn't do it. Failing to hold her back, he decided to make the best of the situation by growing with her. Together the Goulds wrote a paper called "Individual Growth and Marital Consequences." Now he is enjoying the New Freedom stage because he no longer fears that his wife's changes might mean abandonment.

"We now seem to have emerged from under the black cloud of those years, both of us quite different from the people we were before," writes Gould. "The sense of vitality we have now, together and apart, speaks for itself and tells us we did something profoundly right in muddling through our quagmire. Our children are off to college . . . . We have experienced our fair share of death, tragedies and disappointments — maybe more than our fair share of luck."

Luck plays no small part in bringing a couple safely to New Freedom. Full enjoyment of this stage assumes reasonably good health for both partners, some sort of job, volunteer work or career satisfaction for them both, enough money to enjoy at least a little of the good life, and a satisfactory relationship with stable offspring.

Given at least some of these essential components of happiness, a couple can renegotiate not only how their time is spent together and apart but also some of the basic rules of their marriage. Almost always, renegotiation causes a temporary upheaval and can be dangerous to the marriage if either partner refuses to listen, learn and cooperate in welcoming and facilitating change. What is being renegotiated is very often a set of nonverbal agreements upon which the marriage may have been based from the very beginning.

Common Agreements

The most common agreements people make when they get married are on traditional roles or divisions of labor. Typically, the male agrees to work in order to financially support a household, and a female may or may not work but agrees to do most of the housework and childcare. When these partnership agreements are rigidly structured, trapping people in gender-related roles for too many years, it is most often the female who will try to break out of her role after the children leave home. Sociologists say that's when most mid-life marriages begin to crack.

A fifty-year-old housewife, married for twenty-five years, told me, "As long as I stayed home, John was content and I could do anything I pleased. It was when I set my sights on a late-life career that he got very nervous. If we had been unable to sit down and quietly hash it out, I think that would have been the end of us."

Also married for twenty-five years, a waitress confided, "I was forty-six years old and feeling that I was too old to be on my feet so much and that this type of job was better suited to a young girl, so I asked Phil what he would think of my taking it easy from now on. And he got all flustered. It wasn't money; I think we had enough money. It was that he was simply scared of how I would change. But I thought about it and decided he didn't have to be scared. I had changed already, without either of us realizing it. So I did quit my job, and I didn't ask him. I *told* him. He could accept that, but only after a couple of sessions where the theme was, 'I am still the same woman, so don't worry.' I think he was scared I was going through a mid-life crisis or something and we'd get divorced."

Two major factors for divorce after twenty-five years or so are conflict about a woman taking a job and a husband's dissatisfaction that his wife isn't doing enough housework. Ironically, almost universally women complain at every stage that their husbands don't do *their* fair share of housework. But this complaint hardly ever threatens the marriage if it comes from the wife. Perhaps this complaint is so commonly expected that it is generally ignored by men and tolerated by women.

One aspect of renegotiation comes when women who want to begin careers after their children are grown start preparing their husband for the inevitable changes. A woman who has learned how to be firm yet gentle in expressing her desires will point out the benefits to be derived from a new job, such as more money for them both, greater self-esteem for the wife and a shared sense of what life is like for working people. It is important to solicit the husband's support and cooperation, to give him time to adjust and to reassure him that the job is *not* replacing him.

One of the subconscious provisions in the original he-works-and-she-stays-home arrangement is that the man usually expects to have a wife who is in one spot (home) and available when he needs her. He wants to return at night and be rewarded for his labors on behalf of the family. The rewards are wifely attention in the form of a switch in the wife's activities from focusing on herself or the children to focusing on him, probably by preparing a hot meal and perhaps serving his favorite drink by the fireside.

In most cases, none of this is unreasonable. It is simply one manifestation of the traditional division of labor. But when a wife suddenly changes the rules after twenty-five or thirty years of marriage, her expectations change, too. Now *she* wants a supportive mate in one spot where he can be reached, and when she gets home at night she wants attention and praise for her own day of labor.

Careers for former housewives are just one common example of a life change that takes place in New Freedom. When wives initiate any movement away from long-standing ways of life, some discomfort — if not an outright clash — is inevitable. The same is true if the husband threatens his wife by retiring or taking a lower-paying job. The way to avoid problems, however, is not for one partner to stifle new-found energy nor for the other to pretend that he doesn't care about the loss of comfort. Like the time arrangement renegotiations advised by Maxine Rosen, career arrangements can be discussed, modified and agreed upon as well.

Each partner must be very specific about what is acceptable and what he or she cannot tolerate. The husband might say, "I'm not thrilled about your new job, but I could handle it if you promise not to work past 5 P.M." The wife's bargain may be, "I can limit my working hours, but I really want you to cook dinner twice a week or meet me at a restaurant twice a week, because I won't enjoy cooking every night after a full day of work.''

Again the couple is very close to reenacting the life they had and the compromises they made when they were first married.

But now maturity is on their side. If each person has successfully learned the lessons of the previous stages of marriage, they will be eager to experiment with concessions the partner says are important. They know such changes help make an old marriage new and inject more excitement into the partnership. Unlike newlyweds, people in New Freedom don't let inexperience in sharing problems or revealing fears stand in the way of bending to a partner's reasonable requests. As long as each person clearly articulates how much change is fun and how much is threatening, growth takes place.

Says Arthur Mandelbaum, an expert on family relations with the Menninger Foundation, ''If the marriage is to survive, partners have to come to a consensus as a couple about what they will be prepared to support in each other and what they will *not* support.''

It takes trial and error, as in earlier stages, to figure out what is acceptable or unacceptable in renegotiating a mature marriage. Now, however, the trial and error period is swift. People can change much faster than they could at earlier stages, perhaps because they subconsciously realize they no longer have time to waste.

One couple who did change successfully — but not without moments of anguish — is Ed and Felicia. Their story shows how renegotiation enriches a long marriage by allowing people to take full advantage of what they have learned about one another's weaknesses and strengths.

Ed And Felicia

She always had a lot of energy and great zest for life, Felicia says in her high, chirping voice. She yanks impatiently on the door of the oven, peers inside and announces that her cookies are finally ready.

''I love to keep busy. If I'm not sewing curtains or rearranging furniture when I'm home, then I'm baking a cake or Ed's favorite cookies. I love to do a whole lot of things," she tells me as she piles the cookies on a glass platter and marches with them into the den. I follow her, balancing a tray with a steaming teapot, cups and saucers, sugar and Felicia's own half-and-half cream mixture.

Ed puts down the newspaper when we come in, his brown eyes gleaming with anticipation. Cookies and tea after dinner are an important part of his daily ritual. "You can do an interview and ask me any questions you want," he has said, "as long as you don't interfere with my dessert routine."

Ed is a man of set patterns, of comforting and comfortable rituals. He is sixty years old and his love of familiar things has not diminished. Felicia is fifty-three. They have been married for thirty years.

"We knew we were very different people, right from the beginning," says Felicia. "I have bundles of energy. Ed is more laid-back, and he always has been that way. I had to shove him through graduate school. I had to nag him into starting his own accounting firm. I had to...."

"Make all my decisions for me?" Ed asks teasingly, finishing his wife's sentence and sealing her lips momentarily by thrusting the cookie platter into her hands.

She grins and turns to me. "Well, no. I didn't make all his decisions. But I tried to, and sometimes he tried to do it to me. And it wasn't until I started my business that we kind of settled into letting the other person explore new ways of life without interference, as long as we both knew what was happening."

Felicia is a handsome woman with a beaming smile and a black pageboy that bobs with each animated turn of her head. Ed is slender and slightly shorter than his wife. She speaks quickly. He chews for long moments on the rim of his reading glasses before he answers questions or makes any statement.

Felicia describes herself as an artist, a writer of poetry, an avid reader of books on psychology and American history, an expert golfer and now a professional home decorator. Ed says he is simply interested in accounting and likes to lie on the living room sofa and doze off to the sound of soft classical music. They have one twenty-seven-year-old son, who is married and who recently told Ed and Felicia that soon they will be grandparents.

"We could agree on being thrilled about *that*," Felicia laughs. "Our marriage has always been rather...uh...touchy," she tells me. She looks at Ed, and he nods in agreement. "We quarreled a lot," she goes on. "I didn't like his being so inactive, and I wanted him to do weight lifting because he has a skinny chest. I also thought he was too timid about his work.

"And I resented always being the one who had to come up with ideas about vacations. I was the one who agitated to go out to a movie or tried to get Ed interested in travel or computers or anything new. But my big mistake when I was younger was that instead of just doing what I was interested in doing, I would nag Ed to try and get *him* interested so we could do it together. It was as if I needed his approval or his companionship or his physical presence in order to do anything. And it was very frustrating."

Ed chuckles softly and takes a sip of tea. I ask if he was frustrated, too.

"Of course," he answers softly. "She was a grade-A nag. I really wanted to just do my thing, which was to be a good accountant and then come home at night and relax and maybe spend a little time playing checkers with my son, and then go to bed at a reasonable hour. I had to fight off this constant barrage of, 'Why don't you take up weight lifting,' or, 'Let's go to the opera.' I don't *like* weight lifting. I *hate* opera. She wasn't letting me be me."

When she wasn't working to improve her husband, Felicia poured her energy into a multitude of home, volunteer and work projects. In the early years of their marriage, she was a buyer for a large department store. When she grew tired of that job, she switched to residential real estate, often clinching several big sales in one week because she never seemed to get tired. She even worked until the third month of her much-desired pregnancy. That was when disaster hit.

"I started bleeding. It was terrible. The doctor said that if I was going to keep the baby to term, I had to stay in bed. In bed! For six months. You can imagine what that did to an active person like me," Felicia says sadly. From his easy chair Ed sighs deeply, remembering.

Felicia says, "I wanted the baby, so of course I obeyed doctor's orders and confined myself to bed except for going to the bathroom and sitting up to eat dinner. But, boy, I was miserable. I did the best I could to keep my mind occupied. Ed brought me a set of charcoal pencils and a sketch pad, and I did a lot of drawing. I wrote poetry and mailed it out to the women's magazines. Some of it got published, too. I read like crazy. I bet I went through at least one book a day, didn't I, Ed?"

He looks fondly at her and smiles. "And she complained like crazy," he says. "The marriage came very close to ending during Felicia's pregnancy. I just dreaded coming home. We had a full-time housemaid to do all the things Felicia couldn't do, and that poor woman bore the brunt of Felicia's complaints all day long. When I came in the door at night, the housemaid always said to me, 'Your wife is really *waiting* for you. Just *waiting*.'

"And, oh, was she waiting. I'd come in the room and out would pour this torrent of complaints about how she was getting stiff from lying there all the time, how she was bored, how I didn't telephone her enough times that day, how I didn't realize how tough this was, how lucky I was that I didn't have to go through such an ordeal.... "

Ed stops, drains his teacup and looks at Felicia. "You just couldn't help yourself, could you?" he says gently.

"No," she answers. "I couldn't."

Their son was born healthy, and Felicia devoted herself to motherhood with characteristic zeal. She breast-fed her baby, went to infant training classes for new mothers, sewed rompers by hand and even built crude wooden toys. When the child entered first grade, Felicia went along as a volunteer teacher's helper.

"That lasted for a little while, and then I insisted that Felicia leave the boy alone and let him have his own experiences," Ed says. "At that point a lot of energy had been deflected away from me to the child, and I wasn't eager to attract her attention again. So I suggested that she get a part-time job."

Felicia became a receptionist in a doctor's office. The doctor, attracted by her vivacious personality and good looks, often invited her to the golf course with him, where he taught her the game and tried to initiate an affair. Felicia turned him down and the job ended.

"I somehow blamed Ed for that," Felicia recalls. "It seemed like I refused to have the affair on account of Ed, so I lost the job because of him. It was part of my thinking that everything I did was tied up with Ed, that my decisions and my successes or failures were all due to him in some mysterious way."

Felicia's commitment to her husband and child, and to the concept of marriage itself, remained strong. She was, however, overwhelmingly dependent on Ed. Ed was unknowingly contributing to Felicia's dependency by allowing it. He says now that such an arrangement probably satisfied some of his own, less obvious dependency needs. But he was similarly devoted to his family and to the process of painstaking growth within the marriage.

Little by little, Ed encouraged Felicia to rely on her own ideas, her own judgment, and to allow him to do the same. When she panicked at this, fearing rejection, he was the spouse who deflected her angry remarks with a gentle reminder that their problems could be discussed. Ed often played the role of the calm partner.

John Gottman, a psychologist at the University of Ilinois who studies marital satisfaction, says it is the husband who typically manages his wife's negative feelings if those feelings are expressed at a time when tension in the marriage is low. If the wife says something negative, Dr. Gottman asserts, the husband is able to counter with a positive statement and keep an argument from escalating. However, when tensions are high and the wife or the husband says something negative, the wife usually takes over the role of de-escalator.

"Men in both happy and unhappy marriages tend to respond to anger with anger (when tension is high)," says Dr. Gottman. "In happy marriages, though, the wives are able to switch to a de-escalating response during intense conflicts."

And when Ed's patience was gone and a fight got serious, Felicia always rose above her own anger and insecurities to grasp a higher goal for continuing their marriage journey. They both agree that despite frequent bickering, the marriage has been absorbing.

"The lows were very low, but the highs were simply a profound delight," says Ed. "Whenever I thought I couldn't stand this woman one more minute, that if she didn't get off my back I'd explode, walk out on her, maybe sock her in the chops, I'd realize that she might bring me grief but she was also the source of my greatest joy in life.

"Our sex life got better and better through the years as I learned to ask for what I wanted. And Felicia was all too happy to respond and to tell me what she wanted, too.

"We tried various ways of communication with each other, and we found that if we talked over our problems when things weren't hot — that is, when we were in a calm period — that nothing seemed like it couldn't be solved.

"I began to see that every problem is an interaction between two people. You can't have a nagging wife without a husband who is willing to put up with nagging. So I learned to get very firm, very assertive, and to put my foot down about the nagging. And Felicia gradually stopped. By the time our boy went away to college, she was pretty much willing to let me alone to be myself — skinny chest and sleeping on the couch and everything."

All this time, says Felicia, she was consciously working on self-improvement. By teaching herself to behave well toward Ed, she learned not only better behavior but methods of internal control that automatically acted to enhance the marriage. She began concentrating on defeating problems, not on defeating Ed. Disagreements became a joint concern to be solved together, rather than a failure on her part or on Ed's part.

By the time they had been married about twenty-six years, Felicia had abandoned the win/lose concept. She felt secure enough to release Ed from responsibility for her emotions, thus giving herself even more room to grow. "I felt strong enough to take responsibility for my own feelings," she tells me.

At that point Felicia and Ed reached the New Freedom stage. They both settled comfortably into an acceptance of themselves and of one another as essentially valuable human beings.

"It was this sense of being valuable, I think, that made it possible for us to adapt to changes in our lives," says Felicia. "For one thing, Ed developed a kidney problem and needed to be the one who was taken care of, when in the past if anybody was sick, it was usually me. And for another thing, I decided to set up my own interior decorating business. That altered our patterns of living. It also meant sinking some money into a new venture. Ed had to trust that I wouldn't screw it up and the money would go down the drain. Also, I would be traveling quite a bit, which is something I never did before. I still had a lot of energy that I wanted to put to good use, and by becoming an interior decorator I had more direction for that energy. The question was, would Ed be able to swallow all this?"

He could. "My initial reaction was, 'Oh, no, not another wacky proposal, not another flurry of activity!' " he chuckles. "But Felicia didn't dump the idea in my lap or start insisting or trying to win me over to her way of thinking on it.

"First she picked a time when we were both relaxed and things were going along pretty well. Then she carefully outlined her plans about starting an interior decorating business, and I could see that she had been giving it a lot of thought. She told me the reasons why she wanted to start the business, how she felt it was right for her and how it would combine many talents she had but could never express in a coherent way.

"She wasn't coming to me and begging, 'Please, may I do this?' She was saying, 'Look, we are partners in life, and I would like your opinion about this thing that I want to do. It's not fixed in stone. I'm going to do it, but the *way* I do it can be modified if there are things about this that make you uncomfortable.'

"It was exactly the right approach. I would hope to ask for her help in just the same way if I want to make any changes in our lives.

"Felicia was very up-front about telling me that her new career would require travel. That really was a part I didn't like. Neither one of us has spent much time away from home without the other, and since I am a routine-oriented person, the idea of being alone at my age wasn't exactly a thrill. So I told her I didn't like the travel part, and we started talking about what we could do about that."

Felicia, munching on another cookie, waves the half-eaten morsel in the air and exclaims, "It was what *we* were going to do, don't you see? It wasn't *me* shoving something down Ed's throat."

Ed accepts her interruption and uses the time to pluck another cookie from the tray for himself. Then he goes on.

"We very calmly discussed various ways that Felicia could make a go of a business like that without having to be away from home too much. And we figured out that one good way was for her to get a partner. We tried that. It didn't work very well, and we went to plan No. 2, which was an employee who would do at least fifty percent of any travel involved. Felicia really wanted to do more travel...."

"But it was a reasonable compromise," she blurts out, "especially since Ed wasn't feeling too well because of his kidney."

"So Felicia got an employee, and the woman was thrilled to travel, and it has worked out pretty well."

Ed finishes his last sentence in a rush before Felicia can interrupt him again. Then he chomps down the remainder of his cookie and smiles triumphantly. He has accepted that part of his wife that will not change and cooperated with the part of her that has changed — and is changing still.

This in itself represents growth for Ed. His movement is quieter and less dramatic but no less real. It is more internal, whereas Felicia's growth is marked by specific change from a wildly energetic person to one who has learned to channel her creativity in one primary direction. The New Freedom is there for both.

In this soaring, uninhibited stage, each partner can be released from self-imposed defense mechanisms that in the past have erected artificial barriers to intimacy.

Says Felicia, "I think I hated my own insecurity, and it came out in nagging Ed, and the more I would nag him, the more I hated myself for it. So it was a vicious cycle. But now I finally feel like a whole, secure person...as much as I'll ever be. So I could break the old pattern of nagging.

"Nagging is really a demand for attention. It was my defense against feeling that I wasn't worthy of attention, so I had to pull it out of my husband. But at this point the defenses aren't necessary anymore. I don't have to nag, and Ed and I can discuss things as partners. That's how we came to an agreement about my new business. It really was a renegotiation, because the marriage was one way before and now it's another way. And I like this way much better," Felicia adds with a smile.

"Me, too," says Ed.

Trauma And Defenses

A large part of a mature person's inner freedom at this stage may come from finally achieving enough distance from childhood to fully break away from old, destructive behavior patterns. Some of these patterns, such as Felicia's nervous need to maintain a high level of activity at all times, are so fully integrated into one's personality that they remain for life. But other patterns, perhaps based on childhood trauma, can be erased by this time and replaced by more suitable behavior.

In childhood, everyone experiences a trauma of greater or lesser intensity. This experience is burned into our subconscious and, depending on the intensity of the trauma and how old the child is when the trauma occurs, results in behavior pattern formation.

Most childhood traumas involve separation from the primary nurturing parent, who, in most cases, is the mother. She may leave for a few days when the child is a preschooler to go to the hospital and deliver a baby brother or sister. This is painful, and children react with enough fear to make it obvious that they dread future separations. Subconsciously they construct defense mechanisms to help cushion the blow of future inevitable separations. But a greater trauma — mother's death when a child is very young, for example — obviously will trigger much greater agony on the part of the seemingly abandoned child and thus create far more elaborate defense patterns.

People react in different ways to different degrees of trauma, of course, but most of our intense defense patterns involve either a desperate lifelong search to reattach to the parenting figure or an unwillingness to form other close attachments because they, too, might result in eventual loss and unbearable emotional pain. A dependent person who attaches himself too strongly to a mate and clings for dear life may be using the mate as a substitute for the lost mother. An emotionally cold person may be that way because it is easier for him or her to remain aloof and unattached rather than take the chance of losing the substitute mate, or "mother" once again. People who experience severe traumas in childhood most often are the people who get stuck in a stage of marriage. The stage at which they stick, or become fixated, is probably the stage which most closely resembles the growth stage at the time of childhood when the trauma occurred.

If a person remains successfully married up to and through New Freedom, however, there is reason to believe he or she has achieved the strength and maturity to have outdistanced most childhood traumas at last. So the personality fixations, or defenses, that were built up and maintained over the years as responses to these traumas can be modified or discarded. This causes great movement within the marriage.

It is often possible to rid oneself of some restrictive defense patterns at earlier stages of marriage. Indeed, it is probably necessary to do so if the marriage is to move forward with any degree of comfort. But if it has been too hard to break the stronger defense patterns in youth, they often come crumbling down in New Freedom simply because the individuals involved are old enough to have forgotten or to have buried the childhood trauma.

Once defenses come down, the fixed arrangements of the marriage, which are often stifling, are also broken. Quite suddenly, with the magical loss of the old scary memory of early trauma, couples can change.

"My husband was always late for dinner and I'd scream and pout about it, but I'd never really do anything constructive," says a sixty-two-year-old nurse. "One day it just hit me to say to him, quite bluntly but with kindness, that lateness upsets me. It was always that way with me; I remember feeling panic when my dad was late picking me up from school and I was all alone in the schoolyard. So I told my husband that after ten minutes of waiting I will begin eating alone. Or, if he didn't show up on time for the theatre, which was also a habit of his, I'd see him after the show. There was no hidden agenda in that arrangement. I didn't feel the need to punish him anymore for being tardy. I just wanted to eat without being starved or be on time to see the curtain go up.

"It worked because after a few times, with no fights whatsoever, he started being on time for the most part. When he's late now it's no big deal because it doesn't affect me."

Snap! Old chains are broken. People probably don't even know how it happened, but they are *free*, and so is the mate.

The couple now finds new ways of relating, and the marriage is filled with discovery. After twenty-five years or more, there are still quite a few pleasant surprises in store.

For example, a sixty-four-year-old husband told me a major change came about in his marriage regarding his favorite sport, skiing. For years his wife tagged along, stumbling on the slopes and trying to coax him into the warming hut for hot chocolate because she was freezing. They usually had some fun, but a lot of the vacation was typically a drag. He couldn't break loose and ski the expert slopes, and she was acting not out of any love for the sport but simply the way she thought a loyal wife should — by accompanying her man when he wanted to go on vacation. For most of their forty-year marriage, this couple remained fearful of separation, with each partner clinging to the other to prevent a recurrence of some early trauma that may have spurred them into dependency.

One year, after three decades of marriage and after she had become old enough to forget her childhood traumas, the wife quite unexpectedly discovered that instead of skiing what she really wanted to do was stay home and read a good book. Her husband was suspicious, worried and even a little threatened. But she was cheerfully sure of herself. He could go skiing or stay home, she said, but *she* would be fine no matter what he did . . . and *she* wanted to stay home.

Puzzled, but too curious to resist finding out what it would be like to ski unfettered at last, the husband went off and found that he, too, was no longer crippled by the fear of separation.

"We both had a ball!" the husband told me. "When we reunited the next week at the airport, I was filled with ski stories and she couldn't wait to tell me about the book. We chatted nonstop over a fancy restaurant dinner. I couldn't define it then, and I still don't know how to say it, but something very special had happened on account of our going our separate ways about that ski trip."

It is New Freedom, the final transition from dependency to self-sufficiency. Of course, if the marriage has lasted this long, both partners have probably made great strides in freeing themselves from internal constraints bit by bit. In New Freedom, the difference is that final, stubborn barriers are able to come down so the liberating process is as complete as it ever will be for the individuals involved.

Because the mate is no longer essential to one's sense of self, a person can be more honest in expressing needs and emotions. In earlier stages most people behave as if it is too dangerous to say no or to take the chance of antagonizing the mate. Conduct has generally been guided in the marriage by the fear that if a person does something on his own or lets the partner act alone, one or the other will simply escalate the solitary behavior and eventually there will be abandonment. In New Freedom, people feel an explosion of relief in knowing that lack of dependency in a mate is liberating, not dangerous.

Dependency is finally unmasked as anti-loving behavior. It originates in early childhood as a feeling of being empty, unworthy and unlovable because one's parents did not or could not provide adequate attention, affection and care.

Dependent husbands or wives suck strength from one another and may continue to do so for many years. But if they are able to build up enough of a sense of self-worth to renegotiate the marriage when they are older, the stage of New Freedom is the full flower of the marriage.

At the center of that flower is self-love. People take real pleasure in the mature, thoughtful individuals they have finally become and turn their attention to nurturing these desirable new personality traits. Often a man or woman enjoying New Freedom quits smoking, begins to exercise, develops new hobbies and reaches out in more loving ways to friends and family. This further helps erase dependency on the spouse, who is also intrigued by the "new you" and is undergoing the same process of self-discovery. All of these events come together to produce a marriage with more growth potential than ever before.

New Freedom can blossom even in a marriage that has experienced unusual difficulties in the past. A couple I will call Johnny and Pearl had abused one another in a variety of ways through practically every stage of their marriage. Yet they were able to slowly but forcefully change enough behavior patterns for self-love to shine through at last. This paved the way for the renegotiations that mark the stage of New Freedom.

Johnny And Pearl

"We were married when we were both twenty years old. At twenty-three we got divorced. Then we dated and remarried each other just before my twenty-fourth birthday. We separated three times before the age of thirty.

"This marriage has been up and down like a roller coaster. We would get very high on each other, then sink very low. Now we are both fifty-eight years old. It has taken us a long time to stop strangling each other. But I guess we had a terrific attraction for one another all along, because here we are feeling just great and having a lot of fun and it's much, much better than being on a honeymoon. It can only get better. We finally grew up."

This was Pearl's first statement to me about her marriage of thirty-eight years. A thin black woman with high cheekbones and hair pulled tightly back from her face in an upswept bun, Pearl has obviously been thinking about this interview and knows exactly what she wants to say. Her husband Johnny sprawls in an easy chair, his head cocked in Pearl's direction. Even while seated, his huge frame dominates the room. He sucks on an elaborate pipe, and the thick, sweet aroma of the smoke drifts through their well-furnished Atlanta home.

"Oh, I think Pearl is right. That's it in a nutshell," says Johnny. "We are two strong, pretty determined people, and we practically spent a lifetime pushing and pulling at each other to make the other person do what we thought was right. Especially me. I have to admit, I wasn't what you'd call a model husband. Maybe I was too caught up with being the black man who made good. You know, I wanted to show everybody that I could be a success. I really bullied Pearl, and when she let me do it, I thought she was pretty easy to shove around. But when our two boys were grown and gone, that lady sure did blossom, and she made me see how strong she had been all along.

"We are different people now. We are a different couple. I don't push Pearl around, and I respect her for it and I like myself a whole lot better. It's very nice."

Johnny and Pearl are both products of Atlanta's energetic, upwardly-mobile black middle class. They were early graduates of local black colleges, and Johnny was one of the nation's first black men to own a large construction company. He learned the trade from his father, who was a skilled carpenter.

Johnny built his first home when he was eighteen and still in college. It sold immediately. He borrowed some money and invested in three more construction projects, which were snapped up by wealthy black businesspeople. That made Johnny's reputation, and before he was twenty-five he was the owner of a construction firm employing more than fifty builders and craftsmen. He invested, built, sold and reinvested constantly, engineering an almost meteoric rise first in Atlanta's black business community and then in national construction circles as well.

All along, Pearl was part of Johnny's success. She kept the books, managed the office staff, ran errands and even authored the clever contracts that gave Johnny a powerful grip on every construction project he approached.

But Johnny didn't want to share his success with his pliant, soft-spoken wife. When she stopped working in order to nurture their two sons, Johnny accused Pearl of being lazy. When things went wrong in the office, he insisted that she return and cursed her each night when she couldn't bring about the miracle of instant improvement. Greedily, he claimed credit for each success and blamed Pearl for each failure.

Pearl's reaction was either to humbly accept the abuse and hope the next day would be better or to punish Johnny with stony silence and weeks of no sex. Sometimes when he shouted at her, she threw a pot, an iron or even a kitchen knife in his direction. She never actually made Johnny the target, says Pearl. She was just letting off steam.

"He was always a screamer, a real bully," Pearl says. "No, it was never physical abuse. He didn't hit me, but he would say things like, 'I ought to knock your head off,' and, 'You deserve a kick in the ass for that mistake!' But mostly it was that he used me and he was really very scant with his praise. Oh, he would be nice; nobody could stand it if a man isn't nice once in a while. He never forgot my birthday, for instance, and one Christmas he came home with a full-length mink coat and put it on me and said, 'I have the most beautiful lady in the world.'

"But that wasn't enough. Even that statement, 'I *have* the most beautiful lady,' was an indication that he thought of himself as owning me. And except for the pitifully ineffective ways I reacted sometimes, I went along with it — God knows why — and I was always all nerves. By the time I was thirty-two, I had very high blood pressure. When I was forty-eight, I had a heart attack."

Pearl's illness prompted a rush of concern from Johnny that was so intense he describes it as "horrible panic." It was then he realized, he says, how dependent he was on the presence of his wife and how helpless he felt at the thought of life without her.

"Pearl's heart attack wasn't life-threatening, but it scared me to no end," Johnny says softly. He takes the pipe out of his mouth and cups both hands around its warm bowl. He shifts in his chair, bending forward slightly, gathering the courage to recall his terror.

"I didn't know it then, but part of the reason for my panic was that it made me realize I was a big nothing without Pearl. Here I was, acting like a bully toward her almost from the very first days of our marriage and pretending as if I was the brains and the brawn and the power behind everything good that was happening in our family, and it was really her who deserved at least fifty percent of the credit.

"But I didn't have the self-esteem to give her any credit. She was a wonderful wife and mother, a fine and beautiful lady, a marvelous cook, an office manager of great excellence. But I treated her like a janitor and an errand boy. I just took all the good for granted and raised hell because of the bad. I wanted her to be perfect, and when I couldn't have perfection I flew off the handle. It was because I was so imperfect myself. I wanted Pearl to make it seem like I was a perfect man by being a perfect woman.

"When she recovered from the heart attack, we went to a marriage counselor together. I would never have done it before. But I tell you, I was really scared, and I didn't want her to have another episode and maybe die on me. And that was the turning point, I guess, because I learned a lot and our marriage got to the point where when the children left home we could sit down and really talk to each other as equals, maybe for the first time in our lives together."

Marriage expert Millie Kagan says abusive husbands are most often people filled with rage who vent their explosive anger on the mate because she represents the person at whom they are really angry: mother.

"The first female in the life of a man is mother," says Kagan. "A little boy who has an abusive mother is unable to express anger against this powerful parent. So he will tolerate the abuses and wait until he is grown to subconsciously take his revenge. Only this time the mother figure is the wife, and the abuser is the now-grown husband.

"And why would any woman put up with a man like that? For one thing, he can keep her constantly off-guard by expressing many nice traits about himself, interspersed with the abuse. It's common, for example, for a man who hits his wife one evening to show up with a big bouquet of roses the next night and gush all over himself telling her how sorry he is and that it will never happen again. Of course, it does. But she falls for it over and over. Also, an abused wife may have a need of her own to *be* abused. He is dependent on anger, and she is dependent on punishment."

Although the early married years of Johnny and Pearl were characterized by just such an unhealthy symbiosis, their entrance into joint therapy after Pearl's heart attack brought the destructive aspects of their relationship into the open. Pearl began to realize her own power, both as a wife and as Johnny's real partner in the success of his company. Her behavior changed. She demanded recognition for her office work and refused to perform chores she felt were beneath her. When Johnny shouted at her, she no longer reacted silently or meekly cowered before the blast of his verbal storm. She developed outside interests of her own and firmly refused to knuckle under to Johnny's demands that she remain at home to cook his meals each night.

Gradually Pearl's growing sense of self-worth forced Johnny to see her as worthy, too. His demands changed to pleas, then gradually ceased. He asked her opinion about business matters, praised her work, said "please" when he wanted something and "thank you" when it was granted. And, Johnny says, he liked the new man he was becoming.

"I could feel it inside. It was a change from being a guy who thought he had to be tough to get anywhere to a guy who got more out of life by not walking all over people. I mean this directly in relationship to Pearl, but it carried over to other people as well. Like when our younger son, Arthur, moved back in with us after he had already graduated from college and had been out on his own for a year.

"Before therapy with Pearl, I would have screamed and yelled and said Arthur was a bum and kicked his ass right out of the house. But I listened to Pearl, and we figured out together how to handle Arthur in a gentle way. It accomplished the same thing without heartache in the family, and it showed that Pearl and I were really man and wife, equal at last."

The return of twenty-four-year-old Arthur came at a time when Johnny and Pearl had terminated their marital counseling and were at least a year into New Freedom. At that point, they had been married thirty-three years. It had taken at least eight years longer than normal for this couple to progress into the final stage.

Arthur came home, says Pearl, because he lost his job with an engineering firm in Washington, D.C., and wanted to look for a better position in Atlanta. Rather than dribble away his savings on rent for an apartment of his own, Arthur cheerfully announced on a Saturday that he was coming home to live with mom and dad, and he showed up on Sunday with two overflowing trunks, an underfed cocker spaniel and a raging appetite for his mother's sweet potato pie. He promptly settled himself in his old bedroom, asked for the car keys and proceeded unknowingly to disrupt the growing harmony between Johnny and Pearl.

"Arthur didn't mean to be bad," says Pearl. "But his coming back home, when he should have been out on his own, meant that Johnny and I had to try to adjust to yet another situation right at the point when we were adjusting to the new phase of marriage we were in. It was good, and I didn't want anything to go wrong. But there was Arthur, staying out late with a different girl every night, playing loud music when Johnny and I wanted to have quiet reading time, taking the car and not asking permission, all those things.

"And I didn't know how to react to him. I didn't know if I was supposed to act like a mother all over again. And it sure wasn't easy treating Arthur like a grown-up, because there he was back in the bedroom of his childhood and doing little-boy things like forgetting to feed his dog. I'd have to do it, and I don't care much for dogs anyway. It was very upsetting.

"Johnny was getting very upset about all this, too, and I could see there was some danger of him reverting to his old ways. He was starting to yell. Not at me, but at Arthur. The two of them got into some heavy fighting, particularly about the car.

"Now, I love my son. But I knew after two months that Arthur definitely had to go. The way we accomplished that, that was the real test for Johnny and me."

The return of grown children into a newly-emerging marriage of maturity is not uncommon in the United States, and statistics show the phenomenon is on the upswing — increasing eighty-five percent since 1970. Most often the return home of children is because of the skyrocketing cost of housing in large urban areas such as Manhattan, Atlanta, Washington, D.C., San Francisco and elsewhere.

Experts like Millie Kagan agree that this is a highly destructive trend. When adult offspring move back home with their parents, it recreates an artificial parent-child situation rather than encouraging an adult-adult relationship. The parent is almost inevitably seduced into his or her old roles, preparing favorite meals and becoming upset when they are not eaten with gusto; worrying about late hours; commenting on their children's sexual encounters; and being drawn into old quarrels over everything from a blaring stereo to a messy bedroom. The son or daughter resists, not realizing that their return home is an invitation to such unwelcome encounters. Tensions rise, and parents who had been enjoying New Freedom are in danger of regressing to an earlier stage when the presence of children disrupted their sex lives and chained them to parental gender roles they have now outgrown.

"We had to get Arthur out of the house, and I give Pearl a lot of the credit for doing it in a very good way," Johnny tells me. He rubs his forehead thoughtfully and grins at his wife, who accepts the praise with a beaming smile.

"One night she said to me, 'Let's go out to dinner, where we can be alone, and we're going to decide together on a plan of action to help Arthur find a place of his own.'

"By that time I was used to Pearl taking comand of a situation like that, but on the other hand it was still a surprise to me when I realized how strong a woman she could be. And it was very pleasing to me, because I admit I was lost and needed some help or else I was going to slip backwards. My old bad traits were coming out of me slowly, like a leaking water bucket.

"So we went out. And we spent a couple of hours setting out a plan. It was real negotiation. We were familiar with that term; our marriage counselor taught it to us and that was the exact word we used at the time, as I recall. So we called on that experience to renegotiate the living conditions that were facing us concerning Arthur.

"Here's what we did. Pearl told me, 'Take out a pencil and paper and we'll write down a schedule.' And I did just that. We decided we would give Arthur $2,000 to get him on his feet. It would be a loan with no interest, to be paid back after he got himself a good job. That money was something he could use to pay rent on an apartment that Pearl would help him find.

"Then we set a date for apartment-hunting. The very next Saturday, it was. We also set a time limit of one month for the apartment to be found and for Arthur to move into it, ready or not.

"And when we had all this down on paper, Pearl said, 'We are going to stick to this plan, because good parents don't waffle around, and Arthur needs us to help him be strong.' Oh, this is a powerful lady!"

Johnny called a family meeting the next evening, and together he and Pearl explained the plan to Arthur. At first Arthur balked, accusing them of lack of love. But after Pearl and Johnny refused to be drawn into an argument, the young man could not help but be impressed with the strength of purpose that radiated from his mother and father.

Says Johnny, "Arthur told us later, 'Man, you guys are *different*. You don't yell anymore. You act like you mean what you say.' I took that as a real compliment."

The plan worked. Arthur found an apartment, a roommate and the correct path for his continuing development as an independent adult. Johnny and Pearl returned to nurturing the stage of New Freedom, which is the richest point in their married life so far.

"I might fall back now and then," Johnny tells me at the end of our interview. "I still have some bad traits inside, and once in a while Pearl also seems to be the person she was before, in taking bad stuff and just looking sad about it without speaking up for herself.

"But there is a difference, a genuine difference, in our lives now. It seems that we are . . . how shall I say it? . . . we are . . . balanced.

"Always before, I was on top and that meant Pearl had to be on the bottom. Now there is no top and bottom. We like ourselves and we like each other so much more this way. It's not all a bed of roses because, like I say, there are times when we fall from grace," Johnny laughs. "But for Pearl and me, these are definitely the best years."

The Work Pays Off

Couples in New Freedom frequently echo that emotion. People in this stage have endured the difficulties of growth through each stage of marriage and have emerged with a rich sense of self-love. That, in turn, allows them to feel and express genuine esteem for the true self of their partners. So these are, indeed, the "best years." There can be no regret that this stage could not be reached before twenty or twenty-five years of marriage or more, because people instinctively realize that true self-love is not possible without the benefit of maturity and many years of experience in stage development with one's partner.

Says Kagan, "This stage in marriage can be extraordinarily successful if each partner feels rich within himself. At last, two people are friends on an equal basis. Neither one is struggling to remake the other in his or her own image. Now the work pays off. The fighting pays off. Living intensely pays off.

"In the earlier stages, a vital marriage between two individuals resembles giant peaks and very low valleys. In Together Again, the marriage is more like traveling along gently rolling hills. There may be problems now and then, of course, because humans will always be human and perfection is a dream. But now (in New Freedom) there is more or less permanent harmony between two people at last."

Conclusion: ONGOING GROWTH

The Marriage Map guides people through familiar yet unexamined territory. Those who look closely at the dangers and confront them honestly have the best chance of traveling through life in a partnership that brings ever-increasing satisfaction.

The map resembles a huge but imperfect circle. At the end of the journey, couples return to what looks like the beginning . . . yet it is so much deeper, richer and more well-informed that although it brings a sense of completeness, it doesn't close the circle but loops upward.

Let us recap the seven stages of marriage.

People begin with *Fantasy Time*, a stage of youthful innocence when one's partner seems to embody all the good traits of humanity and people fight against seeing any faults.

Compromise is a couple's first encounter with mutual disappointment and confusion when illusions shatter.

Reality Struggles defines a stage when people begin accepting undesirable qualities in one another while idealizing the best traits in order to make reality more palatable.

When people enter mid-life and the stage of *Decisions*, they are learning to cope with big problems as a team while at the same time beginning to form a sense of responsibility on their own.

Personal growth takes a big leap forward in the *Separation* stage, a dangerous time when people reassess the marriage and may force a physical or emotional break to get some breathing space.

Together Again brings the couple to a new and more mature commitment to the marriage and sets the tone for dramatic individual growth in later years.

That growth reaches a climax in *New Freedom*. People renegotiate the terms of marriage to fit a lifestyle based on liberation from gender-imposed roles.

No Boundaries

Ongoing Growth is not another stage because it has no boundaries to mark a beginning and an end. It is more of a concept than a time-span. The idea is present throughout this book, but it probably starts bubbling inside people somewhere in the stage of *Separation*, after twelve to seventeen years of marriage. It gets stronger through the next several stages. At the end of about twenty-five years of marriage, when most people have formed both a secure emotional alliance with a partner and with themselves, Ongoing Growth becomes a conscious goal.

People now realize that personal growth is a lot of fun, and they don't want to stop.

Ongoing Growth is thus an extension of New Freedom — an extension one hopes will continue until death. It pulls this book to its logical conclusion: If people keep growing as individuals, their marriages get better and better. One can improve endlessly.

Biographer June Bingham and her politician husband Jonathan are both over sixty-five years old. They describe the pleasures of their long-lasting marriage as a hearty mixture of shared secrets, tennis twice a week, the friendship of grown children and laughter at the antics of grandchildren, and most of all an intimate knowledge of themselves and of one another.

"With all this time, one has perforce learned to know oneself," write the Binghams. "And, if blessed by the survival of one's partner, one also knows him or her in a way not experienced before. One feels truly at home."

The Marriage Map brings couples to that home where they are at peace with themselves and thus with one another. But peace does not imply an end to the now more relaxed pace of growth. Instead, it allows married people to turn away from problem-solving to soaring, extending growth to the upper reaches of self-evolution.

People now have the time and inclination to show their partners some real appreciation. They remember how to say nice things, bring small gifts and put themselves out for their spouses. Most importantly, people struggle to improve themselves because they know such improvement will reflect on the marriage and also benefit the spouse.

Dr. H. Lee Hall, who has been married to Julia Hall for almost fifty years, says they are both aware of the benefits of Ongoing Growth. He characterizes it as a time when both partners are kind enough to do small favors for one another and wise enough to know that they can control only themselves—not the spouse.

"Julia and I are very happy together," he says. "We drive one another to appointments, constantly offering to be helpful. Also, the marriage is good because we give each other space to *be*, to breathe freely. In no way am I responsible for Julia . . . nor would she let me be. And she doesn't try to 'manage' my life. It's an attitude of 'Whatever you do is fine with me.'

"Our work is similar in that we have both been students of the human mind, but she has never thought psychoanalysis made any sense. And I am an analyst. We don't discuss it. Instead we share ideas that aren't work-oriented. She has her way of looking at human behavior and I have mine. They don't have to be the same ideas. All that is necessary is respect for the other's point of view, not agreement.

"I am a solitary person. She is also very self-contained, but not to the point that I am. I simply do not like to socialize. Julia, on the other hand, has a great friendship going with some of the neighbors. That's all right. They come to the house when I'm not around.

"One could go on and on with examples. But the essense of what you need to know is that a healthy, long-lasting marriage is a relationship between two separate, self-sufficient people who respect each other's differences."

A Continuing Effort

After twenty-five years of marriage or more, those differences may take the form of new activities, immersion in a second career or both. People who have gone through the previous stages push themselves now to share ideas and concepts with a spouse, and they make an effort to find activities to enjoy together. But individual interests and activities are still the underpinnings that keep a person — and a marriage — viable. Says Dr. Hall, "Inactive retirement is probably the most horrible thing a person can do to him or herself and to a marriage."

It takes continuing effort to push on as you grow older, to insist on stretching yourself toward yet-undiscovered heights. It also takes some suffering, which is the willingness to put yourself out for a spouse instead of retreating into excuses that you think may be provided by old age, such as infirmity. A sixty-nine-year-old former travel agent, who is now a part-time photographer, tells me, "If my wife needs me to listen to one of her problems, I'll turn off the ball game and listen. That is suffering. Now and then she asks me to talk to her garden club about bird photography. I don't enjoy those gatherings too much, and it's really hard for me because I can only get around with a cane. But I do it for her sake . . . and that is suffering, too.

"Only now it's a different kind of suffering. I used to think in terms of putting up with these things. I would do them but grumble. I'd think about getting even.

"Now I enjoy the suffering in an odd way, because it shows me that I can be kind and unselfish for my wife, so I can continue to improve my own personality. It's a sort of stretching. That is very exciting at my age. Well, it should be exciting at *any* age, but somehow I was always too busy or too concerned with other things to realize that.

"I definitely think this is the most rewarding part of marriage, because you can look back and see that a lot of what tormented you before was just plain silly stuff. I am finally old enough to know what is silly and what isn't. And every day I learn more about how to tell the difference.

"As long as I can do that, I will improve as a person and my marriage will improve. I take nothing for granted. I still want to get better."

The process of self-improvement never ends, so the concept of Ongoing Growth never ends. Its goal is to amass as much self-knowledge as possible, because with self-knowledge comes what Millie Kagan calls self-ownership.

Self-Ownership

"To me, the idea of this period of marriage boils down to not trying to pull from your mate what you lack in yourself," says Kagan. "A person who does not feel whole and significant wants the spouse to be whole for him. If you think the mate is perceived by others as wonderful, you will be wonderful, too, because you own the mate. That is something you can overcome in this period, because you finally own yourself . . . and nobody else."

Thus, the process of traveling with awareness through the stages of marriage endows a person with the security to do two important things: relinquish ownership of the mate and insist on ownership of one's own actions and emotions. At this point, a person makes no attempt to monitor the mate's activities. This brings the "at home" feelings of peace that accompany Ongoing Growth. And it also brings the freedom a person needs to concentrate on expanding his or her own intellectual and emotional horizons.

When individuals concentrate on self-improvement in later years, they are automatically freed from much of the tyranny of worrying about their spouse's health and survival. Of course, they fear their partner's illness and death. But they are not so much afraid of being alone, because they know now that loss of the partner may diminish but will not destroy them.

Men die earlier in this country than women, and many older

females infect the later stages of marriage with loud fears that their husbands will have heart attacks or strokes and leave them to the bitterness of lonely widowhood. But a strong feeling that, "I am whole, with him or without," can wipe away the phobic tendency to control one's spouse through this fear. Women who are inwardly secure don't subject their husbands to grinding demands to go on a diet, do more walking or otherwise change their daily habits. Interest in a partner's health is reasonable, of course; making it the center of one's life is not. People with a strong identity of their own don't attempt to foist their ideas about health — or anything else — upon their mates. They want them to stay vibrant and alive, but if that doesn't happen they know they can stand alone.

Arriving at such inner security takes a great deal of spiritual strength. A commercial artist in his mid-fifties, who is becoming aware of the concept of Ongoing Growth, thinks his wife had that spiritual strength all along. He is beginning to achieve it now.

"I have to fight with myself not to feel slighted when she takes a great deal of interest in things and I'm left out. I think that shows I still have room for some spiritual growth that will fill me up just being myself, whether she is there or not.

"When our daughter got married, for example, my wife really threw herself into the wedding preparations and she had a roaring good time. I was involved, of course, but I wasn't as caught up in the whole thing, and I certainly didn't play as big a part in helping to select the gown, calling up florists, all that sort of thing.

"And I still did some grumbling, like a little kid whose mommy temporarily turns her attention to matters that don't concern him. I may not be strong enough yet to be totally content to enjoy *her* enjoyment and not get impatient for the time when she'll return and be concerned mostly about me.

"I believe, however, that self-containment has always been one of my wife's stronger points. When we were first married, I was on the road a lot. I traveled on the job and I spent a great deal of time being immersed in my work and not participating much in matters of the household. My wife never faltered in going about her business whether I was there or not. I had no indication that she would have any trouble handling anything that came along, because she just radiated a strength that came from inside herself. She believed she was a very capable, competent person, and so she was.

"Maybe that kind of strength runs in the blood. My wife comes from the southern mountains. It's a hard life up there, and the women don't complain or say they can't do by themselves whatever needs to be done. My wife comes from the tradition of honest self-sufficiency. You can call it a spirituality that comes from the land, perhaps, because that teaches you how to deal with some very blunt aspects of human survival. There are no frills in a mountain woman's life. They depend on themselves.

"I can learn from my wife's example. I am still learning. That's why at this point, after almost thirty years, there is still a feeling of growth in the marriage. She and I will keep getting closer because there is great respect for that self-sufficient quality. It is a big reason why we are best friends."

People who describe themselves as experiencing the rewards of Ongoing Growth tell me over and over that a feeling of calmness comes with self-sufficiency. It more than makes up for a decline in physical strength and some numbing of the pleasures of the senses.

"I would extend that to sex," says a sixty-three-year-old woman. "My husband and I have a nice sex life, but not one that was as fiery as in our younger days. I would like to be more sexually active than my husband is capable of right now.

"But that's okay, because touching is . . . well . . . more *holy* to me than it used to be. We are so together in mind that even if we can't have intercourse too often, I get great joy out of just lying in bed and holding his hand and not saying a word but knowing he is beside me. There is a calmness there I can't fully describe.

"I'm not sure if I mean religious feelings of peace. I am talking about feeling holy in a non-religious sense, although I'm sure some people can find passages in their Bible that relate directly to the increased peacefulness that comes with age. I am talking about the ability of the older person to look inside himself, see good there and

share it with a husband or wife. That, to me, brings calm. You do it
alone, but it benefits you both."

For a woman known to me as Doria, advancement to Ongoing
Growth meant calm in a life that had always been plagued by panic.
Doria is elegant and serene at seventy-eight, but she tells me her
earlier years were a whirlpool of anxiety attacks that constantly
disrupted her sixty-year marriage to Ross.

Doria is the oldest person I interviewed. Her story shows that when
self-torment is changed to self-knowledge, even a very long marriage
can blossom anew.

Doria's Story

"I am speaking to you out of the benefit of age, but I don't think of
myself as an old lady," says Doria. "There is always something new
to learn, and when you look at life that way, you stay young."

Indeed, Doria looks ageless. She is tall and still graceful. Her hair
has been carefully tinted to radiate the glow of silver rather than show
the dullness of gray. It is quite long and thick, and today Doria's hair
is pulled back from her regal face, braided and delicately looped into
an elegant topknot.

"Oh, this hairstyle is one of my little beauty secrets," she laughs.
"If you pull up your hair very tight, it lifts the skin of your face and
smooths out wrinkles. It is rather like a non-surgical facelift. One
can't keep up with all the sagging that goes on, my dear, but one *can*
learn to cope. On days when I don't see anyone, I let my hair down
because if you keep it pulled up all the time it gets too thin.

"And I have my nails done in a natural color" — Doria holds up
her hands to display a perfect manicure — "because red looks
absolutely witchy on an older woman. I stay away from pearls. They
have an aging effect. I wear a lot of white and blue, to be colorful but
not flashy.

"There is a regrettable thickening of the waist that occurs at my
age," she goes on, "and no amount of exercise, which I also do, will
hold it back totally. So I have just decided to enjoy myself and I have

joined a wine-tasting club. Wine has a lot of calories, but it is not a vulgar way to get heavy."

Doria leans forward and shakes a tiny silver bell. The tinkling noise bring Doria's housemaid, who pours wine for her mistress and me, offers delicate tea sandwiches, then swiftly leaves the parlor. Doria goes back to describing her many interests and activities, making the point that her wealth is only a bonus to the enjoyment of life she has now. Her real treasure, she says, is not money. It is freedom from anxiety and the solid marriage that has come as a result of that freedom.

"I was brought up as a Southern aristocrat," says Doria. "It has been nice to have the material comforts. But those comforts never sheltered me from feeling frightened all the time, because I was convinced that if you took away the fancy dresses and the jewels there would be nothing to see except an empty girl.

"My parents were proper but not very warm. They kept their distance from me. I was an only child, and I remember being lonely almost all the time.

"To be honest, I am not very well educated. I went to finishing school and all it taught me was piano, sewing, manners and house management. In short, I was taught how to be the perfect upper-class housewife. I married Ross when I was nineteen and he was twenty-two. I don't think I loved him when we got married, but he was a very attractive suitor. He fit all the requirements: He came from a monied family, too, he was rather handsome, he was a gentleman, he had a bright future . . . all of those things mattered greatly in my day.

"I learned to love him. It sounds trite, but it is true. He really *was* a gentleman, and he had the same good heart in his youth as he does today. I admire Ross a great deal. He has a true feeling for people; he is charitable toward the whole human race. I think I would have been a snob if it hadn't been for him. He taught me not to be so selfish.

"But I'm afraid nothing could teach me how to be at peace with myself. We had our two daughters and a lovely home, we were secure and I still found myself subject to anxiety attacks and that terrible childhood feeling that I was really a person of very little consequence. I believe those feelings were responsible for many of the frequent fights between Ross and me. Up until I was about fifty-five years old or so, my inferiority complex brought on a lot of trouble for the children and for poor Ross.

"To be truthful, I was a meddlesome wife and mother. I was at Ross about everything from his business decisions to the color of his ties. After all, I thought he had to show the world that he was a person of impeccable taste!

"But most of my energies were devoted to supervising the girls. 'Do this!' 'Don't wear tacky clothing!' 'You musn't go out with boys of bad breeding!' I was at the girls night and day. God knows why they didn't rebel worse than they did. They certainly got around me by saying, 'Yes, Mother,' and then going off to do exactly as they pleased. That was with Ross's encouragement, and it made me furious. But he would take me aside and tell me that if I didn't stop badgering those girls, they would surely turn against me. And I think he kept me from making that happen.

"I took out my insecurities on Ross in other ways. I hated to be alone, so if he had to travel I absolutely insisted on going with him. There were many times when that was not appropriate and I felt silly on a business trip, but I simply didn't know what else to do. I didn't have much to keep me busy except Ross and the girls, you see, and the idea of managing by myself would throw me into a panic.

"Ross was an attorney, the head of his own rather large firm. When he was about sixty years old, there was some reorganizing of the firm and Ross moved into big new offices. At once I introduced myself into the situation by insisting on decorating Ross's office. Now, I knew he wanted it his own way, and his preference was for a professional designer. I certainly wasn't that person. But remember, I was filled with the anxiety that I would be useless unless I had something to do with everything important that went on in the lives of my husband and children. I wanted to leave my own imprint on Ross's office. It was one of the few ways I had of participating in his professional life. I still thought I had a right and obligation to do that.

"May I tell you a secret? It was a disaster! I am a *terrible* decorator!"

Doria looks at me, raises her thick brown eyebrows, puckers her mouth and begins to laugh. What a joke she has told me about herself. It is funny now because she has outgrown her insecurities at last. This "disaster," as she calls it, proved to be an odd turning point in Doria's life and in her relationship with Ross.

"He took it well, the dear man, but he couldn't conceal his disappointment. All along, whenever he didn't like something I would do, he would sometimes get very angry and I would be terribly threatened. What would happen to me if I lost his love? So I would become contrite and contain my anxiety, hide it from Ross to make him get over the anger.

"This time it wasn't anger he showed but a terrible sadness. It was as if he was giving up, giving in, saying to himself, 'Well, I can't cope with her so I'll have to tolerate her.'

"Ross's sadness affected me in a way his anger could not. Perhaps I was ready to get his message. I went off alone and wept for myself and for him. I could see myself becoming a domineering old biddy whom no one loved, who was simply *endured*. I couldn't stand the thought.

"But what to do about it? Please be aware that this took a long time, but I began forcing myself to live and let live. I would say it took me from the age of about fifty-five to at least sixty. Remember, I had been anxiety-ridden all my life because I had very few feelings of self-worth. One doesn't wake up one morning and have those feelings. It takes a great deal of very difficult enforcement, so to speak. And having a lot of money doesn't help a single bit. You can't buy your self-confidence.

"Oh, I wish I could tell you how I finally did get that self-confidence. I wish there was a magic formula and I could share it with you and everyone could perform a miracle on themselves. But it wasn't a miracle. It was a forced change which I brought about in myself really out of a different kind of fear. I was afraid of being old and alone, old and disliked. I couldn't stop myself from getting old, but I certainly could do something about the things that made others dislike me.

"I took a new kind of interest in people. It had to be outside the immediate family. This time I was determined to be truly helpful to others, not intrusive.

"I joined the Red Cross as a volunteer, and now I am on their board of directors. I have traveled somewhat in connection with that position, and it was a marvelous thing for me to realize that a lady could travel alone quite comfortably. Ross was very proud of me and I certainly was proud of myself. I didn't do all this very naturally at first, but it got easier and easier over the years, and before I knew it I was enjoying myself and I had quite forgotten about meddling in Ross's affairs."

Doria laughs again, this time more softly. She sips her wine, then holds the goblet in her hand and taps it thoughtfully with a small diamond band that encircles her left index finger.

"Ross gave this ring to me last year," she says. "It is very symbolic, I think, of the change that has come over him because of my new-found role in life. He used to bring me gifts after one of his trips, rather as a peace offering so I wouldn't be at him so much for having gone away. He travels even more now, you know. He has retired, but for Ross retirement meant getting involved in politics, and now he goes back and forth from Washington, D.C., on the average of twice a month. But he doesn't bring me gifts when he travels. He will bring me a gift now for no reason at all. I think it is his way of saying, 'I love you.' He hadn't done anything like that for years.

"And Ross has responded favorably in other ways. I truly feel we are both growing and changing. Since I have been this way, interested in other things besides myself and pushing myself on my family, Ross has asked my opinion about ideas he has. He hardly ever did that before. We have long talks because now I have something to talk about: my work with the Red Cross, how it helps people, some of the administrative problems we have, that sort of thing. Why, just the other day Ross said to me, 'We have an organizational mess with this campaign, and you've been through this with the Red Cross, so how did you sort it out? Give me a few ideas.' Oh, I was so pleased!"

Doria finds much in life to please her now. She participates in wine-tasting festivals, indulging not only her taste buds but her hearty sense of self-sufficiency as well, for Ross does not like wine and never goes with her to these affairs. That is all right with Doria. She is able to enjoy being alone now, whereas in younger days the thought terrified her. She chats gaily on the telephone with her two married daughters and goes on shopping trips now and then with her four grandchildren but says she is careful not to spend too much time with her offspring or to relapse into trying to shape their lives.

"I have a life my own, so I can let them have their own lives," she says. "And I am not going to stop cultivating interests and growing intellectually and emotionally. I have a little taste of independence, and it is a wonderful attribute for a person and for a marriage.

"Oh, Ross would never have left me, no matter how overbearing I became. But he would have been sad, and I imagine that sadness would get worse over the years if I remained the same. And I couldn't bear that. I couldn't live knowing he was my husband only out of loyalty or duty. I wanted Ross to *want* to be married to me, and I believe I have accomplished that. I started forcing myself to be independent because I thought it would benefit the marriage. It has done that, but most of all it has benefited me. I believe the two benefits go together. They complement one another.

"My dear, when you reach this stage of life it is a genuine thrill to say, 'I am capable of self-improvement. I can change, and I have a very clear control over that change and how it will come about.'

"Yes. A definite thrill. I would tell young people to look forward to this."

Marriage Is Based On Wanting Change

Doria is one person who has come through a long, reasonably full life with a marriage that will continue to grow even to very old age. If she has any secret to tell about how to make marriage a success, it is this: A good marriage is based on wanting, accepting and sometimes even forcing change.

All the people I interviewed who were making their way through various stages of marriage said progress was possible because they actively sought to make changes in themselves ... and thus in the partnership. When women were nags or husbands overbearing, for example, they tried to modify that behavior as soon as they became aware of it. People who didn't want to change — like August, sitting alone with his chow in Washington, D.C. — could not get through the stages. Most often, their marriages ended.

When someone forces change, like Doria, the result is increased self-esteem and a blossoming of happiness in the marriage. This can happen at any age and in any stage. Most people do it little by little as they gain maturity. With a person's final realization that he or she can stand alone, marriage takes on new meaning. It becomes something you do for pleasure, not because you will fumble or fade away without it.

The stages of marriage, as presented in *The Marriage Map,* are an outline for change. Each person will fill in his or her own details, emerging with a rich life story of how to be a happy couple in an era where coupling has been made to sound unworkable. It is not. For people willing to embrace the challenge and excitement of change marriage can be a lifelong adventure.